*The New Local Government Series*

*No. 27*

# THE POLITICS OF
# LOCAL GOVERNMENT FINANCE

*The New Local Government Series*
Series Editor: Professor Peter G. Richards

# THE POLITICS OF LOCAL GOVERNMENT FINANCE

TONY TRAVERS

London
**ALLEN & UNWIN**
Boston          Sydney

**Allen & Unwin (Publishers) Ltd,
40 Museum Street, London WC1A 1LU, UK**

Allen & Unwin (Publishers) Ltd,
Park Lane, Hemel Hempstead, Herts HP2 4TE, UK

Allen & Unwin, Inc.,
8 Winchester Place, Winchester, Mass. 01890, USA

Allen & Unwin (Australia) Ltd,
8 Napier Street, North Sydney, NSW 2060, Australia

First published in 1986

**British Library Cataloguing in Publication Data**

Travers, Tony
    The politics of local government finance. –
    (The New local government series)
    1. Local finance – Great Britain
    I. Title   II. Series
    336′.014′41   HJ9423
    ISBN 0–04–352215–7
    ISBN 0–04–352235–1 Pbk

**Library of Congress Cataloging-in-Publication Data**

Travers, Tony.
    The politics of local government finance.
    (The New local government series; no. 27)
    Includes index.
    1. Local finance – Great Britain.
    2. Intergovernmental fiscal relations – Great Britain.
    I. Title.   II. Series.
    HJ9423.T73   1986   336′.014′41   86–3331

    ISBN 0–04–352215–7 (alk. paper)
    ISBN 0–04–352235–1 (pbk.: alk. paper)

Set in 10 on 11 point Times by Computape (Pickering) Ltd, Yorkshire
and printed in Great Britain by Billing and Sons Ltd,
London and Worcester

# CONTENTS

# FOREWORD

This book is based on work undertaken at the North East London Polytechnic in recent years. I am grateful to the polytechnic and to its Rector, Gerry Fowler, for their support.

Others have contributed by their comments and criticisms, notably Professor George Jones of the London School of Economics, Martin Pilgrim of the Association of Metropolitan Authorities, Rita Hale of the Chartered Institute of Public Finance and Accountancy, Robin Pauley of the *Financial Times* and John Carvel of the *Guardian*. To Professor John Stewart and John Gibson of the University of Birmingham, I am grateful for ideas and discussions which have become incorporated in the later chapters. I would also like to thank a number of officials at the Department of the Environment, who have been consistently kind and helpful when dealing with demands for information and statistics, as have Ian Ward and Peter Williams (Association of County Councils), Peter Derrick (Association of District Councils), Bernard Rofe (London Boroughs' Association) and Steve Hughes (Association of London Authorities).

Finally, I would like to thank Jackie Ferris for her efforts in typing the manuscript, and, in particular, my colleague Tyrrell Burgess for many hours of discussion and thought on the issues raised in the book.

**TONY TRAVERS**
*London 1986*

# INTRODUCTION

It would be wrong to see the present crisis in the relationship between local and central government as something sudden and unexpected. The decay of the system of local government finance has been allowed to accelerate by successive governments since the Second World War. White Papers, Green Papers and official inquiries have described a range of problems, while generally avoiding proposals for radical reform. Governments have regularly re-stated the importance of healthy local democracy without taking steps to ensure its preservation.

Since the start of the twentieth century, Parliament has vastly increased its demands for services provided by local government, despite recent transfers of some provision to central government and its agencies. Local authorities have had to expand their provision without access to a single new tax. Central government, on the other hand, has taken for itself a large number of new taxes and other income sources.

Britain is a nation without a written constitution, with great concentration of power in the hands of central government. The balance of powers between parts of government is determined by Parliament, though with convention and precedent being crucial to the day-to-day relationships between different parts of government. Local government's powers to raise a tax and spend money on the provision of services were granted by Parliament. However, these powers included discretion about the detail of taxation and expenditure.

This discretion is being reduced. Central governments, both Labour and Conservative, have sought to reinterpret the relationship between central and local government. In doing so, power has shifted towards the centre. There have been a number of reasons for this shift. The most important of these have been: first, that the deterioration of the system of local government finance has led to demands, particularly from the Treasury, for new powers to influence or to control local spending. Second, the shift from a prolonged period of growth in the years from the mid-1950s to the early 1970s to a period of economic stagnation has meant that governments have changed their demands upon local authorities. After years of continuous expansion, local government has found itself asked for substantial cuts.

Third, the reduction in resources available for services (in particular education) has created pressure from government departments, politicians and pressure groups for greater control over what individual councils spend. Fourth, the rapid expansion of the media (in particular national news and current affairs programmes) has created much greater awareness throughout the country of the standards of service provided by different councils. The increased publication of comparative statistics and studies has tended to strengthen the interest in national standards.

Finally, with the increased polarization of politics, the political divide between national government and local authorities (and even between the same party at national and local levels) has become wider. This has meant that the Government's priorities for the national economy have become increasingly different from the policies of a large number of powerful councils.

This book concentrates on the first of these issues, in particular in England and Wales. Both the legislation and the system of local government finance in Scotland are different from those in the rest of Great Britain. These have been considered recently elsewhere.[1] Northern Ireland has a much less powerful system of local government than that elsewhere in the United Kingdom.

The growth in concern about the local tax base is examined, as is the use of the grant system to reduce such concern in the short term. The attempts of successive governments during the 1960s, 1970s and 1980s to find new income sources and to reform the grant system are analysed. The failure of these attempts to achieve reform is shown to have led to an increase in central control over spending and taxation.

The progress from greater influence over spending (using the block grant system) via increasingly severe penalties for exceeding centrally imposed targets to the setting of a limit on individual authorities' rate poundages is traced in detail.

The major reason for increased central control (and the consequent decrease in local discretion) is, as this book shows, the consistent failure to reform local government finance. Central government's inability and lack of decisiveness have led, and are continuing to lead, to the same central government taking greater controls. There can rarely have been so deplorable a paradox.

NOTES: INTRODUCTION

1   See Arthur Midwinter, *The Politics of Local Spending* (Edinburgh: Mainstream Publishing, 1984).

*Chapter 1*

---

# A BRIEF HISTORY OF LOCAL GOVERNMENT RATES AND SPENDING

### (1) LOCAL GOVERNMENT AND THE NATIONAL ECONOMY

Local government expenditure, financed by rates, grants and charges, became a much larger part of the national economy during the years at the end of the nineteenth century and for most of the twentieth. In 1870 total local current and capital expenditure made up about 3 per cent of the gross domestic product (GDP). By 1974–5 this had grown to 15.7 per cent, though it has fallen back somewhat since then to 12.1 per cent in 1982–3. (See Table 1.1).

Between 1870 and 1880 local government spending expanded rapidly while GDP grew slowly. Local government's share of GDP grew from about 3 to 5 per cent. From 1880 to 1900 the ratio of current and capital expenditure to GDP remained constant while both spending and GDP grew very quickly. The nineteenth century was a period of considerable growth in local government activity. Quarter sessions governed the county areas, as they had done for many years. The administration of the poor laws and of public health was undertaken by town councils, Sanitary Boards and Boards of Guardians. In 1871 a Local Government Board was created to oversee the administration of the poor laws and sanitary laws. In 1874 the sanitary duties of local authorities were greatly extended, while all public health laws were revised, codified and superseded in the Public Health Act 1875. Education provision – by School Boards – was extended during the 1870s to the point that compulsory elementary education was universal. The franchise was extended in 1884, while in 1888 an Act created the county councils to replace government by the quarter sessions.

The last quarter of the nineteenth century was important because it saw the shaping of modern local government, both in terms of structure and in a growth of functions. A complex range of different bodies providing a patchwork of services (or no services in some areas) was formed into a unified system of local democratic provision. From 1900 to the First World War current expenditure continued to grow as a proportion of GDP, while capital spending started to fall after 1905. After the war both current and capital expenditure rose quickly. In 1932 current spending by local authorities hit a peak of just under 13 per cent of GDP, a level not achieved again for almost forty years. Capital spending remained around 3 or 4 per cent of GDP from the mid-1920s through to the early 1960s. Current spending fell as a proportion of GDP from 1932 till 1950, before rising gradually for the next twenty-five years.

Thus local government spending has become a bigger proportion of the economy during the past hundred years, though with significant periods when current or capital spending (or both) have been falling as a proportion of GDP. The trend and changes from time to time cannot easily be explained by changes in the economic or political climate. Periods of rapid growth have occurred under the political control of different parties.[1]

The gross current spending figures underlying these proportions show local authorities in England and Wales spending £30 million in 1870–1, rising to £47 million by 1888–9, the first year of operation of the county councils set up in 1888. By 1900–1 spending had increased to £82 million, with education, highways and poor relief being the major areas of activity. At the outbreak of the First World War spending was £153 million, and by 1939–40 it was £579 million. By this time education, health, poor relief, housing, cleansing, police and the public utilities were each areas of significant expenditure. Gross current spending by local authorities topped £1 billion for the first time in 1953, and, by the time that grants and rating were reformed in 1959–60, it was up to £1,866 million.

Income rose as expenditure increased, though the sources of the income to fund current spending changed as the total grew. In the 1870s rates made up about 50 per cent of income, with grants accounting for very little. By 1888–9 income was £48 million, of which more than half was rate-borne, with grants just up to 10 per cent of gross income. At the start of the First World War, income had grown to £153 million, funded by rates (48 per cent) and grants (15 per cent), with fees and charges accounting for about a third of the total. Rates fell to just one-third of income by 1939–40, with grants up to 30 per cent. As fees and charges also made up about one-third of all local authority income at this time, the three income sources were roughly the same at the outbreak of the Second World War.

During the war rates made up a smaller part of income (by 1944–5 the proportion had fallen to 27 per cent) though it rose somewhat after that, hovering at about 33 per cent through the late 1940s, the 1950s and 1960s.[2] Tables App.2 and App.4 show revenue and capital expenditure respectively, while Tables App.3 and App.5 show revenue and capital income. Figures for earlier years are for England and Wales. Those for 1958–9 onwards show England only. Tables App.7 and App.8 show the proportion of income from various sources.

The rating system which evolved during the nineteenth and early twentieth centuries has remained remarkably unchanged, while the payment of central government grants has developed very considerably. The next sections examine the development of rates and grants up to the middle of the twentieth century.

## (2) RATES

Rates had existed, often being collected to pay for a single local item of spending, for centuries before they were brought together as the single rate demand that ratepayers receive today. Taxes similar to rates had existed as early as the thirteenth century. For example, in 1250 there was a dispute in Romney Marsh over the repair of sea defences to protect adjacent land.[3] The dispute was solved by measuring the length of wall to be repaired and giving the duty to repair the wall to landowners in proportion to their share of lands in need of protection. This case used the area of land. Following a later one, repairs were apportioned according to the quantity and value of the land. Similar payments for benefits received still exist: metered water charges and payments for commercial refuse collection being the clearest examples.

Closer parallels to modern rates can be found in such levies as church rates. As early as 1340 an Act of Parliament stated that every parishioner was to contribute to the repairs of the parish church in proportion to his land in the parish and to the number of animals kept there. The idea of greater payments by the rich than the poor was well established; gaols were built, plague victims relieved and the victims of highway robbery reimbursed under a range of local statutes. Assessment was a matter for local individuals, and could be made by reference to wealth and income as well as property of various kinds.

Rates became a property tax (i.e. with no reference to income) so as to become easier to levy and more comprehensible. A number of statutes improved the basis of assessing rates, leading to the Poor Law of 1601, which is widely quoted as the starting-point of the modern rating system. However, the basis of the rates to be levied was not finally settled (the basis being the annual value of land and buildings) for more than two hundred years after the 1601 Act: only in the Poor Rate Exemption Act 1840 were rates finally levied purely on fixed property.

Rates accounted for a much larger yield than income tax during the nineteenth century, only being overtaken after the First World War. Local government was responsible for a large part of all public expenditure, and the cost of providing new services, such as education, was added to the poor rate. Other services were paid for out of newly imposed rates such as the 'general district rate' for services provided under the Public Health Acts. The borough rate, which was levied by municipalities for civic purposes, was usually collected as part of the poor rate. Most of these rates were merged into a single general rate in 1925.

Since that date the fundamental principle of rating has been that each ratepayer should contribute towards the cost of local services according to the rental value of his or her property. The higher the rent a property will attract, the higher should be the ratepayer's contribution to the cost of local services. Until the Local Government Act 1948 these values were determined by each authority individually. Since 1950 values have been determined by the Inland Revenue. Valuations were intended to take place every five years under the 1948 Act, though in fact they have occurred only in 1956, 1963 and 1973.

(3)  GRANTS

Government grants in aid of services were introduced much more recently than rates. The earliest, which was given to a significant number of authorities in 1835, covered the cost of taking prisoners to their place of trial and met half of the cost of prosecutions at assizes and quarter sessions. Later in the nineteenth century, police and the administration of justice were the main services to receive grant, though by the start of the twentieth century each major locally provided service was partly supported by grants. Grants were thus used by central government to pay for part or all of a local service.

As the number of grants increased, so did their variety and complexity. By 1918 education was supported by fifty-seven grants, calculated on a number of bases.[4] The Royal Commission on Local Taxation concluded in 1901 that the very complexity of the grant system at that time meant that there was no public demand for its reform. Grants were paid for out of assigned revenues (the income from a range of licences, and taxation on wine, spirits, tobacco and carriages).

The 1901 Royal Commission had divided services into two types: those which had to be provided to conform with national policy and those which were a matter of local decision (or of direct benefit to those who financed them). The former were those such as police, highways and education, while the latter varied from authority to authority. The report of the 1901 commission advocated that half of the cost of the 'national' services should be paid for by the Exchequer.[5]

Within the Report a majority advocated that assigned revenues should be kept to pay for the grants, while a minority, led by Lord Balfour, proposed that the grants should be paid for out of general taxation. The minority also proposed that grants should be distributed on the basis of a needs formula, coupled with equalization of rateable values. In addition, if spending was deemed necessary above the level implied by the needs formula, it would be met by a percentage grant. Thus with a minor modification Balfour had proposed something very similar to the 'block grant' which was introduced in 1981–2 in England and Wales.

The Royal Commission's proposals (majority and minority) were ignored. Assigned revenues gradually formed a smaller part of total Exchequer grants. Percentage grants (i.e. where a proportion of any approved spending was supported) grew in importance. A number of 'specific' grants paid in support of particular services (where fixed amounts of grant had to be spent on the service concerned) were also continued. The education grant was increased in 1902 and in 1906. The Departmental Committee on Local Taxation[6] in 1914 accepted the Balfour formula though only for education, including the equalization proposal. (However, it also criticized the equalizing aims of the Balfour scheme on the grounds that if an authority was providing a 'national' service like education, then the fact that the authority was wealthy or not did not matter.)

The Departmental Committee's proposals were also ignored. Assigned revenues became part of general government income, with amounts equivalent to the existing assigned revenues being passed on to local government. In 1929 industry was partly de-rated and agriculture wholly de-rated (it had been partly de-rated on earlier occasions since the 1890s), which meant that additional central grant was needed. This reform produced the impetus for more general reform of the grant system.

The Local Government Act 1929 introduced a new grant system which for the first time made an attempt to take account of authorities' different spending needs and rateable resources. Specific grants remained for education, police and housing, with a new general grant replacing the income from industrial and agricultural rates, remaining assigned revenues and a number of specific grants. The new grant was to be distributed on the basis of a very complicated formula which took into account population weighted by children under 5, rateable value, unemployment and sparsity.

The 1929 grant system was a less radical version of the Balfour formula. The Treasury was satisfied that the number of percentage grants (which were deemed to encourage spending) had been reduced. But the pressure for increased specific grants increased once more. New grants were given for midwives (1936), physical recreation and training (1937) and air-raid precautions (1937). The war extended the use of specific grants. The National Health Service Act 1946 gave a 50 per cent grant towards local health spending. Housing and fire services were also encouraged with specific grants. By 1948 the Government felt it necessary to reform the grant system once more.

The Local Government Act 1948 made a massive step forward towards the modern concept of equalization. Earlier legislation had made limited attempts to assist authorities with low rateable values. The 1948 Act was to lead to all authorities with below-average rateable resources to have their effective rateable values increased by the Government.

This 'equalization grant' was paid to county and county borough councils that had a rateable value per head of population below the national average. The method used to pay such grants was to treat the Government as if it were a fictitious ratepayer possessing whatever rateable value was required to bring an authority's rateable value up to a chosen level. Initially (in the Local Government Act 1948) the chosen level was the average rateable value per head of England and Wales. Therefore every authority could budget on the basis of having at least the same rateable value per head as the national average.

There was a significant complication added to the basic equalization grant system. Instead of using each authority's actual rateable value per head to calculate the equalization grant, rateable value per head of *weighted* population was used. This weighting was a vestige of earlier systems of grant. Between 1948 and 1957 actual population was weighted by the number of children under 15 and by a sparsity measure. This was achieved by giving double weighting to each person under 15 and to one-third of the population required to bring the population per mile of roads up to seventy. For the purpose of equalizing spending needs, the 1948 Act reverted to specific grants. Each service had its own grant, which meant that the bulk of Exchequer support was given in percentage grants. The Treasury was faced once again with a grant system that gave extra grant for extra spending and thus, it was argued, an incentive to higher spending.

During the next ten years, specific percentage grants became an increasingly important proportion of Government support. Spending in cost terms (i.e. compared with price movements in the economy as a whole) fell in the first two years after the 1948 grant system, but then grew strongly up to and beyond the next reforms in 1959.

The grants for each service were paid under detailed rules about what spending was or was not accepted for grant purposes. Monitoring this system was bureaucratic and complex and inevitably involved central interference in local administration. Departments attempted to measure spending needs of authorities on each service as a basis for deciding which spending was reasonable and ought therefore to be supported. There was little success inn measuring needs, and percentage grants appeared to be vindicated by the difficulty in finding acceptable measures of what 'ought' to be spent.

The 1948 system did, to some extent, equalize rate poundages. The variation between the rate poundages charged from authority to authority reduced dramatically in 1949. Many low-rateable-value authorities enjoyed huge cuts in their rate poundages and bills. Those with above-average rateable values per head gained nothing. Poundages were thus equalized, although, at the same time, rate *bills* paid in different authorities actually diverged.

With the implementation of the 1948 Local Government Act the shape of the modern grant system had been moulded. A grant was paid to assist authorities to provide such service, thus giving Government support to local spending and taking some account of the need to spend in each authority. Another grant was supporting authorities which had below-average rateable resources. With grant by now an important part of local government income, debates about the uses of grant and the method of its distribution became a regular feature of the next thirty years.

NOTES: CHAPTER 1

1  See a further analysis of these issues in C. D. Foster, R. Jackman and M. Perlman, *Local Government Finance in a Unitary State* (London: Allen & Unwin, 1980), ch. 4.
2  Figures taken from (i) B. R. Mitchell and P. Deane, *Abstract of British Historical Statistics* (Cambridge: Cambridge University Press, 1962), and (ii) Ministry of Health, later Ministry of Housing and Local Government, later Department of the Environment, *Local Government Financial Statistics* (previously *Local Taxation Returns*), annual series since 1934–5.
3  See E. Cannan, *History of Local Rates in England* (London: King, 1927).
4  See D. N. Chester, *Central and Local Government* (London: Macmillan, 1957).
5  Royal Commission on Local Taxation, Report, Cd 638 (London: HMSO, 1901).
6  Departmental Committee on Local Taxation, Report, Cd 7315 (London: HMSO, 1914).

---

# Chapter 2

# THE 1957 WHITE PAPER

## (1) A REVIEW OF LOCAL GOVERNMENT FINANCE

Early in 1956 the Minister of Housing and Local Government (Duncan Sandys) announced that a full review of local government finance was to be undertaken. He claimed, in reply to a question in the House of Commons on 8 May 1956, that this review was the most thorough of its kind since 1929. He explained that much research was being undertaken inside and outside government, with that by the Royal Institute of Public Administration and by the Institute of Municipal Treasurers and Accountants being most significant.

The Government's main conclusions were announced in the House of Commons on 12 February 1957 in advance of detailed discussions with the local authorities' associations. The conclusions were that the Government did not think it practicable to devise a satisfactory new source of local income by the introduction of a local income tax or by any other addition to the one of the other national taxes. Nor did the Government want to earmark either the whole or part of any national tax for use by local authorities. The solution lay in improving the rating system, combined with a radical recasting of the grant system.

Improvement of the grant system was seen as requiring a reduction in the number of percentage grants (i.e. grants paid by the Exchequer as a straightforward percentage of any spending incurred by an authority on a service) and an increase in the proportion of support given through a general grant (i.e. a lump of money paid to an authority without stipulation as to which services it should be spent on). Percentage grants had been seen (particularly by the Treasury) as an incentive to higher spending and by local authorities as leading to much central checking and control.

## (2) GOVERNMENT PROPOSALS

The 1957 White Paper claimed that the 'main aim of the proposed changes [was] to increase the independence of local authorities in the raising and the spending of their money so far as it is practicable to do so'.[1] It went on to say that for some years it had been a declared objective of governments to simplify and reduce departmental control and that local authorities are responsible bodies competent to discharge their own functions and ... they exercise their responsibilities in their own right ... It follows that the objective should be to leave as much as possible of the detailed management of a scheme or service to the local authority and to concentrate the Department's control at the key points where it can most effectively discharge its responsibilities for Government policies and financial administration.[2]

The detailed proposals did indeed mean a significant shift of control from central to local government. In describing the new grant arrangements, the White Paper explained:

the Government must still remain responsible for laying down national policy and ensuring compliance with basic standards in the several services which are aided by grants ... the maximum local discretion will be given in the method of providing the service: the reward of efficiency will accrue wholly to the benefit of the local population.[3]

Grants to be absorbed into the new general grant were those for education (other than meals and milk), health, fire, child care, planning, road safety, traffic patrols, registration of electors, physical training and recreation, residential and temporary accommodation and school crossing patrols. By changing these from specific to general grants, the proportion of all grants-in-aid which were not tied to specific services increased from one-sixth to almost two-thirds.

Grants were to be negotiated for two-year periods, though the amounts could be changed from one year to the next, in particular if inflation proved higher than expected. The total of grant and its distribution would be announced in a White Paper after discussions between the local authorities' associations and the Government.

In determining the total of general grant for any period, the Government explained that it would take into account:

(a)  the latest available figures of spending by local authorities on the relevant services;
(b)  factors influencing the future demand for services (i.e. social and demographic trends);
(c)  the need to develop services;
(d)  the state of the national economy; and
(e)  foreseeable pay and price variations

If circumstances changed after a grant had been set, the Government would consider a revision.

The general grant was to be paid to county and county borough councils, with amounts fixed in advance. A formula was devised including three elements: first, a 'basic share', secondly a 'supplementary share' and thirdly a 'rate product deduction'.

The basic share was an amount per head of population, plus an additional smaller amount for each child under 15 years of age. The supplementary share included amounts for schoolchildren, children under 5, old people, high density, sparsity, declining population and for authorities in Greater London. The rate product deduction took the product of a 12*d* rate off the sum of the basic and supplementary shares.

An equalization grant – that is, a grant which was paid to equalize authorities' different rateable values per head of population – had been paid in one form or another since 1929. The 1957 White Paper proposed to keep such a grant, though it would be renamed the 'rate deficiency grant'. This was operated in a similar way to equalization grants, but because of the new weighting factors proposed in the general grant the weighting factor for children in the rateable resource equalizing grant was to be dropped. The weighting for sparsity was to be retained and somewhat increased.

Two other changes were proposed. First, the grant would in future be based on rate products rather than rateable values because the Government felt that rateable value might in some areas be unreliable. Secondly, the rate deficiency grant was to be paid to a larger number of councils. Up to 1957 equalization grants had been paid only to county and county borough councils. The county received grant not only on the basis of its own spending but also on that of its constituent districts. However, within each county (whether or not the council was eligible for equalization grant) amounts per head of population were paid out of the county precept to the district councils. This achieved limited within-county equalization. Under the new proposals, capitation payments by county councils were to be abolished and new rate deficiency grants would be paid to those county district and metropolitan borough councils which qualified. County boroughs would continue to receive grant as before, while county councils would receive grant only in respect of their own spending.

Apart from these changes proposed to the grant system, the Government also stated its intention to re-rate industry and freight transport. In 1957 these were rated at only 25 per cent of their net annual rateable value. The White Paper proposed to increase these payments to 50 per cent. In addition, rate payments and payment in lieu of rates by the nationalized industries were in future to become rate income.

(3)   STRENGTHENING LOCAL AUTONOMY

These changes to the grant and rate systems were designed by the Government to strengthen the independence of local authorities. By moving from percentage grants (tied to spending on certain legally defined areas of services) and by increasing the tax base of local government, there was undoubtedly a move away from central control. The Government proposed to take advantage of the changes by reducing the level of grant support in total.

Following the proposed expansion of the rate base and the desire to increase local autonomy, reducing grant was a reasonable next step. By 1957 the ratio of grants to rates was 6:5 compared with 6:7½ thirty years earlier. Grants had been bigger than rates as an income source from about 1950 onwards. At the same time, rates had increased their yield more slowly than either direct taxes, indirect taxes or incomes. More importantly for the Government, re-rating of industry would cut the yield of income tax, profits tax and surtax. The White Paper therefore argued 'that some reduction of grants must accompany the re-rating: and . . . there is a strong case for a reduction equivalent to the total product of re-rating'.[4]

In order to smooth the transition from specific to general grants, the Government proposed to reduce grants by an amount £10 million less than the gain of £30 millions because of the re-rating. The £20 million reduction in grants was to take place largely by a reduction in the amount available for the general grant but partly by abolishing a number of tiny, historic grants. As recently as the late 1950s grants of £1,000 each were distributed between all authorities in England and Wales for 'grants in aid of the compensation to dairy farmers for destruction of infected milk' and for 'portable wheel weighers'.

The possibility of increasing local independence by the introduction of a new tax for local government had been ruled out 'after a thorough investigation'[5] by the Minister of Housing and Local Government (Henry Brooke) in his statement of 12 February 1957. Assigned revenues (i.e. allocating part or all of one or more national taxes to local government) had also been ruled out. The Government could manoeuvre only within the confines of the existing system.

The Opposition welcomed the proposals to strengthen local government, but was critical of the failure to re-rate industry up to 100 per cent. This was seen as an essential if the local rate base were to increase sufficiently so as to stop the drift towards greater grant income. Many Opposition members believed that the autonomy offered to councils by the new system would lead to less being spent on services like health and education.

(4) LEGISLATING FOR CHANGE

A Local Government Bill was published on 20 November 1957. This included proposals contained not only in the Local Government Finance White Paper, but in two others besides. The Bill ran to 78 pages, consisted of 64 clauses and 9 schedules and was divided into three main parts, dealing with, respectively,

(a)   re-rating and the introduction of the general grant;
(b)   the creation of Local Government Commissions for England and Wales; and
(c)   the delegation of responsibility for some services by county councils to the larger borough and urban district councils.


The proposals for the grant system and to re-rate industry which had been discussed in the White Paper on finance were included in the Bill. There was to be a transitional period following re-rating during which the gains and losses to individual authorities arising from the increase in industrial rating would be 'damped'. The Minister of Housing and Local Government would also have powers to reduce the general grant of an authority by any amount he thought appropriate if he was satisfied that an authority had failed to maintain reasonable standards in providing the services which ranked for grant. In applying this sanction, he would have to have regard to 'the standards maintained in other areas' in the service concerned.

For the Opposition, Arthur Bottomley claimed that the Bill failed to meet the financial difficulties of local authorities, because it neither fully re-rated industry nor gave local authorities the full benefit of the additional income from such re-rating as would take place. The substitution of a general grant for the existing specific grants would hamper the development of services, he argued.

Attempts by the Opposition to postpone the introduction of the general grant until after the next general election were defeated, though at the report stage in the House of Commons, fourteen Conservative MPs voted against the Government on the grounds that their constituencies (seaside resorts) would be badly affected by the new proposals.

During the third reading of the Bill in the Commons, J. R. Bevins (Parliamentary Secretary at the Ministry of Housing and Local Government) reiterated the Government view that the proposals would lead to a more objective, responsible and effective way of developing local services. He argued that fears that education would suffer under the new arrangements were groundless, as public opinion would not tolerate any interference with education standards. As far as re-rating industry was concerned, Mr Bevins claimed that the Government could not go further than a 50 per cent rating level, because industry could not bear the resulting extra costs. The legislation was passed and the new system of grants and rating operated from the start of the 1959–60 financial year onwards.

(5) CONCLUSION

The 1957 White Paper and the preceding review of local authority finance were undertaken because of the Government's desire to reduce local authority dependence on percentage grants and because of a desire to increase local government autonomy. Such ends were not inconsistent; moving from percentage to general grants would remove a degree of central government influence over spending priorities. It would also reduce the need for auditing, as percentage grants needed considerable amounts of checking so as to ensure that grant was being paid in respect of appropriate spending.

The changes introduced in the Local Government Act 1958 were therefore important to local government. They established the principle that the bulk of central government support should come as a general transfer from taxpayers to ratepayers, rather than the Government encouraging particular kinds and levels of provision. The 'general grant principle' has been the focus of discussion about the grant system ever since.

Arguments advanced by the Opposition during the passage of the 1958 Act were also to become a regular feature of the central–local debate in later years. Although supporting the idea of greater local independence, the Opposition was afraid that less central direction (because of the change from specific to general grants) would lower standards of provision. Indeed, there has been a tendency for opposition parties to support greater local discretion and control, yet there has been widespread support (from within the same parties) for greater central involvement in spending levels, standards and for more specific grants, particularly while in government.

The ideas put forward in the 1957 White Paper and the discussions which took place during the parliamentary stages of the Local Government Act 1958 have been regularly reconsidered since then. A White Paper in 1966, a Green Paper in 1971, the Layfield Committee in 1976, a Green Paper in 1977, a Green Paper in 1981 and a Green Paper in 1986 have, in turn, examined similar ideas and arguments. The succeeding chapters examine the development of the debate.

NOTES: CHAPTER 2

1  *Local Government Finance (England and Wales)*, Cmnd 209 (London: HMSO, July 1957), para. 5.
2  Ibid., para. 5, quoting from the First Report of the Local Government Manpower Committee, Cmd 1870, 1949.
3  Ibid., para. 13.
4  Ibid., para. 28.
5  House of Commons, Official Report (12 February 1957), col. 1078.

———————◆———————

# Chapter 3

# THE 1966 WHITE PAPER

### (1) LOCAL GOVERNMENT AND THE NATIONAL ECONOMY

The year 1966 marks the start of a period of sustained and growing concern with local authority finance. Issues raised by the Government in the White Paper *Local Government Finance England and Wales* in February 1966, like those in the 1957 White Paper, have become regular topics for debate ever since. Rates, grants and charges were briefly considered.

The first paragraph of the White Paper, written during a period of economic expansion, suggests a quite different attitude towards the public sector from that which emerged from 1976 onwards:

> Local authorities are responsible for a wide range of services vital to the community. They include public and personal health; housing and re-development; education; welfare and child care; police and fire; land planning and transportation; provision for recreation. Few people would argue that the scope of these services should be reduced; on the contrary the demand is for wider-ranging services and for higher standards. Even to maintain existing standards would mean steadily rising expenditure as the number of those to be cared for grows, and wages and salaries and other costs rise. Better services involve even higher expenditure and have to be paid for.[1]

The White Paper was thus written at a time of rising expectations about the scope and effect of public services. At the same time provision was being expanded rapidly in other areas of public spending. Between 1964–5 and 1968–9 overall public expenditure grew by 29.9 per cent in real terms,[2] with growth in 1965–6, 1966–7 and 1967–8 being 6.7 per cent, 6.6 per cent and 9.0 per cent respectively. Table App. 2 shows local authority expenditure rising rapidly in the 1950s and 1960s.

The national economy was also growing at this time; by 11.1 per cent between 1964 and 1968.[3] Thus, public spending was increasing more rapidly than the gross national product. Within public spending local authorities were increasing their current spending more quickly than central government.

Pressures on the rates were bound to increase, even though the

Government was stepping up the level of grant support. The Committee of Inquiry into the Impact of Rates on Households (the Allen Committee) concluded in February 1965[4] that 'domestic rates are less now than before the last war, as a proportion of all local authority expenditure, or of all personal incomes, or of total taxes. The proportion however, has been rising in recent years.'[5]

Not only were rates increasing as a proportion of local authority expenditure and of incomes, but poorer people were paying disproportionately high rates: 'Rates are certainly regressive in their impact on one-person and two-person households. In the lowest income group, rates represent some 5% of income (after taxes and benefits) of the one-person households and account for up to one-third of all taxes on expenditure.'[6]

The possibility of domestic rates being replaced by an income tax was considered, because the committee concluded that the impact of rates could not be shifted from the occupier. If rates were to be replaced by an equivalent income tax, then 'those in the lowest income groups would gain at least in the short run'.[7]

Allen's findings were in line with criticisms of the rating system which had been the original pressure on the Government to investigate it. But the report gave considerable statistical weight to the criticisms, though it also pointed out that most households were well able to pay their rate bills.


(2) THE PROBLEM AND THE GOVERNMENT'S SOLUTION

The 1966 White Paper used the Allen Committee's report as its starting point. It quoted a number of statistics from the report which showed that rates were regressive and that they were increasing more quickly than incomes. That rates were to be reformed rather than replaced was made clear in the second paragraph: 'Even so, after allowing for the rapidity of the rise, the sums involved are hardly large enough to be a major source of difficulty, if the liability were distributed on any sort of logical principles; the total collected in house rates is not much more than half the yield of the tobacco duty.'[8]

The Government explained that it had made a careful study of possible sources of local government revenue to replace rates. It concluded that 'within the present structure of local government' there was no prospect of any significant reform of the financial system. Because there were so many small authorities, all taxes other than rates were deemed not to work. It would be possible to envisage such reform only if there were bigger authorities which were more likely to contain both industrial and rural areas, and thus a more equal share of the tax base.

The arguments in favour and against retaining the rates were made in the White Paper. On the one hand, they were cheap to collect, difficult to evade and undeniably local in character. On the other, they lacked buoyancy and were regressive. Possible solutions to these problems were discussed to moderate the harshness of rate rises through increases in central government grant; to make changes in the rating system; or to reduce local government spending.

Local expenditure could have been reduced significantly only by cutting services or transferring responsibility for some provision to central departments. The Government made it clear that it wished to improve standards of provision, not to reduce them. It also rejected suggestions that the responsibility for providing particular services should be transferred from local to central government simply to ease the burden on the rates. In the Government's view whether a particular service should be provided centrally or locally should be decided by asking how it might best be provided. Applying this test, it was satisfied that there was little room for such transfers.

The second possibility, changing the rating system, was largely ruled out because such alterations could not be made quickly. Capital and site value rating were ruled out because each would require a full revaluation. Even a revaluation on the existing basis could not be completed before 1973 'because of the shortage of valuers and the increasing commitments of the Valuation Office'.[9]

Other, minor reforms of the rating system were proposed. In future, rates were to be charged (in part) on empty properties because property which remained empty for long periods was 'an affront to all right-thinking people'.[10] This proposal was not expected to yield much extra revenue. In addition, a Rating Bill, which was designed to provide rate rebates for domestic ratepayers of limited means and to give all ratepayers the right to pay rates by instalments, was already before Parliament. These changes were intended to solve some of the problems highlighted by the Allen Committee.

But the most important possibility discussed by the White Paper was an increase in the proportion of local government spending met from Exchequer grants. By 1966 grants met just over half of rate- and grant-borne expenditure, though this proportion, according to the Government, was 'the result of historical accident rather than any considered approach to the needs of local government'.[11]

There were three distinctive kinds of grant each of which has been mentioned in the earlier chapters: specific grants, the general grant and the rate-deficiency grant. Specific grants 'were to aid or promote the development of particular services'; the general grant, which was the biggest of the three, was distributed largely according to population, with some weighting given to factors like young and old people, schoolchildren, density and sparsity. The rate-deficiency grant attempted to compensate for differences in rateable resources between local authorities by increasing the rateable values of those authorities with below-average rateable values per head of population up to the national average figure.

The Government made clear that it intended to increase the level of grant support as the solution to the rates problem:

> the paramount need is not so much to encourage or assist the development of particular services as to ensure that the total cost of all services does not place an impossible burden on ratepayers and in particular on householders. The best way of securing this is not by a once for all transfer from rates to taxes, which would mean a rate holiday followed by a resumption of the previously rising trend, but by a progressive increase in the proportion of expenditure met from grants.[12]

The last few paragraphs of the White Paper were devoted to describing the Government's proposals. A new system of 'rate support grants' would be introduced from 1967–8 onwards. Authorities would be asked to submit estimates of proposed expenditure for the next two years. The Government would examine these in the light of 'the need to develop services and of the Government's declared aim of containing the growth of public expenditure'.[13] In this way, the Government would decide a total of relevant spending and fix a grant total which would rise steadily from year to year. 'The aim would be to keep the average increase in rate poundages more nearly in line with the growth of the economy, as measured by the gross domestic product.'[14]

The major part of the extra grant was to be devoted to reducing the rates of householders. Assuming that then current trends continued, the Government hoped to ensure that domestic ratepayers would have to pay rate rises in future years of only one-half of what they otherwise would have been. This solution became known as the 'domestic element'.

The rest of the new grant support would go either to new specific grants (for urban redevelopment, the reclamation of derelict land and acquisition of public open space) or to a new grant in aid of rates generally. The latter was to be distributed to major authorities on the basis of demographic and environmental factors and was to be known as the 'needs element'. The rate-deficiency grant was retained, though renamed the 'resources element'. Thus was the Rate Support Grant born.

Having described the new system, the Government went to some lengths to distance itself from it in the White Paper, suggesting that further reform would be necessary:

> These proposals are not presented as a long-term solution; they would be quite inadequate as such. Their purpose is to reduce the burden of rates and produce a fairer distribution of Exchequer

assistance among local authorities, and so to strengthen the system of local government finance until there has been time to re-examine the whole position in the light of whatever conclusions emerge from the work of the Royal Commission on Local Government.[15]

### (3)   THE FIRST RATE SUPPORT GRANT

The Local Government Act 1966 introduced the Rate Support Grant (RSG). The first Rate Support Grant Order was published in December 1966, detailing how the new system would work in its first year. As proposed, the grant level was set in relation to a relevant spending total which took account of current prices, likely future price movements, fluctuations in demands for services and 'the need for developing those services and the extent to which, having regard to general economic conditions, it is reasonable to develop those services'.[16] Unforeseen rises in pay and prices could be funded (at least in part) by increases in RSG.

The Government used the first RSG Order to stimulate increased spending and to fund centrally an increasing proportion of such spending. In mid-1966 prices relevant expenditure was planned to increase from £2.44 billion in 1966–7 to £2.66 billion in 1967–8 and £2.83 billion in 1968–9. Grant was planned to increase from about 50 per cent in 1966–7 to 54 per cent in 1967–8 and 55 per cent in 1968–9.

The needs element of the new Rate Support Grant was to be distributed according to a number of factors listed in schedule 1 of the Local Government Act 1966. The bulk of the grant available (over 60 per cent) was distributed per head of population, with extra amounts for young people, education 'units', density, sparsity, road mileage, declining population and for authorities within the London County Council area. Education units were calculated according to a formula, distributing 23 per cent of total needs element, so population and education units distributed over 83 per cent of the total needs element.

The resources element, like the rate-deficiency grant which it succeeded, built up the rateable value per head of authorities whose resources fell below the national average rateable value per head. The domestic element was planned to reduce the rate poundage paid by householders by 5d in the £ in 1967–8 and 10d in the £ in 1968–9. New specific grants were introduced for urban redevelopment, the acquisition of open space, the reclamation of derelict land and for the payment of authorities with an unusually high proportion of Commonwealth immigrants.

The needs element for 1967–8 was planned to be £1,027 million, the resources element £204 million and the domestic element £23 million. Specific grants totalled £127 million, making aggregate

Exchequer grants 54 per cent of relevant expenditure. The process of diffusing opposition to rate burdens had started.

(4)  CONSEQUENCES OF THE 1966 WHITE PAPER

Richard Crossman made it clear in his diaries[17] that the 1966 proposals were little more than a short-term political reaction to the unpopularity of rates. The White Paper was rushed out in February, in time for its proposals to be used in the general election of that year.

Whereas the 1957 White Paper and subsequent legislation had sought to make local authorities less dependent on grant and to widen the rate base, Harold Wilson's Government sought to do the opposite. The regressive nature of rates (as identified by Allen) was to be lessened by rate rebates. Thus the effect of rate bills (and increases from year to year in the rate burden) was reduced for many ratepayers.

The domestic element reduced householders' rates whatever the circumstances of those paying. Moreover, the amount of such relief was to be increased annually. Finally, extra grant was to be pushed into the rest of the grant system: either to specific grants or to the needs element.

In the short term, this did indeed slow down the increase in rate bills. Table 3.1 shows local authorities' income from rates in each year from 1964–5 to 1970–1. There is a clear slowing down of rate increases in the three years following the introduction of the new grant system. At the same time, grant increased much more quickly after 1967–8. This change may also be observed in Table App. 7. The percentages of expenditure made up by rates and grants are different in the two tables, because 'relevant' expenditure (used in Table 3.1) is *net* spending, while expenditure underlying Table App. 7 is gross (i.e. includes spending funded out of fees and charges).

Table 3.1   *Relevant Expenditure, Rate Income and Grants 1964–5 to 1970–1: Great Britain*

| Year | Relevant expenditure £m | Rates £m | Grant £m | As a percentage of total relevant penditure | |
|------|------|------|------|------|------|
| | | | | Rates | Grants |
| 1964–5 | 2,263 | 1,107 | 1,156 | 48.9 | 51.1 |
| 1965–6 | 2,579 | 1,258 | 1,321 | 48.8 | 51.2 |
| 1966–7 | 2,872 | 1,415 | 1,457 | 49.3 | 50.7 |
| 1967–8 | 3,141 | 1,474 | 1,667 | 46.9 | 53.1 |
| 1968–9 | 3,345 | 1,561 | 1,784 | 46.7 | 53.3 |
| 1969–70 | 3,722 | 1,692 | 2,030 | 45.5 | 54.5 |
| 1970–1 | 4,216 | 1,839 | 2,377 | 43.6 | 56.4 |

*Source*: Committee of Inquiry into Local Government Finance, Report, Cmnd 6453 (London: HMSO, May 1976), table 26.

The figures in Table 3.1 show that in 1967–8 spending rose by 9.4 per cent, while rates went up by 4 per cent and grants by 14.4 per cent. In 1968–9 the figures were: spending up 6.5 per cent, rates up 5.9 per cent and grants up 7.0 per cent. Grants were gradually increasing to fund additional real spending.

This shift of burden from ratepayers to taxpayers may have reduced the pressure to reform the rates, but it did not solve the underlying problems with local authority finance. In principle it could not have done so. If Government subvention was to be increased each year so as to reduce by half the rate rise which would otherwise take place, within a few years the burden on the Exchequer would have been enormous. Services were still expanding, and (though the Government could not have known it) inflation would be very much higher in the early 1970s.

The short-term solution adopted by the Labour Government was a badly missed opportunity. The possibility of strengthening local government's tax base (by the introduction of a new tax) was specifically ruled out by the 1966 White Paper. The opportunity to reduce grant and take pressure off the rates was lost. This loss was particularly culpable because the late 1960s were a period when institutional reform was viewed with less scepticism than in the late 1970s and early 1980s. A relatively buoyant economy would have assisted any change. In fact, the 1966 White Paper system has continued ever since without reform of the basis of local government finance.

NOTES: CHAPTER 3

1  *Local Government Finance (England and Wales)*, Cmnd 2923, (London: HMSO, February 1966).
2  *Public Expenditure 1968–69 to 1973–4*, Cmnd 4234 (London: HMSO, December 1969), table 1.1.
3  See *National Income and Expenditure*, 1983, edn, table 1.11.
4  Committee of Inquiry into the Impact of Rates on Households, Report, Cmnd 2582 (London: HMSO, February 1965).
5  Ibid., Chapter 15, para. 346.
6  Ibid., Chapter 15, para. 347.
7  Ibid., Chapter 15, para. 348.
8  *Local Government Finance (England and Wales)*, op. cit., para. 2.
9  Ibid., para. 10.
10  Ibid., para. 11.
11  Ibid., para. 12.
12  Ibid., para. 14.
13  Ibid., para. 15.
14  Ibid., para. 15.
15  Ibid., para. 20. (The Royal Commission on Local Government in England was to be set up in May 1966.)
16  Rate Support Grant Order 1966, House of Commons Paper 252 (14 December 1966).
17  Richard Crossman, *The Diaries of a Cabinet Minister* (London: Cape/Hamish Hamilton, 1975), Vol. 1, pp. 251, 303.

---

# Chapter 4

# ROYAL COMMISSIONS AND STRUCTURAL REORGANIZATION

## (1) THE ROYAL COMMISSION ON LOCAL GOVERNMENT

Immediately after the 1966 general election, though before the first financial year of the new grant system, the Government set up the Royal Commission on Local Government, chaired by Sir John (later Lord) Redcliffe-Maud.[1] The Government had stated that full reform of local authority finance could not take place until after the structure of local government had been reorganized, and therefore the commission's terms of reference barely touched on finance. A separate commission examined local government structure in Scotland.

The terms of reference were:

> to consider the structure of Local Government in England, outside Greater London, in relation to its existing functions; and to make recommendations for authorities and boundaries, and for functions and their division, having regard to the size and character of areas in which these can be most effectively exercised and the need to sustain a viable system of local democracy; and to report.[2]

The new structure proposed for local government was for 'unitary' authorities which would provide the bulk of services (i.e. education, social services, health, housing and environmental services), while 'provisional' councils would settle the strategy and planning framework within which the main authorities would operate. The areas around Manchester, Birmingham and Liverpool were to have a different system in which the upper tier had greater responsibilities.

These proposals had consequential effects for local authority finance. The Report stated:

> there will be relatively few authorities, each large enough for efficient management and, we hope, with more resources of their own. There will be no statutory delegation between different levels of local government. A source of frustration and ... of extra cost will thus disappear. Joint authorities will not be numerous. All this will simplify local finance.[3]

The proposed local authorities were to be more nearly equal in their rateable values per head of population. The rateable values or the existing local authorities varied from £87.7 to £15.8 per head, while the commission's proposed authorities would have varied from £65.8 to £28.4 per head. There would be other advantages. Overheads, it was argued, would be cut when more than 1,000 separate authorities were combined into 89 new councils. The departments of the new authorities would be able to meet central Government 'on equal terms', while inter-authority financial comparisons would be easier. Provincial councils would find it easier to maintain relations with central government and the nationalized industries.

Despite the fact that the terms of reference omitted a direct mention of finance the report of the commission devoted a section to the subject. Chapter XIII of the report examined the recent growth in local spending. The reasons for growth given by the local authorities' associations (and agreed by the commission) were: first, central government pressures on local authorities to develop their services; second, an increasing public demand for higher standards; third, the rising population and its greater mobility; fourth, the disproportionate increase in numbers of the old and young; and fifth, inflation and rising costs. The new authorities proposed by the commission would, it was hoped, increase efficiency and thus help reduce the pressures on councils because of spending growth. In addition to chapter XIII, a research appendix considered the future of local government expenditure. This appendix[4] looked at the existing pattern of local authority services, at trends and demographic changes, and put projections about future spending in the context of the whole economy. It concluded: 'the present exercise has shown that the recent growth of local government expenditure is out of proportion to the growth of national expenditure and, in a sense, local government has had what can only be described as its own sustained boom-period with relatively little effective competition'. If local government was to go on enjoying this 'boom' then either the national economy would have to grow faster, or other areas of public spending would have to be reduced, or the public sector as a whole would have to expand.

A section on 'the future of local taxation' made a telling point about local government's financial problems: 'since the present local government system took shape at the end of the last century many new taxes have come into being, most of them more productive, progressive and elastic than local government's sole tax, the rate. All of these new taxes have been appropriated by central government.'[5] The commission was clear that a country desiring local self-government should first decide what functions it wished local authorities to perform and then equip it with an adequate tax system.

Referring back to the 1966 White Paper, the commission noted that the Government had said that the new structure which emerged from the review of structure should provide a more promising context for drastic reform of local government finance. The report went on to claim that the proposed pattern would indeed make such reforms possible: 'without such complementary financial reforms the new local government will be cramped and handicapped as a self-governing institution. We therefore urge that the opportunity offered by reorganisation be taken to examine fundamentally the short-comings of the present local taxation system and remove them.'[6]

Nevertheless, government grants would continue to be required whatever new tax or taxes might be introduced. The commission also accepted the Government's right to manage the economy and local government as a part of that economy: 'Local authorities must accept their role as partners with national government in the provision of services; they must conform to current national policies and recognise the necessary limits to their fiscal freedom; they must be allies of the government in long and short-term economic management.'[7]

Having provided insight about central government's 'appropriation' of all recent new taxes, the commission also brought a new view (not considered seriously before) about the possible additional local income sources. It was accepted that each would have disadvantages: 'arguments can be produced against the allocation to local govern-ment of any one tax, whether existing or new'.[8] What should be sought was the balance of advantage which would give authorities a wider and more buoyant tax base. The objective should not be to raise more money from local taxpayers but to reduce the level of government grant. Rates should be retained, though regularly modernized. Finally, the commission proposed that agricultural property and land should be re-rated.

A system of capital expenditure control was also envisaged; the Government would determine capital spending totals for each major service for five years in advance. Discussions would then determine the distribution of this spending between authorities, with the provin-cial councils ensuring that capital allocations fitted with the provincial plans. There would be a small unallocated margin given to each authority to be used at its discretion.

In the end, the commission's structure of provinces and unitary authorities was not enacted. First, a Labour government (in February 1970) and then a Conservative one (in October 1970) published different proposals for structural reform. The Tories also issued a White Paper on finance in July 1971. The commission's structural proposals, while accepted by Labour, were much changed by the Conservatives. Its financial discussion was not taken further.

(2)  ROYAL COMMISSION: COMMENTARY

Given that the Royal Commission was not intended to examine finance in detail, some of its conclusions were extremely valuable. The consideration of finance which took place did so because of the part of the commission's terms of reference which talked of 'the need to sustain a viable system of local democracy'. By considering local government finance in a White Paper in early 1966, and then following it with an examination of structure starting three months later, the Labour Government effectively separated two issues which should have been considered together. Finance was considered (separately from structure) again in 1971 by the Conservatives and in 1974–6 by the Labour-appointed Layfield Committee.

If local government is to be 'viable' then both its structure and finance need to be appropriate. The Government tied the Royal Commission's hands, leaving it with only structure to change. If it had been open to suggest reforms to rates and grants, and the possibility of new income sources (which the commission would clearly have wanted), then it is possible that the structure proposed would have been different. Looked at differently, if Redcliffe-Maud had known that local government finance would remain unreformed for at least another fifteen years, another structure might have been proposed.

While the commission pressed for reform of finance, it accepted the Government's right to have overall control of local government to assist their management of the national economy. The idea that local government must follow the direction of national economic policy and operate to achieve objectives set down by the Treasury was accepted, though the possibility that it could conflict with the commission's other desire to give councils the widest possible discretion is not discussed. This aspect was an omission in a report which proposed the setting up of provincial councils with specific objectives to plan and develop large areas of the country.

A disagreement between, say, a Labour-controlled North-east province and a Conservative government would have led to the province having to accept the Government's economic view in the commission's proposed economic relationship. Perhaps if Redcliffe-Maud had examined structure and finance, the report would have given the key area of local discretion (and its importance to effective local democracy) more consideration.

(3)   THE LABOUR GOVERNMENT'S RESPONSE

Labour's White Paper *Reform of Local Government in England* was published in February 1970, after several months of discussion and conferences on the Redcliffe-Maud proposals. It broadly accepted the proposals, with the proviso that two metropolitan counties were proposed in addition to the three suggested by the commission. The plan for provincial councils was overtaken by the creation of the Crowther Commission on the Constitution,[9] which led the government to wait for that commission's report before proceeding with this part of the Redcliffe-Maud package.

Part of the White Paper dealt with 'relations between central and local government'. Much of this relationship is concerned with finance. The Government expressed its view (as governments regularly do) that it believed in greater freedom for local authorities, though within the framework of policies laid down by Parliament. The bulk of existing intervention, it was claimed, consisted of reconciling the claims of different authorities and dividing between authorities the part of the national resources allotted to local authorities. 'The extent of the intervention will automatically diminish with the reduction in the number of authorities ... moreover, the smaller number of authorities will make for a more intimate partnership and a more effective dialogue.'[10]

Thus it was believed that local authorities would be made more independent by the implementation of the structural plans. But the Government went on to say it was 'determined to take positive measures to reverse the trend towards centralisation'. First, it was intended to improve the control of capital by moving from project control to control over programmes as a whole. Secondly, an unallocated margin (as proposed by the Royal Commission) would be introduced within which authorities would be free to spend as they liked on capital items. Finally, the Government announced that there would be a Green Paper on finance to deal with controls, finance and taxation.

The commission had recommended that the new local authorities it proposed should be given an additional general power to spend money (without a limit) for the benefit of their areas and inhabitants. The Government pointed out that such a power already existed to allow expenditure up to the equivalent of a penny rate product in this way. Any extension of this power could, it was argued, lead to duplication or waste.

In June 1970 Harold Wilson called a general election at which the Labour Party was defeated. The proposals for both structure and finance in the February 1970 White Paper were therefore lost. In February 1971 a second White Paper was published, containing the Conservatives' plans for local government reform.

## (4)   THE CONSERVATIVE GOVERNMENT'S PROPOSALS

The new proposals rejected the idea of unitary authorities, retaining and extending a two-tier structure of authorities. But the new authorities were to be bigger than those which existed at the time. The Government wanted to increase from three to six the number of metropolitan counties and to create mergers of town and countryside (as Redcliffe-Maud had suggested).

The structure and functions of local government in England and Wales outside London were finally reformed by the Local Government Act 1972. The new system operated with effect from 1 April 1974 onwards. A separate reorganization took place in Scotland in 1975. The number of local authorities in Britain was reduced from over 1,500 to 522. The reorganization in England and Wales produced the following structure:

    6   metropolitan counties
   36   metropolitan districts
   47   non-metropolitan counties
  333   non-metropolitan districts
    1   Isles of Scilly
  ---
  423

Scotland was reorganized into 9 regional councils, 53 districts and 3 island areas. London, which had been reorganized in 1965, continued to be based on 1 county (the Greater London Council) and 33 boroughs (including the City of London).

The functions given to the new councils in England and Wales in the metropolitan areas were different from those in the non-metropolitan areas. Table 4.1 shows which authorities undertook which function from 1974 onwards (the division of functions in Greater London remained unchanged). Parish councils continued to exist after reorganization in England, though in Wales a system of 'community councils' was set up to replace parishes. A further reorganization of local government took place in April 1986, when the Greater London Council and the six metropolitan county councils were abolished. The powers of these authorities then passed to joint boards (of boroughs and districts), to Government-appointed bodies and to the borough and district councils.

Like all previous and succeeding governments, the Conservatives in 1971 stated their attachment to strong local democracy: 'The Government are ... determined to return power to those people who should exercise decisions locally, and to ensure that local government is given every opportunity to take that initiative effectively, speedily and with vigour.'[11]

The section on finance in the White Paper was very short. It made the point that reorganization of structure offered a good occasion to reform finance. A separate review of finance was being undertaken. Again, there was a statement about the financial relationship between central and local government of the kind that has appeared in almost every official document on the subject for many years: 'the Government will need to retain general controls over local authority activities but, subject to this, the aim will be to devolve to local government as much responsibility as possible'.[12]

Table 4.1   *Main Functions of Local Authorities in England and Wales*

| Function | Metropolitan county(g) | Metropolitan district | Non-metropolitan county | Non metropolitan district | Greater London council(g) | London boroughs |
|---|---|---|---|---|---|---|
| Arts and recreation | • | • | • | • | • | • |
| Cemetries and crematoria | | • | | • | | • |
| Education | | • | • | | | •(a) |
| Environmental health | | • | | • | | •(b) |
| Fire service | • | | • | | • | |
| Housing | (c) | • | (d) | • | •(d) | •(d) |
| Planning | • | • | • | • | • | • |
| Police | • | | • | | (e) | (e) |
| Rate collection | | • | | • | | • |
| Social services | | • | • | | | • |
| Traffic and transport | •(f) | | •(f) | | •(f) | |

*Notes*:
(a)   Education provided by boroughs in outer London. In inner London education to be provided by the Inner London Education Authority (which has a special committee of the Greater London Council).
(b)   Some parts of environmental health (e.g. litter control, refuse disposal) run by county councils.
(c)   County councils given certain reserve powers to provide housing subject to a request by a district council and/or approval by the secretary of state.
(d)   London boroughs responsible for provision of housing. Greater London Council given strategic role (e.g. slum clearance, provision of housing for Londoners in areas outside London, rehousing borough tenants across borough boundaries).
(e)   Greater Lonndon (except the City of London) and certain adjacent areas policed by the Metropolitan Police force. This force directly responsible to the Home Secretary. City of London retained own force.
(f)   Some parts of traffic and transport (e.g. lighting of footways, off-street parking) run by district councils.
(g)   The Greater London Council and the metropolitan county councils were abolished in 1986. Their powers were transferred to joint boards, to Government-appointed bodies and to London boroughs and metropolitan districts. The Inner London Education Authority became a fully elected single-purpose authority from 1986.

The Conservative Government accepted in this White Paper, as the Labour Government in 1966 had done, that finance and structure could be separated without difficulty. The end of the section on finance stated that the Government was satisfied that the structural reforms could go ahead without prejudicing alternative financial arrangements. The possibility that potential financial reforms might have influenced the proposed structure was not discussed. It seems likely that even at this time the Government had decided to make few changes to the finance of local government.

(5)   THE 1971 GREEN PAPER ON FINANCE

The Government's review of finance, entitled *The Future Shape of Local Government Finance*, was published in a Green Paper in July 1971. It contained seven pages of discussion about the possible ways in which finance could be reformed, followed by a series of longer appendices which went into considerable detail about trends in local government spending, additional sources of local revenue, improving the rating system and the future of the grant system. The purpose of the review of finance was 'to preserve and strengthen the financial responsibility of local government and to minimise detailed intervention by central departments'.[13]

### Local Spending and Income

The Green paper spelled out (as the 1966 White Paper and the Royal Commission had) the economic problems facing central and local government. Local authorities were taking an ever-greater share of national resources, while pay and prices in local government rose faster than in the rest of the economy. Rates, on the other hand, rose more slowly, largely because of the policy followed after 1967–8 of increasing rates as nearly as possible in line with earnings. Increased grants had been used by governments to fill the widening gap between spending and rates.

The rate of the increase in local government spending was still considerable. Government-planned increases in 1970–1 and 1971–2 were of between 4 and 5 per cent in real terms each year, about twice the growth rate of the whole economy. If this trend continued, there would be a need either for continuing increases in the grant percentage or for rates to go up faster than earnings. On the trends at that time, grants would have to be 60 per cent of relevant expenditure in 1974, rising to about 66 per cent by 1985 (in fact they reached 66½ per cent in 1975–6).

The Government considered whether this rising grant percentage might erode local autonomy, but concluded that loss of freedom was not inevitable: 'while a high-percentage *specific* grant which is paid as a precise share of actual expenditure may have this effect, a *block* grant need not involve detailed intervention by central government, and so long as it is not increased or reduced to reflect actual expenditure, it can have, in some respects, the opposite effect'.[14]

Rate rises were not seriously considered as a way of paying for increasing spending. Such rises would lead, it was claimed, to resentment on the part of ratepayers and difficulties for local authorities. The third possibility discussed was a new source of local revenue. If a new income source could be found which would yield roughly a quarter of that of rates, the grant percentage could have been cut from 60 to 50 per cent in 1974. But if the new tax were to allow the grant percentage to be frozen at about 50 per cent while keeping rate rises at the same level as increases in earnings, the yield of the new tax would have to grow more rapidly than any other national tax had done in recent years.

The possibility of raising charges was also considered. The Green Paper mentioned both 'trading services' (e.g. water supply, cemeteries, airports) and others which produced income (e.g. charges for disposing of trade effluent, payments for health and welfare services, school meals charges). But it was concluded that there was little room for radical change: 'to charge for an essential service such as dustbin emptying which is provided on a standard basis to all ratepayers would bring little advantage since rates already provide the most convenient and the fairest method of spreading the cost'.[15]

Finally, the Government looked at the possibility of transferring services from local government. Either whole services could be transferred to the centre, or local authorities could continue to act as agents for services which were the responsibility of central government. However, this move would conflict with the oft-stated desire to devolve power from central to local government. Also, any arrangement which separated administrative from financial responsibility to any degree 'would be open to strong objections both of principle and practice'.

A specific example of a suggested shift of control was used to underline the Government's objections to the shift of functions to the centre. Teachers' pay had been (and still is) a regularly proposed candidate for central funding:

> On the other hand it is a cardinal feature of our educational system that local authorities are responsible for the satisfactory staffing of their schools, and thus for the employment and conditions of service of their teachers. Leaving local authorities with these responsibilities while passing the bill to central government would sharply divorce financial from managerial responsibility. It would also hinder the development at local level of better forward planning of educational expenditure, which requires that all the services involved – teachers, buildings, and equipment – should be taken into account on a common basis when expenditure decisions are taken.[16]

Thus the Green Paper effectively ruled out rate increases, transfers of services and increases in charges as ways of improving local authorities' financial base. It was clear that rates were to continue as the main local tax source. Reform would involve introduction of an additional source of revenue, the improvement of the rating system and perhaps changes to government grant arrangements.

## (a) New Income Sources

Appendix 2 of the Green Paper looked at ways in which central grants and local rates might be reduced by introducing a new income source. The Government warned that if a new income source or sources were introduced it would be more difficult to estimate the impact of local taxation on the whole economy because the Government could not predict the mix of taxation to be used by local authorities in a particular year:

> a local authority is not in a position to take account of the effect of its decisions on the national economy, whereas the central government is able to relate the levels of individual taxes to the need to preserve a balance of taxation appropriate to overall economic management. It will always be in a better position than any individual local authority to take account of the relative effects of various types of taxation on the economy as a whole. In some countries in order to meet this problem a limit is imposed on the rate at which a particular tax can be levied by local authorities, but this generally leads to all levying up to the limit. The tax then ceases to be locally variable and becomes a variant of government grant.[17]

Each source of revenue examined in the Green Paper was analysed under three headings: administration, suitability and economic effects. 'Administration' meant the cost of running the tax and the possibility of having a large range of local levels. 'Suitability' meant the yield and buoyancy of the tax and whether the tax would create a perceptible relationship between taxation and spending. The dangers of conflict between the operation of the tax and national economic interest were also considered under this head. The potential yield would have had to be at least enough to make it possible to reduce government grant from 60 to 50 per cent, while the tax base should be buoyant enough to allow it to grow at least at the same pace as rates. 'Economic effects' meant the impact of a tax in national not local terms, and the possibility of the Treasury correcting for any undesirable side-effects.

This occasion was the first when a government document had given detailed consideration to new local income sources, and the first of several when the advantages and disadvantages of such sources were to be discussed in Green Papers, White Papers, departmental papers and Select Committee reports. The arguments for and against each tax have remained remarkably similar in the years since 1971 (until 1986), and will thus be considered in some detail at this point, though they will also be mentioned again in later chapters. The taxes considered were: local income tax (LIT), local sales taxes, local employment taxes, motor fuel duty, car licence duty and (in a separate section) reforms to rating.

*Local income tax*    The first revenue source considered was a local income tax. A number of problems were discussed – for example, rearranging the Pay As You Earn system so as to allow each authority to tax its residents rather than the people working in its area. There might also, it was agreed, be problems working out each authority's income base on which the new tax would be levied. In addition 'a massive administrative effort would ... be needed by the Inland Revenue, or the local authorities, or employers, or by some combination of all three, if the tax was to work satisfactorily'.[18] Finally, if profits were included in the local income tax, there would be immense problems in allocating them between authorities.

But an LIT would increase the number of people paying tax to local authorities. The yield would be substantial; an additional 3 points on the standard rate of income tax would pay for cutting grant from 60 to 50 per cent. On the other hand, the Government felt that there would be little scope for regular increases in the tax rate and that the real scope for local variation would be less than appeared.

The economic effects of an LIT would reduce the scope for the Government to influence the national economy, so it was argued. There would be little or no effect on industrial or export costs, though areas which were already more prosperous would be able to levy lower taxes than the less affluent areas, and thus increase their advantage over the rest of the country. Comparisons with other countries were deemed of limited use because in most of them local income taxes had existed before national ones and none of them had a system so inflexibly attached to the workplace as that in Britain.

*Local sales taxes*   Local sales tax and value added tax were considered next. The Green Paper observed: 'although major shopping centres and mail order provide exceptions most shopping is done within the local authority area where people live'. There might be difficulties with a local sales tax because of the new administration required and also because of extending the tax to retail services as well as the sale of goods. Yield would be reasonably high; a 2 per cent local sales tax would probably allow grant to be cut from 60 to 50 per cent. But because the rise in retail sales generally lagged behind the rise in local authority cost increases, there would be a need for regular increases in the tax. These increases would be difficult because changes of small fractions of a percentage point (e.g. to raise the local tax from 2 to 2.25 per cent) would be cumbersome. While the Government expected that the difficulties of conflict with national economic objectives would be smaller than for LIT, there was at the time a serious problem created by the impending change from purchase tax to VAT at the national level. This problem, it was argued, would not be solved by attempting to introduce both central and local VAT at the same time.

*Local employment taxes*    The third tax examined was a local employment or payroll tax. It would be administered by employers themselves adding a flat-rate percentage tax to any national employment tax (e.g. National Insurance contributions). A flat-rate percentage tax charged on employees was dismissed as being no more than a crude and inequitable form of income tax. Liability to tax would be determined by where employees worked, rather than where they lived or where their records were kept.

As with the first two taxes considered, yield would be large and buoyant. A 2 per cent payroll tax would have brought in enough money to cut grant by the desired 10 percentage points, though the rate of tax would have to be raised from time to time because the rise in the numbers employed would probably not increase in line with the gap between local spending and rates. A payroll tax would not be perceptible, as the burden would tend to be passed on in increased prices. As with income tax, poorer authorities would need to levy a higher rate of tax than the better-off.

A payroll tax, the Government believed, would have less effect on the cost of living than a sales tax, and thus a smaller effect on consumption. It would, however, have a greater effect on industrial costs and consequently on the balance of payments. A 2 per cent payroll tax in 1971 would have added £100 million to export costs which could not be offset by charges elsewhere.

*Motor fuel duty*    Motor fuel duty had been put forward by the Royal Institute for Public Administration to the Royal Commission on Local Government as a way of providing local government with increased income. Local authorities could either collect the duty themselves, or have it passed on by the Government. There would be extra administrative costs if the local authorities were to administer their own scheme.

At the time, a transfer of about one-third of motor fuel duty could have compensated authorities for a reduction in grant from 60 to 50 per cent, though perceptibility would be weak in areas where there were many purchases by people from outside an authority. The Government saw motor fuel duties as vital to the regulation of the economy; and thus the larger the share of the tax given to local authorities, the greater the threat to economic control. Again, areas with large sales of petrol would tend to have lower tax rates and therefore attract more economic activity.

*Car licence duty*    Ownership of motor vehicles was seen as another possible candidate for local taxation. In 1971 the local authorities were agents for central government in the collection of vehicle duty, though the system was in the process of being transferred to a central computer. Local vehicle duty would have, according to the Government, to be collected centrally and then passed back to authorities, and it could not be undertaken before 1980.

Yield from the existing rate of duty would have allowed a cut in central grant from 60 to 53 per cent – a higher rate of duty could have reduced the percentage to the Government's 50 per cent target. As the rate of growth in car ownership was slowing at this time, it appeared likely that the rate of duty would have regularly to be increased. While the duty on private cars would be perceptible, there might be problems in taxing cars used partly for business. There would be additional administrative costs and possibly attempts by motorists to register cars in low-tax areas. There would be no significant economic effects of a local vehicle duty.

*(b)   Rating Reforms*
Having analysed a number of entirely new taxes, the Government looked at ways of increasing the yield of rates. First, the possibility of 'super-rating' was considered. It would work by increasing non-domestic rate poundages faster than those for householders. There would be no extra administrative costs. Either non-domestic ratepayers as a whole could be required to pay a certain pecentage above the rate poundage paid by the domestic ratepayers, or increases in the rate poundages for domestic property could be fixed at a proportion of the increases for non-domestic ratepayers. The latter form would entail a progressive, and cumulative, kind of domestic de-rating on top of the domestic element of RSG.

In order to cut grant from 60 to 50 per cent, non-domestic property would have to pay a super-rate of 50 per cent on top of existing rates. To fill the gap between spending increases and the rise in rates and grants, the Government estimated that rate poundages for non-domestic properties would have to rise by about 1½ per cent a year faster than for domestic ratepayers if grant was to be held at a constant proportion.

Super-rating would be a tax on investment and would add to industrial and commercial costs. Much of its burden would not fall locally and it would not therefore be perceptible. The Government concluded that it would be necessary to prescribe nationally the maximum level of super-rating.

A second reform to rating considered was a surcharge on earning non-householders. It would have the advantage of reducing the criticism of rates which argued that a large number of people did not contribute directly to rates. The example of a family of wage-earners living next door to a single old-age pensioner was given to support the fairness argument. The Government then disputed this criticism of rates, pointing out that earners pay towards the cost of central grants to local government. In addition, identifying those earning and resident would be very difficult and expensive. There would have to be exclusions (i.e. children and pensioners). If the yield from such a tax were equivalent to 20 per cent of current domestic rates (which the Government considered a maximum), for each additional earner per household the yield would have been no more than 2 per cent of the existing total rate call. About the same yield would have been achieved, it was estimated, by a poll tax of £10 for each earner. Administrative costs would be high.

A third possible rating reform was to change the basis of rates from rental to site values. Rates were (and remain) a tax on the occupation of land and buildings and were charged on the *rental* value of property. With site value rating, rates would be levied on the market rental of the site, on the assumption that it was available for the most profitable permissible development. In favour of site value rating was the argument that the economic rent of the site was created not by the owner but by the community, so that it is fair for the community to recover a share of this value by taxing it. Site value rating would encourage the more effective and economic use of land while it would not tax improvements.

The Government lined up several powerful counter-arguments. First, site valuation would not tax the current resources of a ratepayer, but instead his or her potential resources. This change would exacerbate criticisms already made of the rates that they do not reflect ability to pay. Secondly, it would tax land values in many cases where it was impractical to use the land. Thirdly, the tax would fall on the owners of land rather than on the occupiers, thus weakening the relationship between local taxation and representation. Finally there were problems with administration (e.g. valuation and ascertaining ownership). The Government argued that comparisons with other countries were inappropriate, largely because of the system of planning control which would be crucial in the decision about the value of a particular site.

The fourth possible way of achieving an addition to rate income was the reimposition of rates on agriculture. The Government admitted that re-rating for agriculture was an anomaly and that circumstances were very different in 1971 than when de-rating took place. In addition, the Royal Commission had proposed agricultural rating. However, because of the size of the task of valuing farm property and the time such a valuation might take, it was proposed to leave agriculture in its privileged position.

Having considered new income sources and additional rate income, the Green Paper looked at ways of improving the existing rates and grants. Rates could be improved by extending the scope of rebates and by moving from rental to capital valuation. Alterations in the treatment of empty property were also briefly discussed. The future of the grant system was analysed in a separate appendix.

*(c)   The Grant System*

The appendix started by considering the relative weight to be given to specific and general grants. The Government stated its view that a return to specific grants would be inconsistent with the intention that local government reorganization should bring greater freedom from detailed controls by central government. Thus the Green Paper advocated that as much of central government assistance to local authorities as possible should be given in the form of 'block' grants (i.e. unattached to a particular service), and that as many of the existing specific grants as possible should be absorbed into the block grant.

The purpose of the grant system as a whole was spelled out in paragraph 4.12 of the Green Paper:

> although the Government are seeking to give local authorities as much discretion as possible, they must be concerned with the total demand on national resources arising from the decisions of individual authorities taken as a whole; and must seek to influence these decisions by the amount of grant provided to augment local revenues. In each grant settlement therefore the Government's primary interest will be the prospective total of local authorities' current expenditure; but they will also be concerned in the share to be borne by local taxes and what contribution should be made from national taxation by way of grants.[19]

The Green Paper then went on to consider the objectives of spending need and rateable resources equalization and how they might best be achieved. The objective of the needs element was described as 'the distribution of grant in such a way that the cost for each local authority of providing a standard level of service should be a standard amount per head'. But the Government admitted the impossibility of precisely measuring spending needs and of providing the standard level everywhere. Library facilities in cities and the countryside were cited as an example of the latter problem. Nevertheless the Government made it clear that it would like to produce a more complex formula which it was hoped would reflect spending needs more accurately.

The resources element was intended to achieve an equal rate poundage for a standard level of spending per head. 'Thus if, after the deduction of the needs element and of all grants other than the resources element, the expenditure per head of the authorities which receive resources element were uniform, so would be their rate poundages.'

The Government then considered the existing equalization of rate poundages and the possibility that a better alternative might exist. The Green Paper paragraph about rate poundage equalization raised the argument about the fairness of one kind of equalization as against others which has rarely been considered by government in public:

> equalisation of rate poundages does not necessarily equalise the burden on ratepayers. The wide variations in the rental values of domestic properties through the country lead to similar variations in rateable values, with the result for example that the rateable value of a 3 bedroom Parker Morris house in a northern industrial town may be only half that of a similar house on the south coast. The range for comparable dwellings can be as much as 1 to 3, excluding central London; whose high values would further extend the range. Thus, if rate poundages were equal, the occupant of the house in the north would be paying only half the rates paid by the occupant of the house in the south. It is true that there are also regional variations in the level of wages, but these are not by any means as great; the range of variation in average industrial earnings between regions is only about 14 per cent. Thus the occupier of a house in the south is likely to be paying a substantially higher proportion of his income in rates than the occupier of a similar house in the north of England. To take full account of these variations a revised system might attempt to equalise not rate poundages but rate payments by comparable domestic ratepayers, by bringing into the distribution formula not only rate products per head of population but also variations in the rateable value of standard council houses and variations of average industrial earnings in each county or region.[20]

The regional variations were far less significant for non-domestic ratepayers, for whom the Government considered the existing rate poundage equalization system would suffice. If the equalization base for householders were changed, there would then be a problem because of the different equalization bases in use. This problem might be solved by differential rating of domestic and non-domestic ratepayers.

Having considered the assessment of spending needs and the basis of rateable value equalization, the Green Paper turned to smaller, administrative matters. First, the possibility of moving from biennial to annual grant settlements was examined. While this change would mean a greater burden of negotiation on both central and local government, it could lead to more flexibility and to a closer relationship between the grant system and the public expenditure surveys. Secondly, the possibilities of paying needs element to non-metropolitan district councils and other changes in the payment of grants were considered.

## (6) CONCLUSION: STRUCTURAL REFORM AND FINANCIAL STAGNATION

Efforts at financial and structural reform between 1966 and 1974 were successful only in part. The 1974 reorganization of local government was the most significant structural change since the end of the nineteenth century. Judgement about the success of the reorganization is not a part of this book. It is worth observing, however, that by 1984 the Conservative Government was convinced that county government was not needed in the six metropolitan areas (or in Greater London). Opposition parties had also developed far-ranging plans for the further reorganization of local government.

After the limited reforms following the 1966 White Paper, the possibilities of financial reorganization outlined in the 1971 Green Paper led to even less change. Despite the fact that there was considerable sympathy in government for institutional change (as the structural reform proved), the Government approached financial reform with utter caution. Discussion of potential new taxes was couched in terms of difficulties rather than advantages. Agricultural re-rating, a reform which would have enjoyed widespread support, was ruled out on flimsy grounds (i.e. the difficulty of valuation), which doubtless masked considerable opposition from the powerful farming lobby. For a Government which was embarking on an enormous structural reorganization, the tone of the Green Paper was indeed feeble.

Although the Conservative Government's proposals were for a structure and division of functions that were different from those proposed by the Royal Commission, the new map of local government did mean that the average size of authorities would be very much larger than in the old system. In addition, the Royal Commission had made its proposals on the assumption that local government's financial base could be strengthened once a new structure was in place.

Thus, there was support for major institutional reform, while a reorganization of local government was about to create bigger authorities with more equal tax bases and the Royal Commission had proposed structural reform on the assumption that financial reform would follow. Finally, at this time public spending was still growing very rapidly. The Government planned further growth, which meant that any financial changes could have been implemented at a time when (as far as was then known) the system as a whole would be expanding. This implementation would have been far easier when the economy and local authority spending were growing than it would have been in later years when contraction had started. The 1966 Government had been in a similar position, yet the need for financial reform suggested by the publication of the White Paper in 1966 and the 1971 Green Paper did not result in any action to change the basic framework of rates and grants.

Despite the failure of the Government to take action following the 1971 Green Paper, the document itself is interesting because it was the first lengthy official description and discussion of possible reforms to the rating system. It went much further than the 1966 White Paper and, indeed, than the 1981 White Paper on *Alternatives to Domestic Rates*. Also, it was the first contemporary government document to mention poll tax. Yet, like all other government examinations of local government finance, its tone and content suggested immense conservatism and a deep concern not to cause any change which might be unpopular with local taxpayers.

Concerning the possible new taxes for local government, all kinds of objections were raised. Perhaps the most destructive to change, both then and since, is the idea that no change to the tax system can be made quickly, so no change should be made at all. This assertion was used as the argument against agricultural re-rating. Although the arguments for re-rating agricultural land and buildings were strong, 'it would impose a substantial task of valuation on scarce professional staff . . . and could probably not be completed before the 1980s. The Government do not therefore propose to make any changes at present in the treatment of agriculture for rating purposes'.[21] As almost any change of local authority taxation would take some years to introduce (or at least, officials have always argued that this would be the case) the argument used here against re-rating farming would stop – and has stopped – all other possible reform ever since.

On the other hand, the idea that part or all of the education system could be centrally funded was ruled out on the grounds that it would conflict with the idea that local authorities should become more responsible for services they provide. The possibility of the removal of education funding from local government has continued to be suggested from time to time (most notably in annex B of the 1981 Green Paper on *Alternatives to Domestic Rates*). Arguments against the removal of education to the centre have become less persuasive as the Government has latterly been more content to remove parts of local government provision and hand them over to other institutions.

The Green Paper briefly considered a number of trends which have become more significant in recent years. For example, different bases for rating (other than imputed rental values) were considered, while the Government conceded that any new tax which had a centrally imposed limit set on the maximum rate would be no more than a kind of grant. The Government accepted that the needs of equalization should not impede the consideration of new tax sources.

The importance of 'block' grants (i.e. grants paid to authorities without any central direction about how they were to be spent) was emphasized. Recommendations were made in the Green Paper that improvements should be made to the needs equalization part of the grant system, while the Government also touched on the possibility that perhaps rate *bills* rather than rate poundages should be equalized.

Some of the 1971 Green Paper proposals have, subsequently, been accepted. For example, the changes to spending needs assessments discussed in the appendix on government grants did indeed take place from 1974 onwards. A White Paper on the Rate Support Grant[22] published in January 1974 explained that

> no formula can hope to represent these differences in need perfec-
> tly. But it is clear that the present system needs updating in the light
> of changes over the years in the pattern of local government activity
> and of the future changes that reorganisation will bring. For the
> present, the Government consider that the best available indicator
> of spending need is the pattern of recent past expenditure.

But the assessment of spending needs on the basis of past expenditure was soon criticized by lower-spending authorities on the grounds that it encouraged authorities to spend higher (and thus would feed back into higher future needs assessments). By the time that the Conservatives were re-elected in 1979, there was considerable pressure – in particular from lower-spending, Conservative-controlled, shire and district councils – to get away from assessments based on past spending. Block grant (discussed at length later) incorporated a new method of spending need assessment which largely avoided direct reference to past spending patterns.

Another consequence of the 1971 Green Paper was the move to annual grant settlements from 1974–5 onwards. While this led to less predictability for recipients it was expected to allow greater year-to-year flexibility for both the Government and local authorities. Also, the hope that settlements could more easily be related to the Government's public spending survey each year could now be realized. These changes eventually led (after 1976) to the ever-increasing involvement of local authorities in the Treasury's Public Expenditure White Paper and to less stability in each year's RSG settlement for individual councils.

Finally, the idea that grant should be paid to each tier of local government was accepted in 1979–80, though it was not until 1981–2 and the introduction of block grant that every county and district authority received grant directly to equalize for variations in spending needs and rateable resources.

The Local Government Act 1974 replaced the existing legislation (the Local Government Act 1966) dealing with government grants to local authorities. But the system established in 1966 was not significantly altered. The changes to such things as spending needs assessments, and attempts to use RSG in a way which involved greater central direction of resources during the years between 1974 and 1979, exaggerated the concerns already expressed with the system. Finally, the 1974 Act introduced the Transport Supplementary Grant as a new grant for current and capital transport spending.

Improving and strengthening the finance of local government was recognized as important by the Conservative Government which reorganized local authority structure in 1974. This importance was, in the end, deemed secondary to avoidance of change in local tax burdens and service levels and to the problems associated with changing the tax system. Small changes in the system of finance would not lead to major year-on-year effects. In addition, the fact that any major reform of finance would be unlikely to take place within the life of the government made major reform appear hopelessly long-term. Local authority finance went unreformed into the aftermath of the 1974 reorganization and the succession of national economic crises in the mid-1970s.

NOTES: CHAPTER 4

1   Royal Commission on Local Government in England 1966–9, Chairman the Rt Hon. Lord Redcliffe-Maud, Report, Cmnd 4040 (London: HMSO, 1969).
2   Ibid.
3   Ibid., para. 511.
4   Ibid., Vol. III, appendix 6.
5   Ibid., para. 524.
6   Ibid., para. 527.
7   Ibid., para. 531.
8   Ibid., para. 536.
9   Royal Commission on the Constitution, Report, Cmnd 5460 (London: HMSO, October 1973).
10  *Reform of Local Government in England*, Cmnd 4276 (London: HMSO, February 1970).
11  *Local Government in England: Government Proposals for Reorganization*, Cmnd 4584 (London: HMSO, February 1971).
12  Ibid.
13  *The Future Shape of Local Government Finance*, Cmnd 4741 (London: HMSO, July 1971).
14  Ibid., para. 1.9.
15  Ibid., para. 1.17.
16  Ibid., para. 1.22.
17  Ibid., appendix 2, para. 2.6.
18  Ibid., appendix 2, para. 2.20.
19  Ibid., appendix 4, para. 4.12.
20  Ibid., appendix 4, para. 4.26.
21  Ibid., appendix 2, para. 2.79.
22  *The Rate Support Grant 1974–5*, Cmnd 5532 (London: HMSO, January 1974).

# Chapter 5

# THE GRANT SYSTEM AND RATES
# AFTER REORGANIZATION

## (1) INCREASING INSTABILITY

The 1974 local government reorganization in England and Wales was not greeted with enthusiasm. In addition to criticisms of the new structure, there were allegations of big increases in staff numbers, and in particular of administrators. Rates rose by over 25 per cent in 1974–5, which was one of the chief reasons cited by the Layfield Committee for the emergence of a 'crisis' in local government finance. These new concerns were added to the existing dissatisfaction with local authority finance.

The Layfield Committee (which is considered in the next chapter) took evidence at a time when rates and grants were becoming very unstable by comparison with the past. In 1975–6 the Government increased the grant percentage to 66.5 per cent (compared with 60.5 per cent in 1974–5) in an attempt to keep rate rises down. In the event, rate rises in 1975–6 averaged about 30 per cent, which was well ahead of the rate of inflation.

In addition to the use of grant to attempt to depress the increase in rates, the RSG became of greater interest for a number of other reasons during the years from 1974 onwards. First, the level of grant attained in 1975–6 (66.5 per cent) was the highest ever. Second, the method of assessing spending needs within the needs element was based on an analysis of past spending patterns from 1974–5 onwards. Third, grant became more susceptible to manipulation by the Government. Finally, the economic crisis which continued through much of the mid-1970s led the Government to cut the grant percentage from 1976–7 onwards in an attempt to reduce the volume of local authority current spending.

A grant percentage of 66.5 per cent was far higher than in earlier years. Figure App. 4 and Table App. 9 show how the grant percentage had risen continuously. The steady increase in the proportion of local income derived from government grants increased concerns (expressed by Layfield) that greater central control might follow. The size of the grant became an issue in itself.

Adoption of the new method of assessing spending need involved a more complex technique than that previously used. Although the new procedure had been proposed by a previous government in the 1971

Green Paper, the new method was unpopular with lower-spending councils. This unpopularity was intensified when there was a significant shift of assessed spending need towards the city areas and away from the shire counties. These issues will be discussed in more detail later.

The Government decided to use RSG (in particular the needs element) to assist other policy initiatives. In particular, the inner-cities policy of the Labour Government led to manipulation of the grant system which caused a shift of needs element into the city areas. Both the needs element and London Rate Equalization arrangements were used to shift considerable sums of grant into the urban areas.

Having regularly used the grant to attempt to keep down rate rises in the years from 1966 to 1975, the economic crises of the mid-1970s convinced the Government to cut the grant so as to discourage expenditure. From the peak of 66.5 per cent of relevant expenditure, grant fell to 65.5 per cent in 1976–7 and to 61.0 per cent in 1977–8. In addition, the Government penalized local government in 1976–7 by holding back £50 million when revised budgets exceeded planned spending levels by between 2.5 and 3 per cent.

The operation of the RSG between 1974 and 1981 became more controversial and came to involve much greater complexity. Details of the system will be considered next.

(2)  OPERATION OF THE GRANT SYSTEM

The details of each year's grant arrangements were published in an annual Rate Support Grant Order. This covered the three elements of grant known as the needs, resources and domestic element and, in addition, the specific and supplementary grants paid to local authorities. The name 'Rate Support Grant' became used to describe either the three elements alone or the three plus the specific and supplementary grants. Often (and correctly) the term 'aggregate Exchequer grant' was used in describing all the grants included within the RSG Order.

The process of negotiation between central and local government which evolved during the 1970s existed, with only small changes, beyond the introduction of block grant in 1981–2. Each year negotiations took place between central government and local authorities about the amount of total local government spending in the next year, about the grant percentage and about the distribution of the aggregate grant. From 1975 onwards a 'Consultative Council on Local Government Finance' became the official forum for discussion. This body was chaired by the Secretary of State for the Environment, and had as members secretaries of state or ministers from each government department with an involvement with local government (i.e. Education and Science, Health and Social Security, the Home Office,

Transport, the Treasury and Environment), supported by their senior civil servants. The local authorities' associations were represented by senior elected members from constituent authorities and officers from the London headquarters of the associations.

The Consultative Council was set up as the forum for negotiations between local and central government. The procedures for negotiation have remained much the same in the years since 1975. Each year the council gave a remit to its officers, who then undertook detailed work under the control of the Official Steering Group. This work took place in a number of sub-groups. The most important sub-group was the Grants Working Group, which was concerned with the detail of each year's grant distribution methodology. Another important sub-group was the Forecasting Working Group, which along with its own sub-groups was responsible for discussions about the detail of each year's RSG. This machinery continues to operate (with some modifications and name changes) in the system of grants which has operated since 1981–2. Figure App. 11 shows the 1976 negotiating machinery, while Figure App. 12 shows the 1984 arrangements.

The work done at officer level in these groups began in the spring of each year, when the Consultative Council gave the remit for the following year (i.e. for slightly more than a year ahead). In April or early May details became available about the level of spending and rates in the financial year just started. Discussions about spending and grant for the next year then took place in the early and mid-summer, before the publication of reports from the various sub-groups in July. In these earlier years (i.e. before the introduction of block grant in 1981–2) negotiations took place over a more relaxed timetable than has subsequently been the case.

Following the work done by officers, the secretary of state decided on a total for local government current spending for the next year. This decision was generally taken just before the time of the RSG settlement in November or December each year. Having set a total of expenditure, the Environment Secretary decided the level of aggregate Exchequer grant. This decision, like that about the overall level of expenditure, took place in the light of the most recent Public Expenditure White Paper and any changes the Treasury might have made in the intervening period. The aggregate Exchequer grant (which is generally expressed as a percentage of 'relevant expenditure')[1] was then divided into several parts. First, the specific and supplementary grants were removed. The remaining part of the aggregate grant was what is usually known as the 'Rate Support Grant'.

RSG was, as has been explained, divided into three parts: the needs, resources and domestic elements. Domestic element was set first. The total cost of the relief to all householders was then taken from the RSG available. The remaining RSG was then divided between the resources element and needs element in the ratio of 1 (resources) to 2 (needs).

Needs element was to be calculated using different factors from those used between 1967–8 and 1973–4. In those years, as was outlined earlier, grant was distributed according to population, with extra amounts for social and demographic factors.[2] From 1974–5 onwards the Government considered that the best available indicator of spending need was the pattern of recent past spending.[3] This change in the method of calculation did not mean that needs element would be directly related to an authority's own expenditure in the previous year, but that authorities with similar populations and other characteristics should have similar assessed spending needs.

A statistical technique known as 'multiple regression analysis' was used to assess spending need. The rationale for moving from the relatively simple system which had operated up to 1974 to the new regression-based approach was that successive governments had accepted that needs element was not giving sufficient recognition to the problems of city areas with declining populations. The pre-1974 needs element, by using a formula which was largely distributed in relation to population and school population, had ensured that areas with falling population (in particular the inner cities) had lost grant.

Because it was judged unreasonable to base authorities' needs elements on their actual past spending, some other form of assessment was sought which took account of previous spending patterns without being directly tied to them. Multiple regression analysis was chosen because it allowed factors which were judged likely to create the need for expenditure to be compared with actual spending patterns. On the basis of the regression analysis, a formula was calculated which allocated needs element. This formula consisted of an amount per head plus amounts for 'education units', 'social services units', sparsity and for authorities in urban or semi-urban areas. The units for education and social services were made up by reference to likely demand for provision in particular services (e.g. primary and nursery pupils, home helps).

The new factors used to distribute needs element were more numerous and less comprehensible than those used in the years before 1974. In the first year of the new system (1974–5) there was a relatively small formula. It consisted of a number of basic factors (e.g. £16.62 multiplied by an authority's 1972 population) plus some more complex indicators (e.g. £112.95 multiplied by the number of 1972–3 eduction units in excess of 200 per 1,000 population). The use of separately calculated 'units' for education and social services made the system less simple than it had previously been, even an untrained mind could resonably understand roughly what was going on.

By 1980 the needs element had become unbelievably complicated.

Table App. 16 shows the 1979–80 RSG needs element factors for non-metropolitan counties and metropolitan districts. The RSG Order 1978 (for 1979–80) included pages of factors for each type of authority, expressed in an unreadable way. A single example will make the point:

(i) The number of men 65 years of age and over and women 60 years of age or over living alone in their area at the date of the 1971 census, multiplied by the number of persons 65 years of age or over living in their area on 30 June 1977 and divided by the number of persons 65 years of age or over living in their area at the date of the 1971 census, insofar as the resultant number exceeds 2.73 per 100 of the population of their area;

Multiplying that number by £355.6.

Each type of authority had a formula involving twenty or more such factors. These were derived from the multiple regression analysis mentioned earlier. On the basis of this formula, each authority in receipt of needs element could calculate its needs element.

Resources element had been used from 1967–8 to 1973–4 to supplement the rate base of authorities with below-average rateable values. From 1974–5 authorities with rateable values per head below a centrally set 'national standard' level would receive assistance. The national standard level for 1974–5 was set at £154, which was well above the previous average level. This increase in the 'standard' level meant that resources element (and thus resources equalization) became a more important part of the grant distribution from 1974–5 onwards.

The needs and resources elements taken together were designed to equalize for authorities' varying spending needs and rateable resources. Because of the raising of the national 'standard' rateable value per head to £154 in 1974 (it rose to £178 by 1980–1), the rateable resource base of authorities was more fully equalized after 1974 than before. Those who believed that the new method of needs assessment used from 1974–5 onwards was an improvement on the simple system also believed that expenditure need equalization had been improved. Much further research was undertaken between 1974–5 and 1979–80 in the attempt to refine and improve spending needs assessment.

Although the national system achieved a greater degree of equalization, authorities in Greater London were treated somewhat differently from the rest of England and Wales. The difference arose because of London's very high rateable values. Logically, the equalization objective of the needs and resources elements ought to have implied a 'negative' resources element and would have removed the enormous rateable value advantage which London enjoyed over the rest of the country. But because negative grants were not allowed, authorities with above-standard rateable values (including many in London) simply received no resources grant. Any above-standard rateable values per head were therefore an advantage to the authorities concerned.

Part of London's rateable value advantage *was* removed through the 'claw-back' of part of London's needs element. This reduction of needs element was set by the Government on a judgemental basis. In addition to this treatment of London's high rateable resources, needs element operated slightly differently in the capital from the rest of England and Wales. Needs grant entitlements calculated on the basis of the national regression analysis were made to outer and inner London. These entitlements were then pooled. Separate needs assessments were then made for the Greater London Council, the Metropolitan Police, the Inner London Education Authority and the inner and outer boroughs. Thus, both the boroughs and precepting authorities in London had a needs element entitlement. But for legislative reasons, needs grant was paid only to the boroughs, with the precepting authorities' entitlements paid to each borough in proportion to its population. On top of this, there were special London Rate Equalization arrangements which took part of the rateable resources advantage of the wealthiest central London boroughs and redistributed it to the other boroughs.

The possibility of changing London's claw-back offered the Government a way of influencing grant distribution in addition to changes in needs element. If the claw-back was increased, London would receive relatively less grant, and the rest of the country more. In fact, the Government chose in the late 1970s to reduce the claw-back and thus give London a bigger share of the national needs element.

The domestic element continued to give the secretary of state the power to prescribe differing amounts in the £ as domestic relief for different rating authorities. The Government decided to use this power to protect domestic ratepayers to some extent from big rate rises arising from the reorganization of local government. These rises were even bigger than they looked, because the 1974–5 rates excluded water and sewerage charges. The latter services were transferred from local government to Regional Water Authorities in 1974. Compared with the previous level of 6 pence off domestic rates, the level of domestic element was increased to a minimum of 7 pence in 1974–5 with greater amounts in those areas where domestic ratepayers would otherwise have been liable to exceptional increases in rates because of the reorganization.*

A number of specific grants continued to be paid (e.g. for police, Commonwealth immigrants and improvement grants). A new 'supplementary grant' was introduced for authorities whose area included

---

* The incoming Labour administration in 1974 fixed the domestic element as a uniform 13p off domestic rate poundages in England and 33.5 in Wales.

the whole or part of a national park in respect of the whole or part of any proportion of the estimated expenditure on national parks which the secretary of state considered appropriate. Another supplementary grant was introduced (under the 1974 Act) for transport. This operated from 1975–6 onwards.

The new needs element was considerably more complex than the previous arrangements. From 1974–5 onwards, more effort was put by the local authorities' associations into the annual negotiations for RSG in an attempt to influence the outcome in favour of particular groups of authorities. The process of negotiation which proceeded each RSG settlement became more important in the years following 1974, because of this increased use of the grant system by central government to achieve more openly political and economic ends.

At this time needs element was paid to non-metropolitan counties, metropolitan districts and London boroughs. For 1979–80 and 1980–1 only, part of the needs element paid to non-metropolitan counties was given directly to non-metropolitan districts. The split between non-metropolitan counties and their districts was made on the basis of expenditure by each tier in the three previous years (on average). The total of needs element thus available for non-metropolitan districts was then distributed on the basis of population (75 per cent) and assessed spending needs (25 per cent). District council spending needs were determined using average spending in the three previous years as a proxy for assessed spending needs.

Throughout this period resources element on account of spending by both county and district authorities was paid to rating authorities (i.e. non-metropolitan districts, metropolitan districts and London boroughs). Thus while metropolitan districts received needs and resources elements, metropolitan counties set their precepts without any reference to grant. The split of grants in this way (i.e. without direct reference to relative totals of spending by each tier) meant that the rates and precepts levied by counties and districts in non-metropolitan areas, metropolitan areas and London were effected differently by the grant system. Domestic element was simply used to lower the total rate (including precept).

(3) AN ASSESSMENT OF RSG

The RSG (and the needs element in particular) became increasingly unpopular following the 1974 reforms. Greater complexity was accompanied by a greater willingness on the part of central government to switch grant about the country while simultaneously reducing the overall level of grant support.

The 1976 White Paper *Policy for the Inner Cities*[4] made it clear that the Government wanted to use RSG to bring about specific social and economic objectives:

When allocating the needs element of rate support grant, successive Governments have sought to increase sensitivity of the grant
distribution to the differences between local authorities' spending
needs. As a result, more account has been taken of the problems of
urban authorities and a greater share of needs element has been
allocated to London and the metropolitan areas. The Government
intend to ensure that full account continues to be taken of the needs
of authorities with severe urban problems.[5]

Table 5.1 shows how the shares of needs and resources
elements of each group of authorities changed between 1975–6 and
1979–80. There was a considerable shift of grant into London at the
expense of the non-metropolitan areas. The metropolitan counties
and districts received a similar share of grant throughout the period.

Table 5.1

|         | Non-metropolitan areas | Metropolitan areas | London |
|---------|------------------------|--------------------|--------|
| 1975–6  | 57.3                   | 29.4               | 13.3   |
| 1976–7  | 56.1                   | 29.0               | 14.9   |
| 1977–8  | 54.8                   | 30.1               | 15.1   |
| 1978–9  | 53.7                   | 29.6               | 16.7   |
| 1979–80 | 53.4                   | 29.6               | 17.0   |

*Source*: Local authorities' associations, *Rate Support Grant (England) 1982–3*, p. 28.

At the same time as this redistribution of RSG took place, the
Government began to level off and then to reduce the percentage of
relevant expenditure met by RSG. The percentage of grant support in
the years 1974–5 is shown in Table 5.2.

Table 5.2

| 1974–5  | 65.3% (includes special provision) |
|---------|------------------------------------|
| 1975–6  | 66.5%                              |
| 1976–7  | 65.5%                              |
| 1977–8  | 61.0%                              |
| 1978–9  | 61.0%                              |
| 1979–80 | 61.0%                              |

*Source*: Local authorities' associations, *Rate Support Grant 1980–1* (Eleventh Period),
p. 74.

The combined effect of lower grant percentages and redistribution
of needs element towards the cities meant that many authorities
(particularly the non-metropolitan counties and districts) found their

grant share falling and began to push for reform of the system.

The shire counties and districts criticized both the needs and resources elements on the grounds that they encouraged higher expenditure. It was argued that needs element would encourage higher spending because the indicators used to distribute it were calculated by reference to past spending; classes of authorities which pushed up their spending would tend to receive higher needs element in future and would thus spend higher still. Resources element encouraged spending, it was said, because authorities' resource base would be supported by the Government for *any* level of spending. Worse still, any extra resources element paid to high-spending councils as their spending increased would be removed from the receipts of lower-spending authorities. (Resources element was limited in total each year, which meant that if some authorities increased their receipts by putting up their spending, others would inevitably receive less. There was a 'close-ending' adjustment each year to ensure that the total paid out in resources element was the same as the amount available.)

Although such criticisms were often made by the non-metropolitan areas, there was little evidence to support them. Needs element based on regression analysis in principle accepted that higher spending required greater needs element support. So, even if the regression analysis approach to needs assessment *did* lead to some higher-spending authorities pushing up their spending, this would have been consistent with the logic of the system. The Association of County Councils argued that regression analysis should be dropped in favour of simpler and more judgemental methods of assessment.

The Government chose to use RSG far more assertively during the late 1970s. As the economy faltered and unemployment rose, Labour tried first to keep up local spending while subsidizing the ratepayer via higher grants, and later to cut spending by cuts in the grant. Concern with the industrial collapse of the inner-city areas led Peter Shore (the Environment Secretary) to shift the needs element from the non-metropolitan areas into the cities. This meant that the previously uncontroversial annual grant negotiations became the scene of regular arguments between the Associations of County Councils and District Councils on the one hand and the Association of Metropolitan Authorities and the London Boroughs' Association on the other about the make-up of the needs element. The divide between urban and rural areas created by the 1974 reorganization of local authority structure undoubtedly exaggerated the extent of the disagreement between the associations. The rapid move to more complex methods of spending needs assessments was made by the Government in part to cover the increasing political manipulation of the needs element.

Other Government actions at this time confirm the move towards greater central involvement in local activity. For example, the Transport Secretary (William Rogers) changed the distribution of the transport supplementary grant in an attempt to bring about changes in local authority spending on transport. In 1979–80 cuts in TSG were used so as to punish both Oxfordshire and South Yorkshire for levels of bus subsidy of which the Government did not approve. Oxfordshire was subsidizing its buses too little for the Government's liking and South Yorkshire was giving too much subsidy. The next chapter will examine the Government's proposals to change the needs and resources elements: in evidence to the Layfield Committee in 1975 and in the 1977 Green Paper on *Local Government Finance*, the Government proposed combining the two elements into a 'unitary' grant. Such a combined grant would have meant further central influence over local spending (it was in fact introduced in 1981–2, though called 'block' grant).

Central grants to local authorities thus became more political after 1974. The Labour Government between 1974 and 1979 set the scene for greater central intervention from 1979 onwards. Not only had a precedent been set for using the grant for political and economic ends, but the whole question of whether local authorities should be subject to detailed central control had been raised. As resources became less available, a considerable body of opinion built up in favour of ensuring that the remaining money was spent in a way which the Government wanted. This intensified demands for central involvement. The scene was set for the Conservatives' move towards more obvious control from 1979 onwards.

NOTES: CHAPTER 5

1 Relevant expenditure is the definition of local authority expenditure (wider than 'current' expenditure) used as the basis of aggregate Exchequer grant. It includes current expenditure, plus revenue contributions to capital outlay, loan charges and contributions to the Housing Revenue Account, net of any interest receipts.
2 *The Rate Support Grant, 1974–5*, Cmnd 5532 (London: HMSO, January 1974), para. 14.
3 Ibid., p. 11.
4 *Policy for the Inner Cities*, Cmnd 6845 (London: HMSO, June 1977).
5 Ibid., p. 11, para. 48.

*Chapter 6*

# THE LAYFIELD COMMITTEE

Just after the 1974 reorganizations of local government in England and Wales, the Government set up a Departmental Committee chaired by Mr (now Sir) Frank Layfield. This was seen at the time as an immediate response to the very large rate increases in 1974 (see the start of the previous chapter). The terms of reference were: 'To review the whole system of local government finance in England, Scotland and Wales, and to make recommendations.' The committee reported in just under two years. The report and its appendices were, and remain, important both for their conclusions and as works of reference.

### (1) CRITICISMS OF LOCAL GOVERNMENT FINANCE

The report opened by describing a crisis in local authority finance. Pinning a general concern with the rating system specifically to rate rises in 1974, the committee believed that anger at rate rises that accompanied reorganization 'brought to a head many of the reservations and dissatisfactions with the operation of local government finance felt by both the government and local authorities'.[1]

Public complaints were summarized as:

(a)  The rating system: it was suggested that there was no apparent link between rate demands and ability to pay. Lump-sum payments made rates more difficult to pay than other taxes. Also, businesses claimed that because rates applied only to part of their capital costs, rating affected some businesses more than others.

(b)  Incomprehensibility: rateable value was alleged to be difficult to understand, and did not vary in any acceptable way with the capital or productive value of property. Revaluations were too infrequent.

(c)  Rate increases: the largest single complaint received by the committee was the size of rate rises in 1974, though the committee pointed out that within the average there were significant variations.

(d)  Local authority spending: the committee also received many complaints about extravagance by local authorities, with the examples of official cars, members' expenses and hospitality allowances being most frequently mentioned. Lavish standards in capital works were also criticized, as was the 1974 reorganization.

(e) Over-staffing: local government reorganization was criticized by the public for increasing staff and salary levels.

(f) Lack of control over expenditure: the committee was often told that authorities decided what to spend first, then thought about the rate effects. Major projects were undertaken without any consideration about the long-term cost. Direct labour organizations were singled out for particular criticism.

(g) Inadequacy of local authority income: it was suggested that local authorities were slow to take opportunities to increase non-rate income. Undercharging for services, under-use of land and buildings, the retention of hidden subsidies, and failure to secure the maximum return from redevelopment projects were all cited. On the other hand, it was often claimed that the limitations of local authority income, in particular caused by the unpopularity of the rates, starved councils of the resources required to fulfil their functions adequately.

(h) Government expenditure: it was widely suggested to the committee that many of the services currently provided by local government were really national in character, run by councils in the interests of the nation as a whole. It was further suggested that the Government should pay a much larger share of the bill. Alternatively, services could be transferred to central government departments.

However, the committee pointed out that many of those who gave evidence were uncertain where responsibility really lay both for services and for the scale of expenditure on them. A public opinion survey carried out to examine such issues showed that knowledge of the system of local finance was very limited. Over half of those interviewed believed that local government paid for hospitals. Those who knew most about the system tended to be most critical of it. Rates were thought to be less fair than VAT or income tax. The general level of service was thought to be reasonable.

Local authority criticisms of the system centred on rates and on the relationship between central and local government. Councils did not condemn the rating system wholesale, pointing out that many of its difficulties were created by the inadequacy and infrequency of rating revaluations. Particular concern was expressed that the rating system had been undermined because governments had granted partial or total relief to some classes of property, notably domestic, agricultural and that occupied by charities.

A complaint about rating shared by local authorities and many members of the public was its lack of 'buoyancy'. (That is, its yield did not rise in line with costs and incomes without changes in the tax rate.) This lack of buoyancy trapped councils between demands from the Government and public for higher services and the difficulty of putting the tax rate up. Some authorities suggested that a single source of tax based on property was too small a base from which to finance a wide and expanding range of public services.

Local authorities strongly criticized the Government for its contradictory attitude. On the one hand some government departments urged authorities to develop and expand their services. Legislation was promoted, circulars were published and loan sanctions were granted for capital expenditure, thus encouraging expansion or improvement. Simultaneously, other parts of Government were asking for spending cuts and economy. Central government was roundly criticized for its lack of co-ordination. It was claimed that the Government proclaimed the principle of local discretion embodied in the general grant system, while individual departments meddled freely in the detail of individual services. The artificial distinction between capital and current spending was said to create an impediment to effective choice in spending plans.

There was also much concern among local authorities about the whole process of macro-economic control. Public expenditure forecasting was said to be inaccurate and not to take into account authorities' priorities or the costs and consequences of new legislation. Cuts in planned spending were often made suddenly and took no account of the real time needed to make cuts in services. Finally, the grant system gave no indication of likely distribution beyond the next year. Rate Support Grant was not announced until so late in the year that planning was made very difficult.

The committee also examined the Government's criticisms of local authority finance. These criticisms were in some cases judged to concern crucial issues. For example, departments were concerned about the continuing rise in local authority spending, which was greater than the rise in gross domestic product or central government spending. This could not be allowed to continue, the Treasury argued, because it impaired the Government's ability to manage the economy successfully. The Government was also worried about the level of grant. As has been shown, RSG had been pushed up in order to keep rate increases down – which, it was thought, might in turn have encouraged higher spending by local authorities.

## (2)  THE ORIGINS OF DISCONTENT

Having described the major criticisms of local government finance, Layfield went on to look at their origins. It was shown how expenditure had vastly increased in real terms and as a proportion of gross national product. The shift from funding spending out of rates to greater reliance on grant income (described in Chapter 3), the real rise in rates, the increase in manpower and the move to general grants were also outlined. From within these trends, Layfield concluded that a 'crisis' had emerged.

The 1974 rate rises were deemed to be the crucial factor in provoking the crisis over rates, though Layfield expected future years to produce less severe changes. The big rate rises were partly because of inflation, which was the second influence on the crisis. After many years of low inflation, prices rose very quickly during late 1973 and throughout 1974. Local authorities' costs had tended to rise more quickly than those in the rest of the economy, thus pushing rates up even more quickly than rapidly rising prices. Uncertainty caused authorities to build up contingency provision and thus rate even higher.

The criticisms of rating, while contributing to the crisis, were of long standing. The impact of rates was said to be unfair, in ways shown by the Allen Committee, and while rate rebates had mitigated this to some extent, they also reduced accountability. Wide variations in rateable values for similar property and the irregularity of revaluations were also deemed part of the problem.

Rate Support Grant was also believed to have led to a crisis. The 1974 Local Government Act, as we saw earlier, changed the needs element so it took greater account of authorities' past spending behaviour. Grant was redistributed towards the metropolitan areas and away from the rural counties. These shifts compounded the effects of inflation, reorganization and the continuing increase in real spending, and produced unacceptably large rate rises in many areas. The committee also cited examples of authorities which had had widely different rate increases between 1974–5 and 1975–6 while increasing their spending by the same amount.

Reorganization of local government in 1974 had added to the problems of finance. Local authorities tended to take on staff and to pay higher salaries. Many had run down their reserves and others had taken on new capital projects without the usual concern for future costs. On top of all this, there was general dislike of the new structure which, according to Layfield, heightened disenchantment with local government finance.

The last cause of the crisis was rising expenditure. Much of it arose from new legislation and central government requirements. Demographic changes had made the increases even faster by increasing the demand for major services. Layfield also felt that local authority expenditure was such that it could not be cut suddenly, at the command of new central government policy. While future economic upturn might relieve the pressure on the system, it was necessary to ensure that local authority finance was strong enough to withstand future economic uncertainties.

(3)  ANALYSIS

Layfield pointed out that many of the problems of local government finance had been considered by governments and Royal Commissions since the nineteenth century. Numerous Acts had reformed parts of the system, though none had attempted to restructure the whole. Indeed, the committee felt that there had been no settled policy on local authority services or spending. It might have been expected that a single government department might co-ordinate policy.

> The Treasury does not take that role. Since the First World War the department concerned in England and Wales has been, initially, the Ministry of Health, then the Ministry of Local Government and Planning, later renamed the Ministry of Housing and Local Government, and since 1970, the Department of the Environment. The role of these departments in the formulation or co-ordination of government policy on local authority expenditure has been rather limited. Their work has been concerned mainly with the co-ordination and discussion of grants, between the various departments, local authorities and their associations.[2]

The committee then listed a number of questions which were discussed in its report. The questions included, for example: 'What is the function of the government in regard to local authorities' total expenditure or expenditure on individual services? What are the means of carrying out that function?' This and the thirteen others listed at the end of chapter 2 of the report are still crucial in the debate about the future of local government finance.

The report examined local government's place in the constitution; the relationship between central and local government; value for money; capital; fees and charges; rating; new sources of income; grants; macro-economic issues and possible reforms. Perhaps the most important features of the report were, first, its analysis of the relationship of central and local government and, second, its conclusions. They will be examined next, before moving on to consider the views of the government departments which submitted evidence to the committee.

*The Relationship between Central and Local Government*
The committee examined the relationship between central and local government, on the grounds that the financial arrangements devised for local authorities would have to support the desired relationship. This meant having to establish what the relationship actually was. For example, the report discerned a general and continuing intention by successive governments to leave local government with services which had strong local character while removing other services with regional

or national characteristics. It was also felt that the widespread view that there was a need for structural reorganization had in the past influenced the Government when it was deciding about what local authorities could and should do.

The relationship had been changed in the 1960s and 1970s by demands throughout central and local government for improved services. Ministers had used the Public Expenditure Survey system (in which local authorities had at that time taken no part) as an instrument to influence local government. The major increases in spending which had taken place had been largely financed by increases in grants from central government.

Although Layfield felt that it was impossible to establish a direct connection between the proportion of grant and the extent of government intervention, it was 'satisfied that the amount of grant, and, more importantly, the fact that total grant was increasing to make development of services possible, powerfully reinforced the political pressures for government intervention'.[3] This view was widely held in both central and local government.

Intervention by central government had not increased solely as an influence on expenditure. Governments (in particular following the 1966 White Paper) had used the grant system to save ratepayers from the additional costs of higher expenditure on services. The committee recognized the practical considerations which politicians felt important:

The interest in the size of the domestic rate which successive governments have shown since the mid-1960s was not, except perhaps in the last two years, primarily due to the effect of local tax levels on prices and incomes policy or other national economic aims. The concern of governments was based on their political judgement of the size of burdens which could tolerably be put on domestic ratepayers.[4]

The committee went on to consider other ways in which intervention by central government had grown and to suggest that the accountability of councillors to their electors had suffered as a consequence. Capital spending and loan sanctions were singled out as areas where control by the centre had grown, while the attempts to cut back on the growth of local authority spending in the mid-1970s were shown to have led to explicit involvement by government departments in the detail of local spending. To be fair to the Government, Layfield pointed out that the authorities themselves had asked for guidance in making cuts, so as to avoid awkward local decisions. The committee concluded that 'this unwillingness of local authorities to accept responsibility is in our view a direct consequence of increasing reliance on grants to finance local services'.

The committee felt that accountability had inevitably been weakened by the fact that increases in local expenditure had largely been met from central taxation, and because the Government had increased its concern with the total of local government spending. As grant had increased, and its distribution had become less predictable, the relationship between changes in spending and in rates had become erratic. The detailed guidance given by ministers to local government, on top of these changes in the grant regime, were gradually convincing the public that central decisions were of overriding importance in determining local behaviour.

In concluding its consideration of the shift of decision-making to the centre and the effect that it was having on accountability, Layfield stated:

Effective control of expenditure cannot be ensured in a system in which local accountability has been seriously weakened, unless central accountability provides that control. Centralisation of expenditure decisions is the inevitable end to which a system depending on high and increasing grants, and associated with an inflexible and politically sensitive local tax, must lead. There is an alternative – namely to revive local accountability. Local councils would be responsible to their electorates for both the expenditure they incurred and the revenue they raised and, above all, for increases in either. It need not be incompatible with the government's proper concern over the totals of local expenditure.[5]

The committee went on to urge the Government to review the relationship between itself and local government, and to decide whether in future responsibility for the provision of local services was to be placed firmly with local or central government. This decision would, in turn, determine the kind of financial system needed. If no decision was taken, it was believed that there would be a continuation of the shift of power to central government.

If central control was chosen by the Government, there would have to be a considerable reform of local government finance. Responsibility would pass to Whitehall for all major spending decisions, current and capital. In a paragraph which was remarkably prescient, in the light of the planned procedures for decision-making in authorities which the Government proposed should have their rates limited by the 1984 Rates Act, Layfield laid out the likely consequences of central control:

Departments would have to deal individually with all, or at least a large number of, local authorities in considerable detail over a wide range of subjects. They would almost certainly have to require the submission of local authority budgets for scrutiny and approval ...

There would be a substantial administrative task, involving in each case the close liaison of a number of departments.[6]

On the other hand, if there were to be greater local responsibility, local authorities would have to become less dependent on central grant and fund a greater part of their spending from local taxation. Local responsibility would require giving local authorities another tax to supplement their rate income. In addition, local authorities would have to be more explicitly treated by the Public Expenditure Survey, and there would have to be greater certainty (over several years) in the level of grant receipts for individual authorities and a better-integrated timetable for grant distribution and local budgeting.

Greater local responsibility would have a number of consequences. First, the Government would lose some of its ability to influence standards of service. Secondly, local authorities would have to put up with greater pressure from interest groups and ratepayers. Thirdly, the pattern of expenditure would be determined to a greater degree by individual councils. Fourthly, the grant negotiations would be less important. Fifthly, audit would have to be strengthened. Finally, if the Government wanted to change its policy towards local authorities, it would have to get parliamentary approval to do so rather than use financial weapons. The committee thought that pressures for uniformity would avoid wide disparities in service standards.

In the light of this consideration of the central–local government relationship, and the detailed examination of local taxation, grants and other items, the committee arrived at a set of proposals.

### (4)  LAYFIELD'S PROPOSALS

Early in the committee's conclusions, it was noted that the commission which considered the structural reorganization of 1974 had not been asked to examine finance, and that 'as a result, a variety of two-tier organisations was adopted with diverse and overlapping responsibilities which present serious obstacles to the creation of a financial system providing clear accountability'.

It was then accepted that the Government 'needs to be able to ensure that changes in public expenditure, including local government expenditure ... do not prejudice its economic objectives', though the committee went on to argue that control over spending on individual services was not necessary. The committee then examined a number of features of local government finance. These included: rates; local income tax; assigned revenues; central funding of minimum standards; grants; fees and charges; capital expenditure and regulation of local government within the national economy. Support was expressed for changes in some of these areas.

Rates should be retained, on the grounds that there was a good case in principle for a property tax. Both domestic and non-domestic rates should be kept, though it was felt that their contribution as a proportion of local government income should not be increased. The rate base should be widened by the addition of agricultural land and buildings to the list of properties which paid rates, while rates ought in future to be assessed on the basis of capital rather than imputed rental values. It was proposed that a full rating revaluation should take place immediately.

Local authority income could, however, be increased by the introduction of a local income tax (LIT). Layfield saw two possibilities for the future of local government finance: to continue with the existing combination of rates and grants, or to introduce LIT. If the new tax were introduced, it would be given to the tier responsible in each area for the bulk of services, leaving both tiers with rates. The percentage of income met by grants could then be cut.

Assigned revenues were explicitly rejected, because, like grants, they put power into the hands of the centre. The idea of taking part or all of an existing service out of local government was also turned down, on the grounds that a service should be centrally funded only if there were no room for local discretion in providing it.

The committee was sympathetic to the idea of attempting to identify the cost of meeting national minimum standards, which would be financed wholly out of central taxation. In such a system, authorities would be free to provide higher standards at local discretion, though higher spending would have to be borne out of local taxation. But there were serious drawbacks to the idea. First, the dividing line between national responsibilities and local discretion was felt to be unclear; and secondly, a system with so many national standards built into it would almost certainly shift power and responsibility to the centre. In a 'note of reservation', Professor Alan Day dissented from the general view of the committee that minimum standards had no future. His note proposed the adoption of such an approach as a 'middle way' between the centralist and localist solutions offered by his colleagues.

Grants were to remain under Layfield's proposals. It was pointed out that if central control were to be increased, the proportion of income made up by grant could also be raised. The committee favoured the retention of a 'general' grant (as opposed to service-specific grants) and (assuming greater local responsibility) a reduction in the grant percentage. Full equalization of needs and resources could, it was argued, be achieved with a level of about 40 per cent if a 'unitary grant' were introduced. Unitary grant would combine the needs and resources elements of RSG into a single grant.

Unitary grant presented a problem for Layfield. While it would have allowed a reduction in grant percentage while still achieving the existing degree of equalization, it also might lead to greater central control:

> A unitary grant would have an obvious place in a system based on central responsibility where the government would be responsible for deciding the main elements of local spending needs. But it would also have some advantages if an approach based on local responsibility were followed. It would permit the achievement of any degree of redistribution to correct for disparities in needs and resources, up to full equalisation, with a much smaller total of grant than with the present system.

The report concluded that unitary grant could fit either a centralist or a localist approach.

The committee believed that grant should not be used by the Government as a short-term regulator of local government spending. Stability was an essential requirement of a grant system, and distribution should be announced as early as possible to allow planning, with a longer-term aim of announcements of grant for up to three years ahead. Accountability would be enhanced by paying grant to each tier of local government. Distribution would have to continue to take account of authorities' different spending needs and their tax-raising capacities, though such capacity should be assessed by reference to aggregate personal income rather than rateable value.

Fees and charges were also considered as a possible way of increasing local income. If charges were to make up a much larger part of income, there would have to be radical changes in social policy. But the committee nevertheless felt that there might be scope for increasing income from charges, and that a review of policy and practice in charging for council services should be set up.

Capital expenditure was examined, though few proposals were made to reform it. Support was tacitly given for the control of capital spending by continued control over borrowing, because it was felt that the Government needed to control public sector borrowing and the relationship between consumption and investment. There should be no write-off of existing borrowing; nor should the Government fund a greater part of capital spending with grants.

The Layfield Committee concluded by offering the Government a choice between increased central control or more local discretion. Under the former, rates and grants would remain as the source of local income, though grants might be increased. The Government would decide what rate poundages it expected local authorities to levy and any departure from them would be clearly identified as the responsibility of the local authority. Spending could be controlled through the allocation of grant and possibly by the limitation of discretionary spending. Council budgets would have to be submitted for approval by the Department of the Environment.

Central control would give the Government a decisive voice in the provision of local services. Local authorities would retain some discretion in services where there had hitherto been little central involvement, and there would remain the possibility of collective pressure by local authorities on central government. On the other hand, it would be difficult in such a system to reconcile the responsibility of councillors to their electorates with the level of ministerial control. Central government would have to find a way of co-ordinating its approach to local authorities.

Local accountability would require that local authorities raised a much greater proportion of their income locally than had previously been the case. Local income tax would thus have to be introduced, though the Government might feel the necessity to limit the extent to which individual councils could vary the proportion of revenue raised from each of the sources. Grant would be cut. Unitary grant would make grant reductions easier than the existing grants, though spending needs assessments would have to be expressed in such a way as to avoid implying that the Government was seeking to determine particular spending levels for each authority. Unitary grant would be paid so as to take account of variations in spending needs and taxable capacity, though in order to give the Government adequate discipline a level of spending would have to be specified for each authority above which the rate of grant payable would be reduced.

Central government's influence over local government under this system would have to allow the Government to influence the rate of growth of spending. The instruments to achieve this influence might include requiring local authorities to raise 'additional taxation' to finance increases in expenditure beyond a specified point and prescribing the proportion of expenditure on capital to be financed out of revenue income. The committee was quite clear in its conclusion that *influence* rather than control should be exerted under the local responsibility system.

A move towards central control could be achieved quickly; local government had anyway been drifting in this way for some time. Local responsibility would take longer, particularly because of the time taken to introduce a local income tax (which would be at least five years). In the short term, grant should be stabilized and local government should be more closely involved in the Public Expenditure White Papers. Fewer circulars and other statements of central policy should be issued.

In its final paragraphs the committee briefly described once more the choice between more central control and increased local responsibility. It was explained that much turns on the value which is placed on local democracy itself. Central responsibility would tend to undermine the role of the local councillor. Most of the contact between government departments and local authorities would probably be between officials. Local government officers would therefore tend to regard themselves as increasingly answerable to government departments rather than council committees ... Shortcomings in local services could be blamed on the inadequacy of the grant ... Ministers and their officials would become answerable to Parliament for local services.

Layfield left the choice between increased central and local responsibility to the Government. If a vital local democracy was to be maintained, it would require the introduction of local income tax. On balance, it was felt that if local government was to remain local, then the costs of introducing LIT would be worth paying. However, the commitee did not come out directly for either alternative, though it was made clear that a majority was in favour of local choice.

The Layfield Report was written after eighteen months of work. The evidence presented to the committee (and published in eight appendices) is interesting not only for the way in which it influenced the report but also because it included several statements of central government thinking at the time. The Treasury, the Department of the Environment and several spending departments gave their views on such issues as macro-economic control, unitary grant and a separate education grant. Before commenting on Layfield, the views of government departments in several areas of policy will be considered.

## (5)   DEPARTMENTAL EVIDENCE TO LAYFIELD

### (a)   Macro-Economic Policy

In a memorandum by the Treasury entitled 'Local Government Taxation: General Fiscal Considerations', officials spelled out their view of central government's responsibilities to oversee local authority finance. It was made clear that local authorities could not be made entirely fiscally independent or wholly responsible for determining their levels and patterns of spending. The reasons given for this were:

First, local government expenditure is an important component of public sector spending as a whole. But the central government is responsible for overall economic and financial management of the economy, including policies which may have a high regional and local content. It follows that the central government's management responsibilities would be much more difficult to discharge satisfactorily without an effective control over the call on real and financial resources made by local government.

Second, the taxable capacity of the community at large at any given time cannot be further tapped by local authorities without reducing the sources of potential revenue available to the central government.

Third, it is the responsibility of central government to ensure some broad equality in the ability to provide public services throughout the country. Since the resources available to individual authorities do not match their needs it inevitably falls on the central government to help towards redressing the balance.[7]

The Treasury went on to explain that, from its point of view, taxes charged by local government needed to have a substantial effect on demand so as to minimize the task of demand management. Because local authority spending and its financing had implications for the allocation of real resources within the economy, as well as for prices and for monetary and financial conditions, the Treasury needed to relate local authority activities to the requirements of national policies.

### (b)  Freedom of Local Government within the Economy

In another memorandum ('Local Discretion and Central Control'), the Treasury outlined a view of the freedom with which local government could act, which evidently flowed from its views about the need for macro-economic control. By conventional standards the Treasury ascribed a somewhat narrow degree of freedom to local authorities: 'they have some degree of freedom, within centrally determined policies, in the administration of individual policies and in the pace at which they develop them'.[8] Later the Treasury explained:

> under present arrangements each authority has freedom, subject to certain real constraints, to determine its overall level of rate fund expenditure. It is this second aspect of local discretion which causes some concern ... because there is always at any given point of time a large overhang of potential local authority expenditure – to take fuller advantage of permissive powers and to implement statutory obligations more quickly and completely.[9]

The Department of the Environment in its memorandum 'Public Expenditure – Central and Local Government Resource Planning' explained that one of the objectives of the central–local relationship should be to ensure for individual local authorities sufficient freedom to decide on resource allocation within their own authorities while again being subject to the need for overall national economic management. In addition, the Government needed to influence policy, and thereby expenditure, on local services of national importance in accordance with national priorities. Other objectives were that individual authorities should have a sufficient assurance of their resource base to plan ahead, and that central government should retain the ability to make political judgements about the balance between public and private expenditure and about the capacity of the economy to bear public spending.

This analysis suggested three areas to the DoE where there might be changes in resource planning. First, there could be closer involvement between central and local government in spending planning over the period covered by the Public Expenditure Survey. Planning of this kind might involve some movement towards strengthened upper-tier local authorities or even to setting up regions. Second, the Government could reduce the level of central control over capital spending by individual authorities (though retaining overall control). The third area for change was current expenditure.

According to the DoE, desirable reforms would have been:

(i) to give the Government power to restrain the growth in local government spending by letting the full marginal cost of expenditure in any year fall on the ratepayer;

(ii) to allow the Government to restrain the local adoption of policies and plans that would carry implications for future years which were not compatible with the likely level of resources to be made available;

(iii) greater stability in grant distribution;

(iv) great announcements for more than the immediate year;

(v) the acceptance (by the Government) of the need for some inflation-proofing to take account of the lack of buoyancy of rates;

(vi) changes in Government planning so as to make local authority longer-term planning possible;

(vii) a fuller flow of information between central and local government to facilitate better corporate planning.

These proposals were intended by the department to be seen alongside those in appendix 7, which outlined a 'combined' grant to replace the existing needs and resources elements of the Rate Support Grant.

*(c)   A 'Combined' Grant to Replace Needs and Resources Elements*
The Department of the Environment's evidence on 'Central Government Grants to Local Government; Some Possible Changes', published in appendix 7 of the Layfield Committee's report, outlined a combined grant to replace the needs and resources elements of RSG.

This proposal re-emerged in the Labour Government's 1977 Green Paper as 'unitary' grant and finally – as 'block' grant – in 1979 in the Conservative Government's Local Government, Planning and Land Bill. The DoE evidence on the subject is thus important as a pointer to the future shape of local government finance and because it explained how some of the reforms suggested by Government departments in other evidence to Layfield might be brought about.

The department outlined the possible new grant. First, an assessment of each authority's spending needs would have to be made, using a formula applied centrally by the Government. Then a rate poundage would have to be set which the Government would ideally like authorities to charge for spending at the assessed spending needs figure. The grant payable would then be the difference between the authority's spending need and the amount it could raise in rates at the standard rate poundage.

Authorities would not be statutorily obliged to fix their rate at the standard level (and therefore could spend above or below the assessed spending need figure). They would be free to levy a higher or lower rate if their own view of their spending needs differed from a figure given by the central formula. That is, authorities would receive grant calculated as the difference between their centrally assessed spending needs and the Government's standard rate poundage regardless of what they decided to spend. There would be no formula to determine higher or lower rate poundages and grant receipts for spending above or below spending need. All spending above this assessed figure would be 100 per cent rate-borne. There would be no incentive to spend over assessed needs in order to attract more grant.

The department explained:

the prominence of the assessment of spending need and of the standard tax rate in the formula would make clear for the first time the respective roles of the government and of the local authority in the authority's rate-making process. That constitutes the first major advantage of the alternative approach though it carries with it the difficulty that the central machinery for assessing needs would have a heavier responsibility to bear and its judgements would be far more open to public debate than at present.[10]

The DoE felt that the explicit measurement of spending needs would allow more public discussion than the existing system, while the needs assessment would become the basis of grant allocation. An additional advantage of the new grant was that it would be possible to equalize spending needs and rateable resources with a very much lower grant, thus allowing the Government more freedom to decide how far additional grant should be given to keep down the level of local taxation generally.

It would be open to the Government to organize the grant system so that authorities which spent above their assessed spending needs were required to charge the same extra rate poundage for comparable increments of extra spending. If there were no such arrangement, authorities with high rateable values would be in a position to fund spending above assessed spending needs with a much lower rate poundage addition than those with low rateable values. The scheme suggested by the DoE involved setting an additional rate poundage for extra spending above the assessed figure, according to a schedule set by the Government. The extra rate income generated by the additional rate poundage would yield more in authorities with high rateable values than their intended additional spending. Any excess thus collected would be contributed to a pool which would be drawn on by authorities with lower rateable values. The system would allow authorities with high and low rateable values to charge similar rate poundages for similar levels of spending above assessed needs.

If such a system were introduced, it would have given the Government greater control over local authorities. The assessment of spending needs would become much more explicit than in the then existing needs element and would anyway be much more important in grant calculation. The Government could also determine the extent to which spending above assessed needs might lead to higher rate poundages. The Government would therefore have considerable power to say what authorities should be spending and to discourage them from spending above that level. Central control of local government current spending would be increased.

The advantages of a combined grant, according to the Government, would be, first, that it would be possible to achieve full equalization of spending needs and rateable resources. Second, equalization could be achieved at a lower cost to the Exchequer; third, it would clarify the relationship between central and local government, making local authorities clearly responsible for any spending above the assessed needs figure. Fourth, it would remove the 'open-ended' nature of the existing grant system and allow greater regulation by the Government.

The major disadvantage of the combined grant, according to the DoE, was 'that it would have the appearance of a major change in the whole philosophy of the grant system'.[11] The assessment of spending need would be seen as intervention in local authorities' existing powers to decide what to spend. Councils would be encouraged to spend up or down to the assessed spending need figure, though the pressure to spend up would probably be the more powerful. This would probably lead, according to the DoE, to an increase in spending in the short term. The assessment of spending need, which had proved difficult within the existing needs element, would be even more problematic in a system which relied on a more open assessment.

## (d)   The Rates as a Local Tax

The Treasury submitted evidence to the Layfield Committee on the advantages and disadvantages of rates as a local tax. Domestic rates were seen as being quite different from other taxes paid by individuals in that the tax base was fixed. Authorities were forced to increase the rate of tax in order to keep revenue growing in line with rising prices. VAT and income tax had buoyant tax bases.

Yet domestic rates had been shown (in a memorandum written by the DoE) to represent a more or less static proportion of personal disposable income in recent years. The perceptibility of rates was seen by the Treasury as a good quality. The criticism that domestic rates were levied without regard to ability to pay was challenged. Rate rebates, it was argued, lessened the tendency towards regressiveness for the poorest ratepayers. If the incidence of rates was looked at over an individual's lifetime rather than in a particular year, regressiveness was likely to appear less marked because young people often took on substantial housing commitments in the expectation of rising incomes, while retired people continued to occupy accommodation whose size was determined by the needs of children who had then ceased to be members of their parents' household.

Finally, any discussion of abolishing domestic rates would have to take account of finding an alternative. Such an alternative would add to a tax burden which was already rising. The redistribution which might be brought about by new taxes would depend upon which new revenue source was chosen. A local income tax would probably be progressive, increasing the tax burden of middle- and upper-income groups and cutting the burden of the lower-paid. But LIT would also mean that the imputed income enjoyed in terms of the services of a house by owner-occupiers, and those paying less than 'market' rents, would be left entirely untaxed. There would therefore be an additional incentive to occupy more accommodation than was needed, as there would no longer be any encouragement to move as a result of the higher rates now generally charged on larger houses. According to the Treasury, replacing domestic rates with increases in indirect taxes would probably have very little effect on the distribution of income overall.

Business rates were a tax on some, but not all, fixed capital assets. Like other business expenses, they were deductible against corporation tax (or income tax in the case of sole traders). The Treasury memorandum went on: 'it does not appear that business rates have a marked impact on income distribution or on the pattern of economic activity'.

Concluding the section on rates, the memorandum stated:

> In theory the present system of business rates could have some effect on the location of industry and commerce. It is difficult to

judge how far this takes place in practice. Rates are not a large part of total value added by UK businesses – they account on average for about three per cent. Decisions about an appropriate location for investment will be influenced by the availability of labour, communications, nearness to markets and the effects of central government policies.

## (6)  LAYFIELD: CONCLUSION

The report of the Layfield Committee and its appendices remain a comprehensive examination of the whole of local government finance as it was in 1976. Much of what was included in the report remains a good guide to the subject. In retrospect, it seems a pity that the committee did not come out more explicitly for a particular solution. Having surveyed all the evidence, Layfield pointed out that there were two possible directions in which local government finance might develop. First, there could be a move to greater central control; second, there could be a more locally based solution. In the final paragraph of the report, the committee stated that, although it could not be responsible for the Government's choice, 'there is a strongly held view amongst us that the only way to sustain a vital local democracy is to enlarge the share of local taxation in total local revenue and thereby make Councillors more directly accountable to local electorates for their expenditure and taxation decisions'.

The relationship between central and local government, which had not changed significantly for many years, was fairly well understood, even if the Government did not make clear what it was attempting to achieve through this relationship. Subsequent events, including attempts by the Government to achieve greater central influence and control over local authorities, could not have been predicted by the committee. There was not, therefore, urgent pressure upon it to do more than suggest a solution which would strengthen local finances and improve accountability. The choice of whether to do this or not was left to the Government. If Layfield had known the way in which successive governments would attack local autonomy, doubtless the Report would have been made more aggressively anti-centralist.

The shape of things to come was implied by the evidence given to the committee by the Treasury and the Department of the Environment. Both departments suggested a rather limited view of local government powers while making clear the need for greater control over local authorities. National economic objectives had, according to the departments, to override local discretion. In 1976 this was no more than a pious hope. Subsequently the Treasury pressed for greater control over individual authority spending. By 1984 it had succeeded in achieving far greater influence over the spending of individual councils than would have been thought possible in 1976.

The DoE's hopes for the future of the grant system included a combined needs/resources grant and more stability and predictability in grant distribution. The former proposal was accepted by the Labour Government in 1977 (thought not introduced) and finally enacted in 1980 by the Conservative Government. Stability and predictability were, if anything, reduced in the years following 1976, first as the Labour Government moved needs element about the country from authority to authority, and then as block grant made it even less easy for authorities to predict their grant income until just before the start of the next financial year.

The Treasury's views on rates were illuminating. Having made out a case for greater control over local government spending, rates were almost dismissed because they had little effect on business and because they represented a small burden on most householders. Furthermore, the burden on householders would be broadly fair over a lifetime. Finding an alternative to rates would be extremely difficult, it was argued, largely because of their huge yield.

Nevertheless, politicians of all parties kept up continuous criticism of local government finance throughout the years following 1976. Ministers and senior back-benchers in the Conservative Government from 1979 onwards intensified this criticism. The Treasury stuck to its Layfield line throughout; rates were impossible to replace, cheap to collect and not particularly burdensome to individuals and business, yet still the Government and MPs complained about the rates.

The Layfield Report was published in May 1976. It pointed to greater centralization or to more local control as possible ways for local government to develop. In many ways, the committee was foresighted in seeing how the centre would continue to take more control if local authority finance were not to be reformed. The committee also managed to overcome the Inland Revenue's objecting to introducing a local income tax by proposing changes in the tax system and by suggesting that LIT be incorporated in the Revenue's plans for computerization of the tax system.

Having examined the problems of local authority finance in detail, the committee left the Government with a fairly general choice between more local or more central control. With hindsight, the members of the committee might have wished they had been more insistent in opposing continued incremental centralization.

NOTES: CHAPTER 6

1  Committee of Inquiry into Local Government Finance, Report, Cmnd 6453 (London: HMSO, May 1976), p. 3.
2  Quoted by the committee from the First Report from the Expenditure Committee 1975–6, Vol. 1, para. 17.
3  Committee of Inquiry into Local Government Finance, Report, op. cit., p. 66, para. 7.

4  Ibid., p. 67, para. 9.
5  Ibid., p. 72, para. 25.
6  Ibid., p. 76, para. 36.
7  Ibid., appendix 1, pp. 277–8.
8  Ibid., appendix 6, p. 32.
9  Ibid., appendix 6, p. 32.
10  Ibid., appendix 7, pp. 26–7.
11  Ibid., appendix 7, 'Evidence by the Department of the Environment: Central Government Grants to Local Government: Some Possible Changes', para. 3.7.1

----

# Chapter 7

# THE 1977 GREEN PAPER

### (1) LABOUR'S RESPONSE

The Labour Government responded to the huge efforts of the Layfield Committee with a short Green Paper, published exactly a year after the committee's report. The introduction to the Green Paper stated that there would have to be much further work before any final decisions could be taken about reform. But on some subjects, the Government felt that there was 'widespread agreement on the changes that are required', and in such cases the Government made specific proposals for action. Legislation would be produced in due course.

The Green Paper examined the relationship between central and local government, Rate Support Grant, specific grants, capital expenditure, sources of local revenue, value for money and central-local consultation. Unlike the 1971 Green Paper (which made no proposals for action), this one was short and, in some ways, nearer to a White Paper. But like the 1966 White Paper, the 1971 Green Paper, Layfield and other official documents, this one started with an attempt to set out the relationship between central and local government.

### (2) THE CENTRAL–LOCAL RELATIONSHIP

The 1977 Government felt that 'the dilemma which faces central government is to secure and promote an effective local democracy with genuine political choice and at the same time fulfil their responsibilities for the management of the economy and for the standards of public services'. Because the Government had responsibility for the management of the economy as a whole, it was argued that it must concern itself with the total of local government expenditure and taxation. The Green Paper summarized central government's role as:

• to ensure that the local services (education, personal social services, housing, etc.) reflect national priorities and national policies and are provided at broadly comparable standards;
• to ensure that, in aggregate, local government's spending plans are compatible with the Government's economic objectives;
• to ensure that activities of one authority do not have adverse effects on the area of another;

- to promote co-operation between local authority and other complementary services;
- to ensure that the financial arrangements promote efficiency;
- to safeguard the interests of vulnerable minority groups whose interests may get a proper hearing only at national level;
- to encourage and maintain local democracy.

Local government's responsibilities were also outlined:

- to provide services to meet local needs and preferences;
- to provide services in accordance with the statutory duties laid down by Parliament and national priorities;
- to promote greater administrative efficiency – another level of government enables the responsibility for local decisions to be decentralized;
- to provide initiatives leading to the formulation of new policies;
- to operate and develop democracy at the local level.

Having laid out a view of the 'roles' of central and local government, the Green Paper went on to consider the crucial problem which had been identified by Layfield. This problem was the absence of any explicitly established view of the relationship between central and local government and the confusion to which this led over where the real responsibility for local expenditure rested.

Layfield, as was described earlier, argued that the Government should decide whether it wanted a more 'centralist' or a more 'localist' system of control over local government. The Government considered this choice, and disagreed with the committee:

Any formal definition of central and local responsibilities would lack the advantages of flexibility and rapidity of response to new circumstances. It would be likely to break down under the pressure of events. The Government's view is, therefore, that while clarification of responsibilities wherever practicable is desirable, a fundamental redefinition is not necessary as a basis for solving the problems of local government finance. The disadvantages of both the centralist and localist approaches are clear, and the Government do not think there is a clear case for the adoption of either.[1]

The Government also rejected the detailed proposals of the minority of the committee[2] for a simply defined form of allocation of responsibilities between central and local government. The existing financial arrangements were thought capable of 'giving expression to a middle way approach' if they were modified to some extent. The Green Paper stated that the Government intended to discuss with the local authorities' associations how the respective roles of central and local government could be more effectively carried out. Four reasons were given for such discussions.

First, the Government felt that it needed to be able to exert more effective influence over total local authority expenditure. Second, greater equity should be achieved, with ratepayers paying a similar rate poundage for a comparable level of service wherever they lived. Third, the Government felt that local electors needed to have a better way of assessing local spending decisions and of requiring local authorities to account for them. Lastly, the Government wanted additional financial powers to promote particular policies.

In order to achieve the improved relationship between central and local government which was envisaged, the Government considered changes which would have to be made to the grant system. Chapter 3 of the Green Paper examined possible reform of RSG. The system then operating was said to have several drawbacks. For example, although the RSG mechanism enabled the Government to influence total local expenditure, it did so in a non-selective, across-the-board way. Also the method of assessing spending needs in the needs element of RSG was much criticized, while the resources element did not equalize fully for variations in rateable values. Another difficulty was that 'the arrangements do not readily enable ratepayers to understand the way the expenditure of their local authority is financed'.

### (3) UNITARY GRANT

The Government proposed to introduce a 'unitary grant' to replace the needs and resources elements of RSG and to improve the whole grant system. It wanted to do this despite the fact that the local authorities' associations were opposed to the proposal. Appendix 1 of the Green Paper described unitary grant thus:

> The grant allocation to each authority . . . would be the payment which would enable each authority to provide overall levels of service comparable with other similar authorities, if it levied a standard rate poundage. The basic grant would be the difference between the cost to an authority of providing a standard level of service and the revenue it would raise from a standard rate poundage. This means that two figures are crucial: the assessment of the cost to each authority of providing comparable overall levels of service and the corresponding standard rate poundages.[3]

The appendix went on to explain how it would be possible to increase the rate poundage cost for authorities which chose to spend much above the Government's assessment of what they ought to spend. This would allow the Government to bring home to local authorities the importance of attempting to keep local government spending within the nationally planned total. In fact, the unitary grant was precisely the same as the 'combined' grant proposed by the Department of the Environment to Layfield and as the 'block' grant introduced by the Conservatives in 1981–2.

The unitary grant would allow equalization of spending needs and rateable resources with a lower grant total than existed in 1977. The idea of relating equalization of taxable resources to income (as Layfield had suggested) rather than rateable values was rejected by the Government because domestic rate bills would become an amalgam of two different bases of taxation and the logic of the system would be difficult to understand or justify. Poorer ratepayers in richer areas would end up paying more in rates while it would be impossible to compare the rate poundages of authorities with each other.

The new grant could also be paid to each tier of local government, which would mean that rate bills would more accurately reflect relative spending levels. In addition,

> provided the assessment of an authority's spending need is accurate, ratepayers would be in a position to ask, if the rate poundage were above the standard rate poundage, whether their local authority was less efficient or was providing services to a higher level than other similar authorities. Alternatively, if the authority fixed a poundage below the standard poundage, it could be that the authority was more efficient or was providing services to the local [*sic*] level than other similar authorities, and so reducing the burden on its ratepayers.[4]

This fact, in conjunction with improved rate demand notes, would allow increased accountability.

The government concluded the discussion of unitary grant by again acknowledging authorities' concerns that unitary grant (and in particular the publication of explicit needs assessments) would undermine local independence. Discussions would take place to see whether some other arrangement could be found or if unitary grant offered the best possible improvement.

### (4)　OTHER POSSIBLE REFORMS

The Green Paper then considered specific and supplementary grants. It was argued that these might be needed for a number of purposes: to encourage spending on particular activities or services; to compensate authorities which provide services at the request of central government where there is little or no discretion; to supplement general grant in services where need arises very unevenly, and to assist authorities providing services over an area wider than their own boundaries. The

Government felt that there was a case for a small increase in the use of specific grants, in particular for education.

In the section on sources of local revenue, rates were given a vote of support. The Government agreed with Layfield that the advantages of rates outweighed the disadvantages and that anyway there was no preferable alternative. It was proposed, however, to introduce a new basis of valuation for domestic rates. The point had been reached, it was argued, where there was no longer enough evidence of free market rental values to support another valuation on the basis of rental values. Capital values would therefore be used as the basis of the next revaluation. Rental values would continue to be used for non-domestic revaluations because the evidence for valuing these on a capital basis was not as plentiful as for a rental basis. The new basis of valuation could not be introduced before 1982–3 and there would have to be arrangements to mitigate the effects of moving from one basis to the other. Future revaluations would take place at five-yearly intervals. The Layfield Committee's proposal that agricultural land and buildings should be re-rated was rejected on the ground that it would harm the farming industry, put up prices and be more expensive for the Inland Revenue and local authorities to collect, and because any increased rate income would be offset by grant reductions.

All new forms of local taxation were rejected by the Government. Like Layfield, it was agreed that taxes other than a local income tax were impractical. LIT was rejected (despite the fact that Layfield made it clear that a system of local government finance with local control required a new tax source) because the Government did not believe that taxpayers could be made aware of the LIT they paid, because there would need to be new equalization arrangements and because there could be little freedom for authorities to set their own tax rate.

Capital spending was discussed for half a page in the Green Paper. In line with evidence given by Government departments to Layfield, it was stated that local authorities should be freer to determine their own priorities for capital spending. The Government proposed to discuss with local authorities a new system of capital expenditure approvals for expenditure on programmes rather than on projects. Such approvals would be given for one year, with an indication of the figures likely to be approved for subsequent years.

Other proposals in the Green Paper were that the Head of the District Audit Service should produce an annual report dealing with general audit matters such as local authority accounting systems, financial control problems raised by statutory provisions and the soundness of local authority finance. This report should be published and considered by an 'independent institution' which would be set up to consider the reports and to give advice on the need for comparative studies. The government felt that authorities should have the right to continue to choose their own auditors.

Finally, the Green Paper considered how co-operation between central and local government could be improved. It was proposed to examine, with the local authority associations, how the Consultative Council on Local Government Finance (which had been set up in 1975) and its subsidiary committees could be made to work better. Statistical information could also be improved, as could local government's contribution to the annual Public Expenditure Survey process.

### (5) CONCLUSIONS

Much of the thinking in the 1977 Green Paper, like the evidence of Government departments to Layfield, suggests how official opinions were changing. In discussing the extent to which the Government might press its policies about an appropriate level of local spending, the idea of direct control over spending or rates is mentioned, though rejected. The difficulty of across-the-board grant reductions was also described in the Green Paper in terms that were to be used in the years after 1979: 'the disadvantage is that all local authorities suffer a reduction in grant whether or not they have followed Government guidance on expenditure levels and whatever their local circumstances'.[5]

Unitary grant would, it was suggested, give greater Government influence over spending by allowing grant reductions to be imposed in authorities which decided to spend more than their spending needs assessment. This would allow a regulatory feature to be explicit and built into the grant system distribution arrangements. 'Such an arrangement would have advantages over the taking of ad hoc powers, after the event, to discriminate against "overspending" authorities'.[6]

In addition to this power to cut the grant of authorities which chose to spend much above the Government's assessment of their spending needs, the spending needs assessments themselves would become explicit under unitary grant. The Government proposed to explore alternative methods of measuring spending needs, though the resulting figures were not to be prescriptive. It was also proposed to increase the use of specific grants, which would also have tended to move control to the centre.

While the 1977 Green Paper made a significant shift towards a new, more centralist grant, it failed to propose any new local tax. The Green Paper was very thin and contained little thoughtful consideration of the issues discussed in detail by Layfield. As a poor response to a major problem, it set the scene for the next government to change local authority finance with little real consultation. Rates were to be retained, though all possible alternative taxes were rejected. LIT was summarily dismissed on the grounds described earlier. By 1977 the

British economy was growing much less rapidly than in the periods when previous Government documents on local government finance had been published (e.g. 1966 and 1971). The scope for radical action had been much reduced.

Nevertheless, the proposals in the Labour Government's Green Paper met with considerable hostility from the parliamentary opposition and from local authorities. Unitary grant in particular was singled out as an attempt to increase central control over local government. For example, in September 1977 Keith Speed, the Conservative local government finance spokesman, noted: 'The local authorities' associations have already made clear their apprehension over the unitary grant. They fear that the grant in this form would admit much greater interference by Government departments.' He also set out his party's objections to capital values: 'The case against capital values as a basis of rates is even more clear cut. They will exaggerate all the defects of the present system and make it worse.'

At this time, the Labour Government did not have an overall majority in Parliament, and relied on support from the Liberals and elsewhere. Unitary grant and capital valuation were sufficiently unpopular to convince the Government that it would not command a majority for either.

Little or nothing came of Layfield or the 1977 Green Paper. An Advisory Committee on Local Authority Audit was set up, but the major proposals for grants, for a reformed basis for rates and for a new tax base were all left untouched. Nevertheless, the Green Paper (like the Treasury's evidence to Layfield) was markedly more centralist in its intentions than previous documents had been. No fundamental reform was achieved, and a further step towards the final degeneration of local government was taken. Almost every issue outlined by Layfield was ignored or rejected.

The Layfield Committee's view that the financial relationship between central and local government had to be determined, and a set of consistent financial arrangements made, was rejected. The Government felt that the existing arrangements would do, provided small adjustments were made. LIT, which Layfield had made clear was needed if local government was to remain fully locally controlled, was ruled out. Unitary grant, which the committee had said would be most likely to be introduced as part of a more centrally run local finance system, was nevertheless proposed. The tone of the Green Paper suggested that, whatever happened, the Government wanted greater central control over local government spending.

NOTES: CHAPTER 7

1   Local Government Finance, Cmnd 6813 (London: HMSO, May 1977), para. 2.8.

2  Professors Alan Day and Gordon Cameron wrote notes of dissent from the Layfield
   Report, advocating a 'middle way' between 'centralist' and 'localist' approaches.
3  *Local Government Finance*, Cmnd 6813, op. cit. appendix 1.
4  Ibid., para. 3.27.
5  Ibid., para. 3.11.
6  Ibid., para. 3.14.

*Chapter 8*

# THE 1979–83 CONSERVATIVE GOVERNMENT

## (1)  BACKGROUND TO THE 1979 GENERAL ELECTION

The 1977 Green Paper had been published in the first full financial year following the constraints imposed on the British economy after the visit of the International Monetary Fund in 1976. Conditions imposed by the IMF led to pressures to cut public spending from 1976 onwards. In addition to an end to a period of substantial growth, there were other changes taking place during the mid- and late 1970s which are important.

First, the Public Expenditure Survey system (PESC) had been developed in the years following the Plowden Report[1] in 1961. PESC sought to bring together all public spending programmes into one exercise so the Government could assess the effect of such expenditure on the national economy. Local government was increasingly being involved in the 1970s in the planning process even though the Cabinet had no direct control over what councils decided to spend. The setting up of the Consultative Council on Local Government Finance[2] in May 1975 allowed increased interconnection between central planning and local authority activity. Work completed by officials of central and local government for the council on spending patterns and grants is now taken account of in the PESC process.

Second, the Government decided from 1976–7 onwards to apply cash limits to increases in the amount of RSG paid to local authorities in 'increase orders'. Before 1976–7 the Government increased RSG during and after the year in which grant was paid so as to compensate for inflation between the time of the RSG settlement and the end of the financial year. However high inflation turned out to be, grant was increased to the full extent of rising prices. From 1976–7 cash limits were applied to about three-quarters of central government spending and to the RSG. If inflation turned out to be higher than predicted when grant was set, there could be no extra grant for authorities beyond an amount set at the RSG settlement.

Third, the Government started to take a much closer interest in the total of local government spending. RSG for 1976–7 was cut by £50 million (in effect a cut in the cash limit described above)[3] in an attempt to reduce current spending in that year. The Public Expenditure White Paper published in January 1974[4] explained that 'because of the Government's overall responsibility for economic management, they must be closely concerned with the aggregate of local authority expenditure'. Later in the same White Paper, the Government explained that influence over local government spending was achieved through control over grants:

> In this way, and through guidance issued to local authorities, the Government influence the level of current spending. But the ability of the Government to regulate, within a reasonable margin, the total of local authority expenditure (both capital and current) depends essentially on the co-operation which they receive from local government.'

So the climate within which local authorities operated between 1976 and 1979 was one where the Government was taking closer interest in their spending and was involving them more closely in central planning processes, and where attempts were being made to cut public spending as a whole. The proportion of relevant expenditure met by government grant was cut in 1977–8 to 61 per cent, from 66.5 per cent in 1975–6 and 65.5 per cent in 1976–7. Spending was also planned to fall (though only marginally).

Current expenditure by local authorities remained more or less constant in volume terms (i.e. with the effects of price changes removed) in 1976–7 and fell in 1977–8. Capital spending fell in volume terms by 17 per cent in 1976–7 and by 30 per cent in 1978–9. Overall, local government spending fell sharply, though current spending started to rise again in 1978–9. By early 1979 local authority current spending and manpower were at highest-ever levels, although the economic outlook was not significantly different than it had been in 1976. It is at this point that the Conservatives won the 1979 general election.

## (2)  CONSERVATIVE POLICY

The new Government's policy was outlined in its manifesto, then detailed in its first financial statement before being implemented between 1979 and 1983. The 1979 Conservative manifesto stated: 'any future government which sets out honestly to reduce inflation and taxation will have to make substantial economies, and there should be no doubt about our intention to do so'.[5] During the 1979 election campaign, the Conservatives made it clear that major areas of public spending (social security and health) would be protected from cuts while spending on defence would increase in real terms. By implication, reductions would have to be made in areas like housing, education and social services if the overall target of reduced spending were to be hit. Local government, as the provider of such services, would be required to make economies.

Therein lay a difficulty which plagued the Government from 1979 onwards in its relationship with local authorities. The Conservatives were committed to cutting spending on services which were not under direct central control. Local authorities had the power to raise any rates they chose within the law and could, if they chose, spend more than the new administration wanted. The influences open to the Government at that time were exhortation and further reductions in the percentage of local relevant spending funded by the RSG.

Government financial policy, outlined in the Financial Statement and Budget Report 1979–80 (which was published immediately after the election), stated that reductions would be sought compared with the outgoing Labour Government's public spending plans. This attempt to cut expenditure was to continue throughout the period from 1979 to 1983. The reasons for doing it were explained in the 1980 Public Expenditure White Paper:

> the Government intend to reduce public expenditure progressively in volume terms over the next four years. This is a substantial change from the plans published by the previous Government . . . The change of direction is central to the achievement of the objectives set out in the earlier short White Paper . . . These are: to bring down the rate of inflation and interest rates by curtailing the growth of the money supply and controlling Government borrowing; to restore incentives; and to plan for spending which is compatible both with the objectives for taxation and borrowing and with a realistic assessment of the prospects for economic growth.[6]

Policy also emerged as the Government introduced legislation in 1979, 1980 and 1981. This, and the continuing attempt to reduce expenditure, will be examined in the following sections.

### (3) EARLY CHANGES

On taking office in May 1979 the Government immediately announced plans for public spending different from those published in January 1979 by the Labour administration. Labour had planned for volume growth (i.e. growth after the effects of inflation had been removed) in 1979–80 of 2 per cent. The Conservatives set a new plan which was 3 per cent in volume below the one set by Labour (i.e. 1 per cent in volume terms below 1978–9 out-turn). In addition, the Government announced that the RSG for 1979–80 would be cut by £300 million. At a meeting with the leaders of the local authorities' associations on 31 July 1979, the Government announced that the spending plan for the next year (1980–1) was 1 per cent lower than the *revised* plan for 1979–80. This meant that on 31 July local authorities faced a plan for 1980–1 which was 5.5 per cent lower than the one set for that year by the Labour Government in January 1979.

At the meeting on 31 July 1979 the Secretary of State for the Environment (Michael Heseltine) tabled a statement entitled 'Public Expenditure 1980–1'. This described the cuts required in 1980–1, and went on to consider in more detail what this would mean for authorities. The statement explained:

> It is the Government's view that priorities should be given to law and order, and in particular the plans for court, police and pro- bation services . . . The Government was elected to promote higher standards of achievement in education. However, faced with the overriding need to contain public expenditure, the Government recognises that spending on education services cannot be exempt . . . In all the difficult decisions that Local Authorities are going to have to make the Government must point out that the quality of provision is not automatically dependent on the level of expendi- ture.[7]

In announcing reductions, the Government stressed the importance of local autonomy: 'within the overall need for spending reductions, the Government thinks it right to give local authorities the maximum freedom to decide on the allocation of funds in accordance with their own spending priorities'.[8] The local authorities' associations, which at that time were all Conservative-controlled, did not object forcefully to the reductions proposed. Although local authority current expendi- ture did not fall in the way the new Government wished no action was taken by the secretary of state in the attempt to influence the pattern of spending.

The Government's revised expenditure plans were confirmed in a public expenditure White Paper (Cmnd 7746) and formed the basis of the Rate Support Grant settlement for 1980–1, which was announced by the secretary of state at the meeting of the Consultative Council on Local Government Finance on 16 November 1979.

In addition to the Government's announcements about public expenditure reductions, the secretary of state also made it clear that he would take action against local authorities which failed to take heed of the Government's policy of spending reductions. The earliest indication of this intent was given by Mr Heseltine at the Joint Local Authority Associations Conference at Scarborough on 20 September 1979. He said that no Government, of whatever party, would or could tolerate a situation where local authorities pursued their own ends regardless of the expressed views of the Government.

When he announced details of the 1980–1 RSG in November 1979, he expressed his dissatisfaction with the grant system: 'The arrange- ments used to distribute the grant in recent years have proved neither equitable nor sensible. But in the time available it has not been possible to develop any alternative. I have therefore had to make use of the existing arrangements for 1980–1.'[9] The secretary of state went on to spell out the shape of things to come:

> So far as overspending is concerned, while a majority of local authorities have shown a willingness to keep in step with the Government's guidelines on public expenditure, a minority of authorities persist in maintaining levels of expenditure which the present economic circumstances simply do not justify. It is, however, clearly wrong that the Government's contribution through the rate support grant to local authority expenditure can take no account of whether expenditure is reasonable or not. That is now the case. Such is the perversity of the present resources element arrangements that high spending authorities get the same level of support on all additions to expenditure, at the expense of other authorities. This is unacceptable ... I therefore intend to introduce provisions in the forthcoming Local Government, Planning and Land Bill to replace the needs and resources elements of the existing grant arrangements with a single block grant, payable to all authorities.'[10]

Three weeks later, the Government introduced the Local Government, Planning and Land Bill 1979 in the House of Lords. Commenting on the new Bill, Michael Heseltine said:

> This bill marks a significant advance in the relationship between central and local government. It has four central themes:
>
> i.   a better framework for the distribution and control of public funds in place of the present unsatisfactory system;
> ii.  the withdrawal of central government from detailed scrutiny of local government;
> iii. improvement of the general level of information available to councillors and ratepayers to help them play a full and constructive role in their authorities;
> iv.  better value for money in local government.[11]

The Bill introduced 'block grant' to replace the old needs and resources elements (and to give the Government more influence over grant distribution); it also proposed the relaxation or reform of 300 or so controls over local government, and provided for greater publication of information by local authorities and a wide range of smaller changes.

The Government was forced to withdraw the 1979 Bill before it started its passage through Parliament. The Opposition argued –

successfully – that a Bill with major constitutional implications (i.e. the changes in the grant system) should start in the Commons. It was reintroduced early in 1980 in the lower House. The 19980 Bill was somewhat shorter than the original, but the major section dealing with local authority current expenditure was retained. Block grant started on its way to the statute book in the spring of 1980.

Before going on to consider the 1980 Bill, it is worth pausing to examine the earliest months of the administration. A shift in public expenditure policy had been introduced, major changes in the RSG system had been announced, the secretary of state had warned that he would take action against 'the overspenders' and a major local government Bill had been introduced and withdrawn. Mr Heseltine had simultaneously started to reduce staffing in the Department of the Environment and to reduce the number of quasi-autonomous non-governmental organizations ('quangos').

The concept of 'overspenders' had also been revived, having previously been introduced in the Labour Government's 1977 Green Paper. From a general attempt to reduce local government spending starting in June and July 1979, Michael Heseltine changed his position by the Scarborough local government conference in September to hint that the Government could not tolerate authorities pursuing their own ends regardless of his views. By November 'a minority of authorities persist in maintaining levels of expenditure which the present economic circumstances simply do not justify'.[12] On 16 December 1979 the secretary of state talked of 'the problem of the overspenders'[13] when making a statement about the detail of the 1980 RSG.

So from a general reduction in public expenditure, the idea of particular councils 'overspending' emerged within six months. The 'problem of the overspenders' had become the justification for introducing block grant and the 'transitional arrangements' which were contained in the Local Government, Planning and Land Bill, and which allowed the Government to treat some authorities in a different way from others.

(4)   THE INTRODUCTION OF BLOCK GRANT

Block grant, as the most important part of the Bill, received barely any advance discussion. The idea was not new, as we saw earlier, having been proposed to the Layfield Committee by DoE officials in 1975[14] and then having become Government policy in the Green Paper published in May 1977.[15] But, as was shown in Chapter 7, no reform was made to the grant system in 1977 because of the extent of opposition.

In 1980 there was neither a White Paper, a Green Paper nor any other form of consultation. The policy objectives introducing the new grant (in addition to those described by Michael Heseltine earlier) have had to be inferred from ministerial statements and commitments given to Parliament. These objectives will be examined after the Government's original proposals for block grant have been considered.

Block grant was expected to do in one step what the existing needs and resources elements did in two. Needs element was an attempt to compensate for variations in spending need per head of population, while resources element sought to equalize between authorities their different rateable values. Block grant was intended to achieve both kinds of equalization by use of a central assessment of expenditure need and a national formula for determining ratepayers' contributions at different spending levels in relation to the assessed spending need. Grant would make up the difference between actual spending and the calculated contribution by ratepayers.

The original step in distributing block grant, as with the needs and resources elements, was the setting up of a national total of grant. The determination of aggregate Exchequer grant would continue as before. The Government would determine a total of planned spending ('relevant' expenditure) by local authorities for the coming year and decide what percentage of such spending would be supported by grant. The grant would then be separated into its various components. First, a range of specific and supplementary grants (for services like police and transport) would be removed. Second, the domestic element (renamed the 'domestic rate relief grant') would be set and removed. The remaining grant would be block grant. This process would be undertaken separately for England and for Wales.

Having arrived at a total block grant, the distribution mechanism would have to be created. The first step would be the setting of an assessed spending need figure for each local authority in the country. As it was planned to distribute the new grant to all authorities (unlike the needs and resources elements, which were not distributed to all), the process would be more extensive than the preceding arrangements.

The assessed spending need figure (originally known as 'standard' expenditure) would be taken into account when each authority's grant calculation was made. The amount to be paid in grant was the difference between an authority's total expenditure and the amount it could raise by levying a rate on its rateable value. This rate (originally known as the 'standard' rate poundage) would be determined by the relationship between the authority's total spending and the centrally assessed spending need figure.

The Government would determine the relationship between changes in spending and increases or decreases to the standard poundage, taking account of the difference between an authority's budgeted spending and its standard expenditure figure. A similar determination had been implicit in the previous system. But a key difference between the new and old systems was that the Government intended to require a larger contribution from ratepayers for additional spending per head in those authorities which chose to spend more than a fixed percentage above standard expenditure. This, the Government hoped, would discourage high spending.

In order to reduce the changes in grant distribution brought about by the introduction of the new system, the Government proposed to use 'multipliers' to moderate such changes. The details of how block grant could be operated were not known with any certainty at the time that the Local Government, Planning and Land Bill was passing through Parliament. A full description of its operation is included later in this chapter.

The legislative power to introduce the new grant was contained in part VI of the Bill. The Government also proposed in this part of the legislation to introduce 'transitional arrangements' for 1980–1 so that the secretary of state could reduce either the needs or the resources element of an authority which chose to levy a rate higher than that it would have had to levy in order to finance its spending needs after the operation of the needs and resources elements.

During the passage of the Bill through Parliament, ministers attempted to explain the new grant, and to point out its advantages. These are considered next.

On 25 March 1980 Mr King said: 'the principle of block grant is fundamental to the Government's determination to improve the present system of local government finance. Whatever the differences which may exist about the method of achieving it, there is widespread recognition that the present grant system is defective and has to be changed.'[16] Reform of the grant system to reduce defect was one of the Government's concerns.

The Government did not pretend that the system would be simpler than the highly complex needs and resources elements. Lord Bellwin, in the Lords committee stage, said:

> What we are doing first is to make available in a form which people really will be able to see, certainly a complex system, no one seeks to deny that, but at least the black box is open, the things are on the table; you will be able to debate it and discuss it in a way that has not been done before. I am not saying for a moment that it will be easy because it will not, but at least it will be there and it will be seen.[17]

A second feature of the new system was to be its openness, though there would be no reduction in complexity.

Another advantage of block grant was that it would allow 100 per cent equalization of expenditure need and rateable resources, which could not be achieved with separate needs and resources elements. Mr King explained this point thus: 'At present the richer authorities can fund their increasing rate of expenditure at a lower poundage than other authorities. Under block grant that will no longer be true. That is because at the moment the present system is not a true or perfectly equalising system as it is intended to be.'[18]

Block grant was expected to require fewer civil servants to administer than the needs and resources elements: 'It may come as a surprise to the Opposition that we expect to be able to operate the block grant, when it is introduced, with fewer staff – fewer civil servants – than under the present system.'[19] Thus Tom King described the staffing requirements of administering the new system.

Lord Bellwin was clear that the new system would be fairer than the old one: 'The fact is that we believe that a workable system has been developed which will allow an equitable grant distribution to be made for the next financial year.'[20]

Finally, the Government was convinced that the block grant could be used to convince local authorities to act in the national interest. Discussing the 'transitional arrangements' for bridging the old RSG system to the new, Lord Bellwin claimed:

> surely it is right for the Government to spotlight those authorities who are not willing to conform to national policy objectives. I am sure that the country at large thinks it right and proper that those authorities who refuse to cooperate should bear the cost. The Government are entitled to expect the cooperation of local authorities whose individual local objectives must be subordinate to the national interest.[21]

In short, the block grant was intended to reduce defects in the system; to be more open; to allow 100 per cent equalization of spending needs and rateable resources; to reduce the number of civil servants required to work the system; to be fairer as between authorities and, crucially, to impose national government policy on recalcitrant local authorities.

Whereas Michael Heseltine had announced block grant in November 1979 as a way of coping with the 'overspenders', Tom King and Lord Bellwin were more circumspect during 1980 when describing the detail of block grant and its likely effects. As the extracts from the Commons and Lords committees suggest, ministers defended the way in which grant was to be distributed and the fairness of block grant, with little reference to the detail of spending control which had been discussed prior to the introduction of the legislation.

The government did not, as the Bill progressed, show any great confidence that block grant would give it sufficient central control to impose spending cuts on the 'overspending' councils, as this quote from 27 March 1980 suggests:

My department will not be in the business of saying how much each authority should spend, where it should or should not make cuts or on what it should spend money. I have tried to make clear that that is a matter for local authorities. Options are open. They have been canvassed by outside pundits and others who are concerned about the problems of the growth of public spending and ways of curtailing it. We have specifically rejected that approach. We have said that our concern is the distribution of public money. Beyond that I am powerless to do anything about fixing the level of rates ... Local authorities are autonomous. They fix their rate systems. I can comment and urge the need for economy. I have some influence over the distribution of public funds but the ultimate decision on rating and on the volume of expenditure of local authorities is a matter for the councillors themselves.[22]

The Government faced stiff opposition to the clauses in the Bill which would introduce block grant. Even in the months up to May 1980, when all the local authorities' associations were Conservative-controlled, Government supporters in local government were worried that block grant would deprive councils of their freedom. When, after the May 1980 local elections, the Association of Metropolitan Authorities changed to Labour control, opposition intensified.

In a statement, the Association of County Councils listed its reasons for opposing block grant:

(i)   the proposals are unnecessary for influencing total local authority expenditure; nor are they required for the solution of the defects of the present system;

(ii)  they will markedly increase the power of the central Departments to influence local rating decisions;

(iii) they may well have unintended effects on local expenditure and rates;

(iv)  the system is ill-defined in the Bill; the widest of powers are sought through secondary legislation, without adequate safeguards against their possible misuse.[23]

The strength of local authority feeling against block grant brought the three major associations (the Association of County Councils, the Association of Metropolitan Authorities and the Association of District Councils), with the London Boroughs' Association and the Greater London Council, together to produce a joint alternative proposal. This was published on 20 February 1980, during the Commons committee stage of the Bill, and followed an invitation from Michael Heseltine to prepare an alternative.

The associations' paper listed the secretary of state's objectives in introducing block grant and their own objections to the system. They then proposed the retention of the existing needs and resources elements of RSG with two qualifications. First, there should be a new system of needs assessment along the lines set out by the Government for the assessments in block grant, and secondly, an authority's resources element entitlement should be limited.

The needs grant distribution would be based on notional needs assessments, unrelated to the actual spending of individual authorities. Assessments would be limited in their year-to-year variation and would be a single figure for all services. Some statistical techniques would be used in calculating needs assessments. Needs element allocations were to remain close-ended (i.e. the figure notified to an authority at the start of the year could not be varied by spending more or less than the spending needs assessment).

Resources element would also be limited for each authority. In the years up to 1980–1 any authority which received support from the resources element would continue to do so at any level of expenditure. The local authorities' associations' proposal would have continued to relate an authority's entitlement to resources element to its actual expenditure, but with the proviso that there would be a cut-off point at a specified percentage above assessed spending need. That is, resources element would reach a maximum point (when an authority was spending just above its spending needs assessment) and then remain at that level for all higher spending levels.

The associations went on to say that the Bill should allow for the possible introduction of a measure of rateable wealth other than rateable value per head. In conclusion, the proposal stated:

> The associations are convinced that the grant and accountability proposals contained ... meet the Secretary of State's stated objectives in a way which his own proposals cannot. At the same time they can operate within the established constitutional relationships between the electorate, local government, central government and parliament, whereas his proposals fundamentally alter those relationships in a manner which can only be detrimental to local and central government, and to public administration in general.[24]

To have produced a joint proposal of this kind was a considerable feat, and suggested just how much of a threat to local government the council leaders considered block grant. Not only were all the associations still Conservative-controlled at this point, but there had been several years of infighting about the operation of RSG, in particular between the ACC and the AMA.

The government rejected the associations' proposal on 10 March 1980. In a letter to Sir Gervas Walker (the ACC chairman), Michael Heseltine wrote:

I am sorry to say that your proposals on the grant machinery do not meet our objectives ... I have always made it clear that my major objective in introducing block grant was to deal with the problem of the major overspending authorities and the pre-emption of grant that flows from high spending ... Your proposals recognise this problem and suggest a way of dealing with it, setting a cut-off of resources element for expenditure beyond some threshold above assessed expenditure needs. But they provide no consistent link between grant and expenditure for authorities spending above the threshold. Block grant does.[25]

The associations responded with a statement on 11 March. The chairmen of the ACC, ADC and AMA said:

We are bitterly disappointed by the Government's decision to reject our alternative to Block Grant ... The explanation for the rejection of the Associations' scheme is totally inadequate. The local authority Associations' scheme met the Secretary of State's objectives stated in the Second Reading Debate. He has now changed those objectives and gives a clear indication that the Government is bent on achieving greater control over the actions of each and every individual local authority.[26]

The bitterness of this response was remarkable; all three chairmen were at this time Conservatives. But it set the scene for the passage of the Bill through its parliamentary stages and for the relationship between local and central government from 1980 onwards.

In fact, the parliamentary stages of the Bill were not easy for the Government. Block grant had not been worked out in detail, and yet Tom King had to discuss highly technical aspects of the old and proposed systems for several weeks. For example, Tom King stated on 27 March 1980 (in the House of Commons committee) that authorities could not be in the position of losing block grant as their spending increased. On 1 April Mr King confirmed that some high-resource authorities *would* suffer a grant reduction as spending increased. Block grant, it should be remembered, was only part of a long and contentious Bill.

Despite Mr King's noble efforts, the problems the Government faced and the way in which it solved them were widely criticized inside and outside Parliament. A striking example of this was contained in a thumb-nail sketch of the Government's handling of block grant contained in the *Financial Times* of 5 August 1980. The *FT*'s local government correspondent Robin Pauley said:

The Government took ... principles into legislation before any work had been done to test them in detail. As Mr King was promoting his principles in committee, horrified civil servants were discovering that the more detailed work they did, the worse the mire in which they found themselves . . . Block grant, we now know, will not be any simpler, will not be any more logical and will also be full of extraordinary anomalies and potential unfair and discriminatory factors – all of which will need complicated, and sometimes arbitrary and often crude mathematical factors to iron them out.[27]

Block grant was pushed through Parliament during the spring and autumn of 1980. Apart from some changes in nomenclature and limitations on the use of multipliers, the Bill went largely unchanged. The expenditure needs assessments, which were originally to be called 'standard expenditures', were renamed 'grant-related expenditure assessments'. 'Standard rate poundages' were likewise renamed 'grant-related poundages'. These amendments were accepted by the Government so as to make the needs assessments and rate poundages appear less normative.

The changes made in Parliament to the conditions under which multipliers could be used were, however, more substantial. The original Bill stated that

the Secretary of State may provide in a Rate Support Grant Report that the amount of block grant payable to a local authority for a year shall be calculated by deducting from their total expenditure, instead of the product of their standard rate poundage, and the gross rateable value of their area, the product of those sums multiplied by a multiplier determined by the Secretary of State.[28]

The rest of the clause stipulated that multipliers should be used only according to principles applied to all local authorities or to all authorities belonging to the same class.

Although ministers had outlined their reasons for needing multipliers (i.e. to limit gains and losses in grant from year to year, to make adjustments to take account of London's high rateable resources, etc.), there was concern in Parliament that multipliers might be used for purposes other than those outlined by ministers. For example, a future government might use block grant to penalize *low* spenders.

Amendments made in the Commons and Lords sought to limit the chances of this kind of use. First, the legislation was altered so as to ensure that the grant-related poundage *decreased* if an authority chose to spend below grant-related expenditure. Clause 58 (2) of the Act states:

Where an authority's total expenditure is at a level equal to or less than their grant-related expenditure, a given decrease in their total expenditure must produce the same decrease in their grant-related poundage as would be produced by the same decrease in their total expenditure if it were at any other level which is less than their grant-related expenditure. (3) Where an authority's total expenditure is at a level equal to or more than their grant-related expenditure, a given increase in their total expenditure must produce an increase in their grant-related poundage not less than the increase that would be produced by the same increase in their total expenditure if it were at any lower level.[29]

This change meant that the relationship between spending changes and grant-related poundages could not be such as to penalize low spending relative to GRE or to reward spending above GRE with an increased rate of grant. This amendment was introduced at the report stage in the House of Commons by Robin Squire, Conservative MP for Hornchurch and a former leader of the London Borough of Sutton.

The second significant amendment was made to the clause allowing the use of multipliers. This was modified so as to set out in more detail the purposes for which multipliers could be used. Clause 59 (2) of the Act was changed to limit the use of multipliers so that they might only *increase* grant (with the exception of limiting the possible gain in grant to an authority from one year to the next because of changes in the mechanics of the grant).

Otherwise, the opposition of the local authorities, the parliamentary Opposition and several Conservative members of the House of Lords – including the presidents of the ACC (Lord Ridley) and the ADC (Lord Sandford) – failed to stop the Government introducing block grant. Very few changes were made to what had appeared in the original Bill.

It is also worth noting that the 'domestic element' was renamed the 'domestic rate relief grant' from 1981–2, while there were also changes to the method of controlling capital expenditure, relaxation of some controls over local government and a range of other legislative changes.

(5)  TRANSITIONAL ARRANGEMENTS

The transitional arrangements mentioned earlier were also introduced in the Local Government, Planning and Land Act. These arrangements allowed the Government to reduce the resources element of any receiving authority, and to reduce the needs element of any London borough which because of its high rateable resources did not receive resources element. The new arrangements would work for 1980–1, or until block grant was introduced. Authorities would be penalized if their 'uniform rate' exceeded the 'notional uniform rate'. The notional uniform rate was the rate an authority might be expected (by the Government) to charge, given its receipts from needs and resources elements, at the level of its assessed spending needs. The uniform rate was for most authorities very close to their general rate poundage, though some adjustments were made to London authorities to take account of rate equalization in the capital.

When authorities' budgets for 1980–1 showed a total 'overspend' of 5.6 per cent (£740 million) compared with the RSG settlement level, the Government decided to ask authorities to submit revised budgets. Authorities' revisions still left an excess of 2.6 per cent (£300 million), which prompted the Government to take further steps. First, Mr Heseltine announced that £200 million would be held back from the total of RSG available. Second, the transitional arrangements would be used. Third, urban programme grant was to be withheld (in part) from Hackney, Islington and Lambeth.

Withholding £200 million in grant from all authorities, regardless of their behaviour, brought protests from councils which felt that they ought to be let off penalties. Mr Heseltine agreed: 'I greatly regret that I have no statutory powers to do this although next year with the introduction of the new Rate Support Grant system I shall be able to differentiate between the prudent and the profligate.'[30]

In fact, the transitional arrangements *did* allow grant to be withdrawn from authorities which, in the Government's view, were spending excessively. The scheme affected authorities whose 'adjusted uniform rate' was above 155p in the £. Authorities could be exempted (known as a 'waiver') either if their 1980–1 expenditure increase was at least three percentage points below the average for their class or if they met a volume target set by the Government. The City of London was exempted because of its unique circumstances. Twenty-three authorities originally fell within the scope of the new penalty arrangements.

The grant abatement for the authorities which were over 155p but not exempted was an amount equivalent to a 1p rate plus an amount equivalent to one-twentieth of a penny rate for each 1p by which an authority's uniform/adjusted rate exceeded the threshold level of 155p. No authority could lose grant equivalent to more than a 5p rate.

Some authorities subsequently avoided penalties because their out-turn spending fell below the revised budget level. A number of the councils which were penalized sought to have the secretary of state's use of the transitional arrangements judged illegal in the courts. The secretary of state was found to have failed to consult authorities properly in accordance with the law. However, the penalties were enforced once the Government had gone through procedures in a legal way.

(6) OPERATING BLOCK GRANT

The Local Government, Planning and Land Act was given Royal Assent in time for the 1981–2 RSG settlement. From 1981–2 England

and Wales were to have separate RSG systems. So the statements by the Secretary of State of the Environment to Parliament and to the Consultative Council on Local Government Finance announcing the 1981–2 RSG on 16 December 1980 marked the start of different systems in England and in Wales. This account of the system concentrates on England, though a separate section described the Welsh system.

The RSG settlement statement underlined the country's economic problems. The economic situation was described as 'grave' by the secretary of state, and the consequence was that the demands of government on the 'wealth-producing' sector of the economy should be reduced.

The 1981–2 RSG included an overall spending plan for local authorities which was about 1 per cent below the figure which had been included for 1981–2 in the March 1980 Public Expenditure White Paper. This lower spending plan was also lower than spending in earlier years. For example, the 1981–2 RSG settlement plan was roughly 5 per cent lower in real terms than the out-turn for 1978–9 and also 6 per cent below the level of 1980–1 revised budgets. In short, the 1981–2 plan was for significant real reductions in spending. Table 8.1 shows plans and estimated out-turn spending for each year from 1978–9 to 1981–2, as shown in successive public expenditure White Papers and in the Chancellor's November 1980 statement.

Table 8.1

|  | 1978–9 Out-turn | 1979–80 Plan | Out-turn | 1980–1 Plan | Out-turn | 1981–2 Plan (a) | Plan (b) |
|---|---|---|---|---|---|---|---|
| Labour Government | 100 | 102 | — | 103 | — | — | — |
| Conservative Government | 100 | 99 | 102 | 98 | 101 | 96 | 95 |

Sources: Cmnd 7439, Cmnd 7841, Cmnd 8175, The Government's Expenditure Plans 1979, 1980, 1981. Plan (a) for 1981–2 is derived from public expenditure plans, whereas Plan (b) is taken from the Chancellor's November 1980 statement.

Having held the grant level at 61 per cent in 1980–1, the Government cut it to 60 per cent in 1981–2. Of this overall figure, the percentage in England was 59.1 per cent and in Wales 73.4 per cent. The domestic rate relief grant (previously known as the domestic element, and designed to subsidize household ratepayers) was kept at 18.5p in the £ in England (36p in Wales).

Block grant was used for the first time, with its new method of assessing expenditure need, and with an automatic penalty-zone for authorities which spent more than 10 per cent (on average) above the assessed need figure. But even at this early stage, Michael Heseltine began to express doubts about the ability of block grant to hold down expenditure. In his statement to the Consultative Council, he said:

> The new block grant system does not, of course, guarantee delivery of any given aggregate volume of expenditure, since it is primarily concerned with the fair distribution of grant and leaves local authorities free to reach their own spending and rating decisions. This means, however, that the Government must look to local authorities to deliver, as they have done in the past, the reductions in the volume of expenditure prescribed in our expenditure plans. At this stage I do not propose to issue formally a guideline for each authority but I am seeking urgently the views of the local authority associations about what steps need to be taken to secure the delivery of the national target. The Government certainly hopes that it will not be necessary to call for revised budgets again in 1981/2.[31]

Details of the first block grant arrangements were laid out in the Rate Support Grant Report (England) 1980. This gave some of the figures required to work out each authority's grant allocation for 1981–2. Other information, for example population and rateable value figures to be used in calculating grant, was made available to authorities by letter.

As was expected, the new grant would achieve in one exercise what the needs and resources elements had done in two. That is, to equalize the rate poundage cost of comparable levels of spending in relation to a central needs assessment. Therefore, two of the key factors in allocating grant were an authority's assessed spending needs (now known as 'grant-related expenditure') and its rateable value per head. The relationship between an authority's budgeted spending and its grant-related expenditure (GRE) would effect the rate poundage which the Government would assume would be charged on its local rateable value. A high GRE would therefore tend to lead to higher grant receipt, other things being equal, than a lower GRE. Similarly, a relatively low rateable value would mean bigger grant receipts than a high rate base in otherwise similar authorities.

An authority's entitlement to block grant was described in the RSG Report as the difference between its actual spending for block grant purposes and a notional rate income. The latter was to be calculated by multiplying the authority's own rateable value by a rate poundage, known as the grant-related poundage (GRP). The GRP might be modified by the application of a 'multiplier' to yield the final notional rate income. Thus, a formula-based representation of this would be:

block grant = expenditure − (GRP × rateable value × multiplier).

The GRP for any level of spending would depend on the variation of the authority's actual expenditure from its centrally determined spending needs assessment (GRE). If actual expenditure exceeded a predetermined threshold above GRE, the GRP would increase at a faster rate, thus producing lower grant entitlements than would have accrued in the absence of the threshold.

Grant-related poundages were set so that, if an authority chose to spend in line with its GRE, it would be deemed to charge a rate poundage of 134.42p. (This figure was in fact split between tiers of local government so that, for example, the figure for a non-metropolitan county was 116.92p and that for a non-metropolitan district 17.5p.) For each additional £1 per head of spending above GRE, the GRP would rise by 0.56p (equally, if it chose to spend £1 per head below GRE, GRP would fall by 0.56p for each £1 per head). This was very similar in principle to the way in which the needs and resources elements (taken together) operated in 1980–1. A 'threshold' was set, as had been expected, 10 per cent above the national average GRE per head. Once an authority's spending passed the threshold level, its GRP would rise by 0.7p for each £1 per head of spending, though the lower poundage increase (0.56p) would still apply to spending up to threshold. Figure 8.1 shows the relationship between expenditure per head and GRP in 1981–2.

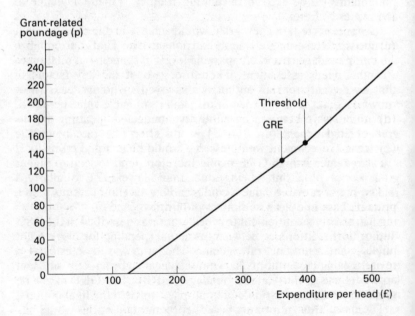

Figure 8.1   *Relationship between expenditure per head and grant-related poundage, 1981–2.*

Setting the threshold at 10 per cent above the *national average* GRE per head was significant. For authorities with above-average GREs (mostly urban areas) the threshold was less than 10 per cent. Westminster, for example, had a threshold only 4.8 per cent above GRE. Those with below-average GREs found that this method gave them a threshold above 10 per cent.

Another feature explained in the RSG Report was the use of 'safety nets'. These were to be used to ensure that grant losses, measured against a 'base position' (which was a Government-calculated estimate of how the new system might have affected authorities in the previous year), would not exceed prescribed limits. The limits added up to a maximum grant loss equivalent to a 13p rate at ratepayer level (i.e. taking account of all tiers of local government). Safety netting would be achieved by use of multipliers.

Multipliers were to be used, as had been explained in the Commons Standing Committee and laid down in the Local Government, Planning and Land Act 1980, for five purposes, including safety nets:

(a)  to limit losses of grant arising from the introduction of block grant because of (i) the new method of spending needs assessments and (ii) the extension of equalization of spending needs and rateable resources compared with the needs and resources elements;

(b)  to limit gains of grant arising from the introduction of block grant;

(c)  to limit losses in grant which would result because some authorities would find themselves spending high in relation to GRE (and thus would suffer the lower rate of grant increase brought about by the higher GRP for spending more than 10 per cent above GRE);

(d)  to preserve London's rateable resource advantage over the rest of England; and

(e)  to make adjustments to the grants of authorities part of whose area lay within the Metropolitan Police District.

The method of setting GREs and GRPs had to be according to principles applied to all authorities. Multipliers had to be set according to principles applied to all authorities in each class of local authorities. GREs, GRPs, multipliers and other details were to be published each year in a report to Parliament. Because of the need to revise these factors during and after the financial year to which they applied, the Secretary of State for the Environment would have to lay supplementary reports before Parliament from time to time.

The calculation of assessed spending need (GRE) was therefore crucial to authorities' grant allocation. Considerable effort had been put into improving the assessment of expenditure need in the late

1970s and in the months immediately before block grant first operated. A Study Team on Expenditure Needs Assessment (STENA)
had reported in 1976. This report was followed up by further work in
sub-groups of the Grants Working Group in the months after unitary
grant had been proposed in 1977. These sub-groups examined four
possible ways of assessing spending needs.

These were: regression methods; simple methods; a unit cost
method and client group methods. The *regression methods* sub-group
had made a number of recommendations for technical improvement
in the use of regression analysis (which had been used in the needs
element since 1974), and suggested further work. The sub-group
which looked at *simple methods* concluded that most of the possibilities which they considered would not be feasible. The *unit cost*
sub-group produced immensely complex and lengthy work which
attempted to build up for each service a unit cost of provision which
could be used to assess how much each authority needed to spend. The
fourth sub-group examined *client-group*-based methods of needs
assessment, which sought to produce a method based on the number
of 'clients' in receipt of local authority services and the national
average expenditure on each client.

In the section on the RSG Report dealing with GREs, the reasons
for moving from the existing system of needs assessments to the new
one to be used in GREs was given. It was explained that, in the old
system, assessing spending needs started from the assumption that the
correlation between the existing pattern of local authority expenditure
and a range of social and demographic indicators would provide the
best possible indication of the need to spend. An analysis was
undertaken which sought to explain the variation in individual local
authorities' need to spend. The analysis was carried out using
a statistical technique known as 'stepwise multiple regression
analysis'.

The RSG report stated that the Government considered the old
method of assessing spending needs unsatisfactory for four reasons:

–   the selection and weighting of indicators purely on the basis of
    their correlation with past expenditure led to results which were
    inexplicable on any commonsense basis;
–   the indicators and the weights given to them varied considerably
    from year to year, leading to big swings in grant entitlements and
    a continuing need for elaborate damping mechanisms;
–   the method of analysis treated all local authority expenditure
    equally, regardless of whether it related to the fulfilment of
    statutory obligations or discretionary improvements to services;
–   excessive spending levels by groups of authorities with similar
    characteristics could feed back into further increases in the level
    of their grant.[32]

The new system of grant-related expenditure was based on the work done by the technical groups and sub-groups discussed earlier. The main features of the new assessments were, first, that indicators chosen to distribute GRE were to be related to the service to which they were relevant. Second, the indicators should be selected on the basis of common sense based on judgement. Third, the expenditure assessment attached to each unit of an indicator should be intelligible; and finally, the sums for individual GRE indicators should add up to a total GRE which could be compared with the total GRE of other authorities in the same class. The Government felt that this approach would be more open and that informed discussion would lead to annual improvement.

Sixty needs components were, in fact, used in 1981–2. These were published in appendix 2 to annex J of the Rate Support Grant Report (England) 1980. Many were plausible determinants of an authority's likely need to spend. 'Residents', for example, was a significant indicator, being worth £55 of GRE for each person living in the local authority area. There were indicators for 'day-time net inflow' of population and 'visitor nights', both designed to assist areas with demands for services from business or tourists. Other indicators included children aged under 5, those aged 5–17 and an additional assessment for those aged 11–17. School pupils of different ages, the elderly, roads, social and environmental factors each received one or more indicators. The GRE indicators used in 1986–7 are listed in Table App.17.

London, in the previous system, was subject to special arrangements which provided for a special within-London needs assessment for distributing needs element to London authorities, for a deduction to be made from London's needs element to offset part of the capital's high rateable values compared with the rest of the country and for the distribution of this advantage between inner and outer boroughs through adjustments to their needs element entitlements. Block grant brought London within the scope of the national arrangements, in that its authorities were to be subject to the same grant-related expenditure system and the equalizing machinery of block grant arrangements. The effect of the latter, if not constrained, would be to remove London's resource advantage completely, which would significantly cut London authorities' grant.

London was therefore allowed to retain part of its rateable resource advantage (as under the old system), which would be distributed between inner and outer boroughs. These arrangements would be given effect partly by multipliers and partly by inter-authority transfers made under the London Government Act 1963. These transfers were to be known, as had earlier similar schemes, as the London Rate Equalization scheme. Multipliers were also to be used to make adjustments to the block grant of authorities just outside the London boundary part of whose area fell within the jurisdiction of the Metropolitan Police.

The effect of the new system made 1981–2 quite different from 1980–1. Both tiers of local government received block grant, whereas payment of needs and resources elements was made to different tiers in different areas. There were inevitably changes in the grant receipts of authorities, and shifts of rate burden from tier to tier and from authority to authority. Metropolitan district rates went up while those in the metropolitan counties fell because of the redistribution of grant. Safety netting lessened the shifts, though only to a limited extent; the safety nets were calculated on the assumption that all authorities spent at GRE. Thus authorities which spent above GRE found that safety nets were much less effective than they appeared at first sight.

For some authorities, the impact of the new grant was dramatic. In particular, those with high rateable resources and low spending needs found that block grant left them worse off. This was because, under the old system, the needs element was a fixed payment, whatever the expenditure or rateable value of an authority. Even if an authority had an exceptionally high rateable value, it would receive needs element. But as resources element was only a deficiency grant (i.e. it made authorities' rateable value per head up to a 'national standard' set by the Government), authorities with resources above the national standard simply received no grant. If resources element had fully equalized, it would have had to be negative (i.e. to take grant away) for authorities with above-standard rateable values.

Block grant, in effect, allowed this negative resources element by reducing the needs element of authorities with above-standard rateable resources. Thus authorities like Westminster, Camden and Crawley found themselves with block grant of zero; their high rateable resources led to a negative resources element effect that outweighed any needs element they would previously have received.

In terms of the new grant, this effect (of declining grant for higher spending) was created because the GRP calculated by the block grant formula for a particular level of spending would, when applied to the rateable value of an authority with very high rateable resources, bring

Table 8.2

|  | Westminster | Lewisham |
|---|---|---|
| Expenditure | £57.894m | £43.734m |
| GRE | £57.894m | £43.734m |
| GRP at GRE | 48.6p | 48.6p |
| Rateable value | £304.634m | £33.503m |
| Multiplier | 0.764971 | 0.700588 |

in more rates than the proposed level of spending. This point can be demonstrated by examining the 1981–2 block grant receipts for Westminster and Lewisham if each had spent at its GRE – Table 8.2.

The difference between the multipliers was due to the arrangements to spread London's resources advantage over the rest of the country so that Lewisham and other lower-resource authorities enjoy some of the benefit from Westminster's high rateable values. In this example, each authority is assumed to spend at GRE. It will thus be assumed to charge its ratepayers the GRP specified in the RSG Report for spending at GRE. Each authority's rateable value is multiplied by its multiplier. The resulting rate income is then taken from total spending. The gap between spending and rates is then made up with grant:

$$\text{block grant} = \text{total expenditure} - (\text{grant-related poundage} \times \text{RV} \times \text{multiplier}).$$

*(a) Westminster*:
block grant = £57.894m − (48.6p × £304.634m × .764971)
            = £57.894m − (£113.256m)
            = − £55.362m.

*(b) Lewisham*:
block grant = £43.734m − (48.6p × £33.503m × .700588)
            = £43.734m − (£11.407m)
            = £32.327m.

As block grant cannot be less than zero, Westminster would have got no grant for spending at GRE, while Lewisham would have received £32.327m.

Figures 8.2 and 8.3 show for Westminster and Lewisham the relationship between expenditure and grant over a range of spending levels in 1981–2. For both authorities, there was a point up to which all spending is grant-funded, though this was well below any realistic likely level of spending. Beyond this point, Westminster's grant declined very quickly (for the reasons outlined above), while Lewisham's grant increased. Lewisham's rateable value was sufficiently low for any additional rate poundage for increasing spending to bring in less than the proposed spending increase. This was even true for spending beyond the threshold.

Authorities with different GREs, rateable values and multipliers had different relationships between spending and grant. Others with high rateable values (e.g. the City of London and Camden) were in the same position as Westminster, while most authorities in England had a relationship between spending and grant more like that of Lewisham. Those with relatively high rateable values tended to have grant which increased up to threshold and declined thereafter.

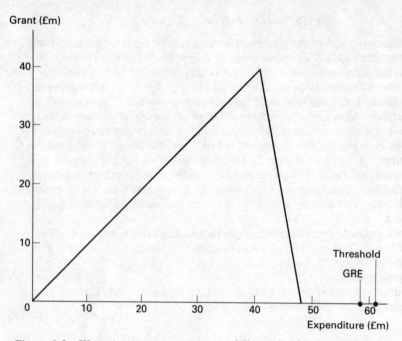

Figure 8.2 *Westminster: grant receipts at different levels of expenditure, 1981–2.*

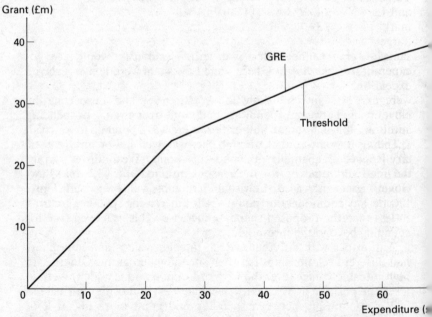

Figure 8.3 *Lewisham: grant receipts at different levels of expenditure, 1981–2.*

Block grant continued to operate in a similar way to that set out in the original RSG Report throughout the years from 1981–2 onwards. Changes were made to some of the components of GRE, while other minor internal adjustments were made from year to year. The addition to an authority's GRP for each additional £ per head of spending above GRE was increased from 0.56p to 0.6p during 1981–2, while the cost of each additional £ per head for spending over threshold was increased from 0.7p to 0.75p. These slightly increased figures were then used in each year from 1982–3 to 1984–5. There were further increases in the additional GRE for each £ per head of spending in 1985–6 and 1986–7.

However, a much more significant change was made early in 1981 which came to overshadow any changes in the internal workings of block grant. In January 1981, after the first RSG had been announced, but before authorities had set their 1981–2 budgets, the Government announced a current expenditure target for each authority in England (though not Wales) for 1981–2. Even at this early time, ministers and civil servants had become convinced that block grant could not deliver the immediate reductions in spending for which they had hoped.

## (7) THE INTRODUCTION OF TARGETS AND PENALTIES

Targets were something quite new. The Local Government, Planning and Land Bill had made no provision for any Government 'benchmark' for local authorities other than GRE. Yet in January 1981 a 'target' was set for every authority in England. It was not set on the same definitional base as GREs (which were expressed in 'total' expenditure as defined in the RSG Report) but in terms of 'current' expenditure. Nor was the target set on the same price base. GREs were expressed in cash, while the new targets were expressed in November 1980 prices.* The target set was 5.6 per cent below each authority's 1978–9 spending in volume terms.

These targets were introduced, according to the RSG Supplementary Report (England) 1982, 'so as to focus authorities' attention on the reduction needed from each authority in order to meet the Government's overall expenditure plans for local government'. The

---

* 'Current' expenditure is spending on goods and services, net of any income to those services. 'Total' expenditure is current expenditure, *plus* items like debt charges, revenue contributions to capital spending and rate fund contributions to the Housing Revenue Account, though minus income from interest receipts and specific and supplementary government grants. 'Current' spending is therefore that which provides direct services like teachers and street lighting, while 'total' spending is *all* an authority's spending which falls to be funded out of rates and block grant. 'Cash' is simply the amount of money spent. 'Volume' is a real-terms measure which expresses spending figures in the prices of a particular date or year. Thus 'volume' terms shows how much the quantity of a service changes from year to year, while 'cash' shows how much was actually spent. The Government changed the basis of public spending planning from a 'volume' to a 'cash' basis in 1982.

Government had realized that the vast difference between the spending and GRE in many authorities (for example, Tower Hamlets budgeted to spend 88 per cent over GRE in 1981–2, Camden 76 per cent and Lewisham 70 per cent) made it unlikely that these would spend at or near GRE). Indeed, if all authorities *had* spent at GRE, there would have been an enormous shift of spending from the metropolitan areas to the shires. Therefore, the Government set targets which related much more closely than GREs to actual spending. For those authorities with vast differences between their GREs and spending, a target of 5.6 below their 1978–9 out-turn current expenditure was much more likely to be attainable. The fact that targets were set on a different price base and used a different definition were only two of the objections made by the local authorities' associations.

Another problem in the view of many authorities was the choice of 1978–9 as a base year. The non-metropolitan counties and districts both complained that some of their authorities had reduced their spending in that year, and were faced with a low base-line compared with authorities which had (compared with 1980–1) relatively high spending in 1978–9. The Government was unmoved by arguments about such allegations of illogicality and unfairness.

Authorities set their expenditure for 1981–2 in the light of the block grant system and of the new targets. The new grant made it difficult to judge precisely how individual authorities were being treated. For example, whereas block grant was paid to all authorities, the old needs and resources elements of RSG were not. But it was clear that a number of authorities lost grant in 1981–2 compared with their position under the previous system in 1980–1 because they chose to overspend GRE by a considerable amount.

Block grant and the publication of individual spending targets did not produce the cut in spending desired by the Government. In a statement to the Consultative Council on 2 June 1981, Mr Heseltine announced that budgets for 1981–2 were 5.3 per cent (£800 million) above the total of targets, in November 1980 prices. At out-turn prices (i.e. including pay and price changes up to the end of 1981–2) the overspend totalled £1,250 million. Spending was back at the level of 1978–9, rather than 5.6 per cent below it.

Authorities were asked to submit revised budgets, by the end of July. The secretary of state also announced that he would take 'further steps' if the response to his request was unsatisfactory. These steps were an increase in the tapering off of grant for spending above the 10 per cent 'threshold' over GRE and the introduction of a system of penalties for authorities which chose to exceed their expenditure target. The Government at this time envisaged such penalties totalling £450 million.

Two changes were therefore proposed. First, the block grant 'taper' for spending over GRE was made tougher. Secondly, an additional system of penalties (known colloquially as 'hold-back' was grafted on to the grant system. Within the scheme of hold-back outlined, authorities which chose to spend marginally above target would get some exemption from hold-back. Those spending from 0.1 to 2.0 per cent above would receive partial exemption, while those spending within 2 and 4 per cent above received a lesser degree of protection.

The statement to the Consultative Council concluded with a reminder, a threat and a promise:

> The whole relationship of central and local government has traditionally rested on the clear understanding that local government keeps within the overall financial policies of the central Government. I believe strongly in the voluntary observance of this understanding ... I have to say also that the Government is deeply concerned about the unfairness of the way in which revenue is raised through the rates. We are therefore currently considering further measures, including legislation next session, which are needed to bring home to local authorities and their electorates the consequences of high spending policies ... Finally, the Government have been considering the problems of the rating system itself. The Government intend to issue a consultation document on the alternatives to domestic rates in the autumn.[33]

It is worth noting that the secretary of state mentioned the electorate in this statement. Hitherto, local authorities had been the sole object of ministerial encouragement. Ministers had by this time moved from a concern for local government in general, via the 'overspenders', to electors in their attempts to induce lower spending. At this time, local authorities were able to levy a supplementary rate during the financial year. The grant hold-back which was announced on 2 June 1981 could have led directly to supplementary rates as authorities made up lost grant with increased rate income, and in that way might have 'brought home' to electors the consequences of particular spending policies.

During the period from June to September 1981, the local authorities tried to encourage the Government to modify the hold-back arrangements. In the middle of this process, on 4 August, Tom King announced that plans for *1982–3* meant local authorities cutting all their 1981–2 overspend while making a further cut of 1 per cent in volume terms.[34]

On 3 September, Michael Heseltine gave the results of the revised budgets exercise. In total these were £15 million *higher* than the original budgets; 257 out of 413 authorities reduced their spending between original and revised budgets, by £196 million in total. But other authorities increased their spending by a total of £211 million.

The overspend of targets was now up to about 5.5 per cent in volume (8 per cent in cash).

Hold-back was to be used, the secretary of state announced. The authorities (in particular the non-metropolitan counties) did, however, win a major concession; an authority which spent below either its target or GRE would be exempt from penalty. This meant that a number of councils – non-metropolitan counties especially benefited from this – that overspent target but which were below GRE were let off penalties. With this and another exemption for authorities meeting the cost of urban riots in 1981, the total hold-back was estimated in September 1981 at £290–£300 million.

DoE civil servants considered a way of achieving the effects of hold-back by reducing authorities' grant by use of multipliers. This involved reducing the block grant of all authorities (by increasing the grant-related poundages at all levels of expenditure) and then using multipliers to increase the grant of those authorities which were spending at or below target or were achieving exemption.

This attempt to circumvent the spirit of the Local Government, Planning and Land Act appeared, as it was discussed within the Environment Department, to go outside the original intention of the legislation. DoE lawyers suggested that a legal challenge against the use of multipliers in this way might be successful, and that new legislation ought to be considered. The Government decided to introduce the Local Government Finance Bill 1981 in order (among other things) to give them the power to operate block grant hold-back.

### (8)  AN ASSESSMENT OF BLOCK GRANT

Before moving on to discuss the Local Government Finance Bill, it is worth pausing to consider the first few months of block grant in operation. Following difficulties experienced by the DoE in carrying the Local Government, Planning and Land Act through Parliament and the need to introduce targets and hold-back, it was clear by now that block grant had fallen well short of what ministers had hoped for it while it was being considered by Parliament in 1980.

The Government had claimed that block grant would lead to a fairer and more 'equitable' grant distribution than was previously the case. The problem in judging the success or failure of the system in these terms was that very different kinds of fairness were tangled up here. First, there was the question of fairness in the distribution of grant between authorities. The new grant was fairer in the Government's terms. One of the objections to the previous system was that authorities which chose to spend high would tend to bring in extra grant, which was, in the Government's view, unfair. The new method of measuring the need to spend would have weakened any tendency which the old needs assessments may have had to push up spending. It also tapered off extra grant receipts in authorities which decided to spend above the 'threshold' spending level over GRE. Although it had never been proved that the needs and resources elements had encouraged higher spending, the Government was convinced that any possibility that high spending was rewarded while low-spending authorities lost grant was unfair. By reducing such a possibility, the system was, in the Government's view, fairer.

Another kind of fairness was involved in the actual build-up of GREs. Construction of needs assessments under governments of both parties has proved an immensely subjective process, with final assessments in each year often being influenced by the need to provide statistical justification for a grant distribution to suit the political demands of the day. In that sense, the needs assessments in block grant might have been deemed to be as fair as those in any other grant settlement in the years up to 1981–2. But the factors used in expenditure needs assessment were more plausible than those in the old needs element. Indicators in the new block grant included many, such as 'residents' or 'children under 5', which were widely agreed to be significant determinants of the need to spend. The weights attached to each resulted from a round of negotiations between central and local government. Although the new needs assessments were in many cases very complex, they were undoubtedly more comprehensible than their predecessors. In the fuel analysis, 'fairness' is a highly subjective concept.

A second major area where the Government had wanted to make the grant system more equitable was in the equalization of rateable values and expenditure needs. Ministers had claimed that 100 per cent equalization was possible with block grant, though this promised advantage remained nothing more than a possibility. Multipliers were used in 1981–2 (and again in each succeeding year) to allow London authorities to retain a part of their resources advantage over the rest of the country, thus broadly replicating the extent of equalization which had taken place in the 1980–1 system. Under the old arrangements, this advantage was maintained by means of partial reduction in London's needs element (that is, leaving part of the resources advantage which naturally occurred). Block grant required that the Government used multipliers to stop the full equalization of rateable values which would happen automatically. This point was discussed more fully earlier in this chapter. The Government agreed that 100 per cent equalization did not, in fact, take place, but argued that it was at least simpler to see what was going on.

Although the Government admitted that the new system would not be simpler than its predecessor, it was claimed that benefits would flow from its comparative openness (though it would have been possible to make the old system more open by publishing more of the details of spending needs assessment). In fact, it was – and is – widely agreed that block grant (and especially the target and penalty systems which have been added to it) was very much more complex than the much-criticized needs element. Block grant was so complicated by the range of multipliers, assessments of spending need, poundage schedules, close-ending and such concepts as 'negative marginal increments' of grant that it remained incomprehensible to the overwhelming majority of councillors, officers, civil servants and Members of Parliament. By the time that targets and penalties had been added to the basic block grant mechanism, any advantages deriving from increased openness had been far outweighed by additional complexity and new arrangements.

The Government claimed that fewer officials would be required in Whitehall to run block grant than the previous system. No figures had been produced by the DoE to suggest that this was true, and given the ever-increasing size and complexity of the arrangements, it seemed unlikely that there had been any staff reduction. It was shown that the DoE had to spend more than twice as much on computer time in preparing for the 1981–2 and 1982–3 block grants as in the previous two years.[35]

But it was as a disincentive to high spending that block grant appeared to have had least success. While it remains difficult to demonstrate direct relationships between changes in the grant system and changes in the pattern of local authority spending, there can be no doubt that spending in 1981–2 overshot Government targets by a wide margin.

As was shown earlier, the total of local authorities' *current* expenditure at the time of their original budgets in 1981–2 was 5.3 per cent greater than the Government had planned. If the sum of 'total' expenditure (the definition used for block grant purposes) planned by the government was compared with the total of authorities' original budgets in April 1981, the overspend was between 9 and 10 per cent. The reason for the greater over-budgeting on 'total' than 'current' was that the former was expressed at out-turn prices and thus included allowance for pay and price rises during 1981–2 whilst the latter included no such provision. That is, authorities budgeted for a greater volume of services than the Government planned (i.e. more teachers and social workers) *and* expected their costs to increase more quickly than the Government would wish.

This overspend may have been because of one or more of a number of factors. First, there was the uncertainty arising from the change from one grant system to another; authorities were unsure how the new arrangements would work and in many cases raised more money from the rates as a buffer against contingencies. Second, no one knew how large the 'claw-back' factor would be to close-end block grant. (Like the previous resources element, block grant allocations depended on authorities' spending decisions. Many treasurers expected a considerable over-claim of the grant available and a consequent large adjustment of grant in mid-year.) Third, the inflation assumptions made by the Government at the time of the RSG settlement (5 per cent for pay, 11 per cent for prices) were widely believed to be too low. Fourth, the Government's planned reductions in the volume of spending in three successive years had been viewed by local government as too great and too fast; the 1981 public expenditure White Paper envisaged local government expenditure in England falling by 7.6 per cent between 1979–80 and 1981–2. Fifth, it is clear that local government believed that interest rates would be higher than the Government predicted. Finally, it is possible that many authorities 'spent up' to their GRE, while others failed to spend down.

As explained earlier, an important feature of block grant was an assessment for each authority of its expenditure need (GRE). Local authorities opposed the introduction of block grant (and the previous proposal for a unitary grant) on the grounds that it reduced their autonomy and increased central control. Publication of a GRE for each council was seen as particularly worrying because it was expected that such a figure would be seen as a norm. In the event, many authorities found that their proposed total spending in 1981–2 was likely to be below their GRE, which led to pressure from opposition groups and others to spend up to GRE (or beyond GRE to the 'threshold' where grant increases started to taper off or, in some cases, where total grant started to fall). Although authorities which overspent their GREs might be thought to be in the opposite position, many of these (for example, Lambeth and Sheffield) were controlled by groups which remained fully committed to their high spending policies despite grant loss. In addition, some of the highest spenders did not receive grant (because of their high rateable values) and were therefore free of any grant deterrent.

Apart from the Government's explicit objectives for block grant, which were largely concerned with making the grant system fairer and more open and giving some influence over the higher spenders, ministers undoubtedly had other, unspoken objectives. At the time that block grant was being introduced, there was speculation in the press and within the local authorities' associations that several ministers would have preferred more direct control over individual authorities' spending than that offered by block grant.

The importance attached by Treasury ministers to the attack on local authorities was made more explicit during 1982.[36] By this time, block grant had been shown not to work in the short term, as Treasury officials and ministers had feared all along. This pressure from the Treasury to obtain greater control over individual authority budgets was kept at bay during the early years of the Conservative administration by DoE claims that block grant would bring spending under control. When in 1982 and 1983 local government spending exceeded plans, ministers who had all along wanted to take more direct control were able to assert themselves. The next sections examine other developments during 1982 and 1983 and the policy and legislative steps towards introducing authority-by-authority rate limits.

(9)   THE LOCAL GOVERNMENT FINANCE BILL

The Government received advice from its lawyers that the powers given by the Local Government, Planning and Land Act 1980 were probably insufficient for the purposes of operating grant hold-back for authorities which overspent their targets. This meant that the penalties announced in June (and revised in September) 1981 could not be implemented immediately. The Government therefore decided to introduce another local government Bill, which would, among other things, give it power to operate hold-back. Because the Bill concerned did not become law until 1982, any hold-back suffered by authorities during 1981–2 and 1982–3 could not be removed from entitlements until after Royal Assent for the new law.

The Local Government Finance Bill, published in November 1981, did more than legalize hold-back. It also contained three major proposals. First, the Government would take power to specify the maximum rate or precept which each authority could set in each year; any authority wishing to spend at a level above that implied by the rate limit would have to raise the additional sum by way of a supplementary rate which could proceed only after approval by ratepayers at a local referendum. The additional rate burden would have been skewed so as to fall disproportionately on domestic ratepayers. If the authority failed to gain consent in the referendum, it would have to have borrowed the additional resources (having first received approval from the Environment Secretary) and then be subject to a lower rate or precept limit in the next year.

Secondly, the Bill introduced provisions which would allow the Government to make adjustments to authorities' block grant so as to impose hold-back. This would give officials and ministers the confidence to penalize authorities that they lacked when operating under the Local Government, Planning and Land Act. The third feature of the Bill was the setting up of an Audit Commission to take over the functions of the DoE and the District Audit Service with respect to audit in local government.

The Bill failed to make any progress in Parliament. Once published, the proposal to force local authorities to hold referendums about spending at levels determined by the Government brought considerable opposition from local authorities and, more importantly, from Conservative back-bench MPs. MPs were concerned not only about the reduction of local autonomy but also about the constitutional implications of the widespread use of referendums. It was the issue of using referendums in this way which forced the Government to withdraw the Bill and introduce another on 16 December 1981.

In a period of intense activity just before Christmas 1981, the Government announced not only the details of block grant with a new target and penalty system for 1982–3, but also the Local Government Finance (No. 2) Bill and the long-promised Green Paper on *Alternatives to Domestic Rates.*[37]

The (No. 2) Bill was a straightforward replacement for the Local Government Finance Bill published six weeks earlier. The clauses of the original Bill dealing with block grant adjustments (or 'hold-back') were retained, as were those about audit. However, the whole section dealing with referendums and spending limits had been dropped. In their place the Bill proposed to abolish supplementary rates and precepts.

During the passage of the Local Government Finance (No. 2) Bill in 1982, few of the substantial problems of local government finance were tackled. Instead, the Government took the powers it wanted to reduce grant paid to authorities which overspent targets, abolished supplementary rates and set up an Audit Commission. This Bill passed through Parliament with surprisingly little discussion of the principles of local government finance. MPs and ministers were largely concerned with the mechanics of budgeting once supplementary rates had been abolished and hold-back had been legitimized.

Abolition of supplementary rates and precepts was, Tom King argued, a stop-gap change until local government finance was reformed following consultation on the Green Paper *Alternatives to Domestic Rates*:

I should like to make it clear that the provision is designed to meet a short-term problem, but that it is in no sense a one year temporary power. Also, it is in no sense a measure intended to avoid the need for the fundamental reform that the Government seek and for which we have published the Green Paper ... Until such a reform is achieved we feel that there is no case for supplementary rates.[38]

The Government was forced to make a major concession. Robin Squire, MP for Hornchurch and a Government back-bencher on the Standing Committtee who had fought hard for local government during the passing of the Local Government, Planning and Land Act, tabled an amendment to clause 4 (which would allow the use of hold-back) which would ensure that the new power could be used only in a form announced in the RSG Report. That is, the severity of hold-back could not be intensified after RSG had been announced. Local authorities had expressed the worry that if there was the possibility of a second wave of hold-back in mid-year at the time when supplementary rates had been abolished, then councils would have to 'rate up' when setting their budgets. This might *add* to local authority spending rather than help to reduce it.

Tom King announced the Government's acceptance of the amendment during the committee stage of clause 1 (which abolished supplementary rates):

> The objective of my Hon. Friend's amendments is to require the Secretary of State to announce the principles of any grant holdback scheme in advance of the year to which it relates so that local authorities know where they stand when they are budgeting. The Government are sympathetic to the purpose of the amendments to similar effect when we reach Clause 4 . . . In regard to 1982–3 I can, therefore, give a specific assurance to the Committee that we do not intend to operate a differential holdback scheme in England of any greater severity than that already announced on 21 December . . . Because there will be no 'super-holdback' scheme in 1982/83 it will be unnecessary for authorities to rate up against that contingency in finalising their budgets.[39]

The Opposition was quick to show delight at the Government's concession, especially as it made a significant change to what was already a 'No. 2' Bill. Gerald Kaufman replied to Tom King thus: 'I congratulate him [the minister] on having won an important battle with the Treasury. On Second Reading I said that the Bill was the Government's seventh thoughts; it now appears that it is the Government's eighth thoughts and that, in effect, we are to debate a local government No. 3 Bill.'[40]

Before considering the operation of targets and penalties in 1982–3, 1983–4 and 1984–5, the Government's search for a replacement for domestic rates will be examined. A Green Paper on *Alternatives to Domestic Rates* had been published just after the first Local Government Finance Bill in 1981.

### (10)   ALTERNATIVES TO DOMESTIC RATES

The Green Paper on *Alternatives to Domestic Rates* was the result of continuing pressure on the Government to take action to reform the rates. The Conservatives' pledge to abolish household rates in 1974, which had been repeated (albeit in a weaker form) in 1979,[41] encouraged Government back-benchers to press for rating reform. This feeling manifested itself, for example, in the publication of a private Bill by Sir Hugh Fraser on 2 December 1981 entitled the 'Rating System (Abolition) Bill'. This proposed legislation commanded support from all parts of the parliamentary Conservative Party.[42] It proposed simply to abolish all rates on the existing method of assessment and was intended to demonstrate the strength of feeling on the back-benches, rather than actually to abolish rates.

The Government's solution to unease about the rates, and to some extent about other worries with local authority finance, was the same as that attempted by previous governments. A consultative document was published. Ministers clearly hoped that this would put off the evil day when a decision would have to be taken. *Alternatives to Domestic Rates*[43] was published in December 1981.

The Green Paper covered much the same ground as had the 1971 Green Paper and the Layfield Committee. Only one of the major 'alternatives' suggested in 1981 (poll tax) had not been given detailed consideration in 1971. Several of the 1971 proposals were not considered in 1981. The problems with the existing system listed in the Green Paper were similar to those touched upon as early as the 1957 and 1966 White Papers. The preface to the 1981 Green Paper explained:

> For some time there has been dissatisfaction with the way in which local people contribute to the cost of local services through the present system of domestic rates. Some domestic ratepayers believe that they pay too large a share of that cost, pointing out that other local people who are not householders are not required to pay rates at all. Many of those professionally concerned with rating and valuation matters believe that the technical basis of the domestic rating system is no longer satisfactory in some respects.[44]

The Government had described a worry about the burden of rating. Yet the concern was different from that expressed in 1966, when the worry was that the poor paid more in rates than the rich and that the rates were generally too high. Now the Government claimed that (because of the rate rebates which had been introduced to reduce the burden of rates on the least well-off) some people were paying little or no rates. In addition, it was argued that individuals who were not householders (and did not, therefore, pay rates directly) were a problem because they could vote for higher local government spending without having to pay higher rates.

The Green Paper considered a number of criticisms of the way in which domestic rates operated. The first of these was that 'the burden of domestic rates is unfairly shared between different types of household or as between people occupying property of a similar kind in different local authority areas'. Secondly, 'domestic rates bear too little relationship either to ability to pay. .. or to the use that is made of local government services'. Thirdly, it was argued that the lack of market information made impossible any further revaluation of rateable values on the basis of imputed rental values.

The Green Paper then went on to discuss what it called 'wider considerations'. In this section, local government's traditional free-doms were discussed, along with the Government's base for influence or control over national economic matters. The relationship between central and local government was summarized in the following terms:

> Local government has traditionally enjoyed a degree of discretion about the amount of local revenue it raises and the amount of revenue it incurs. It is obviously desirable that authorities should be able to tailor local revenues and expenditure to the provision of a level of services on which they decide, provided, on the one hand, that the levels of revenue raised and the expenditure incurred do not prejudice the Government's objectives for the national economy, and, on the other, that local services are provided to acceptable standards.[45]

The Government explained that neither local government nor local ratepayers were in a position to assess the effects of their decisions on the national economy or the economic impact of local expenditure. Central government, it was asserted, had to take a strategic view about such matters when managing the national economy. The Government also explained that it had introduced new guidance backed up by grant incentives (i.e. block grant, targets and hold-back) to encourage authorities to behave in a way which supported national economic policies.

The section on 'wider considerations' finished with a statement which was to prove important when judging the significance of the policy of rate limitation which was proposed in the 1983 Conservative Party manifesto and subsequently taken into the Rates Act 1984. The 1981 Green Paper considered the possibility of taking more central control over local authorities:

> The weaker the influence of the local tax system in restraining expenditure, the more pressure will develop on central government to impose direct controls on levels of local government expenditure. For example, statutory upper limits could be imposed on local authorities' income and expenditure. The case for the Government taking such powers has to be judged against the very considerable constitutional and practical difficulties that would be involved.[46]

The Green Paper went on to consider the main requirements of a local tax. The most important criteria, according to the Government, were:

(a)  Is it practicable?
(b)  Is it fair?

(c)  Does it make those who take decisions on local expenditure properly accountable to local people who pay?
(d)  Can the costs of administration and collection incurred by the taxing authorities and businesses be kept within acceptable limits?
(e)  Are the implications for the rest of the tax system acceptable?
(f)  Does it encourage proper financial control?
(g)  Is it suitable for all tiers of local government?

Each of these criteria was then considered briefly.

To be *practicable*, the source of income had (either alone or with another tax) to be able to produce at least the yield of domestic rates, to yield a reasonable amount in each local authority and to be applicable easily to individual taxpayers. *Fairness* was seen as the acceptability of the tax to the public; if a tax commanded broad public support, then it would be judged to be fair. *Accountability* would be fostered if a tax were to be clearly perceptible to local electors and taxpayers and, as far as possible, be paid as far as possible by people who benefit from local services. Any local tax (or a combination of taxes) must, if it were to be *acceptable*, be capable of cost-effective collection, without putting an unacceptable burden on authorities or employers.

Consideration of any changes in the system of local taxation should also have regard to the implications for the balance of the whole *national tax system* and for the distribution of the tax burden between different individuals and households. This would apply particularly to any changes involving new taxes like a sales tax or an income tax which would overlap with existing national taxes.

Any local tax would have to give authorities a *predictable income* each year, otherwise there might be a need for a build-up of balances or for short-term borrowing. The Government also felt that a tax which was not buoyant (i.e. if its base did not rise naturally with inflation) would have the benefit of increasing the perceptibility to local taxpayers. A local tax should not, however, be 'lumpy'. That is, if the minimum practicable change in the tax rate produced a large variation in tax revenue, local authorities might have to run high balances or to raise the tax rate more quickly or more slowly than they wished to.

Finally, the Government was looking for a tax which was *suitable for all tiers* of local government. A local tax should be capable of producing an independent source of income for each of the tiers of local government, possibly including parish councils as well as counties and districts.

Having discussed the qualities of a local tax, the Green Paper examined a number of taxes and then changes which might reduce the level of domestic rates without introducing a new tax. These will be dealt with in turn.

*Local Taxes: the Government's Views*

Three new taxes were considered in some detail, while a number of others were rejected out of hand. The possibility of reforming the rates was also examined, as were a number of ways of cutting rates by increasing central support. Reformed rates, a local sales tax, a local income tax and a poll tax were each given a chapter, as were 'assigned revenues', increased grants and several other features. In addition, annex B suggested a radical possible alternative method of funding the education service.

*(a) Rates*   Rates were described by the Government as practical (they already existed); as perceptible (the very pressure on the Government to reform or abolish the rates was evidence that people understood what they were paying in rates and were aware of increases in the rates burden); as allowing control over the total collected and as suitable for all tiers. Their effect on the national tax structure was well known. On the other hand, many allegations of unfairness had been made against the rates; for individuals who received no help from rate rebates or other benefits they were judged to bear little relationship to the ability to pay; non-householders were not required to contribute directly to rate bills, while rateable values upon which rates were charged were unevenly spread about the country. Thus rates, even with the equalizing effect of the rate support grant, produce a more variable local tax burden than would a tax with a more general expenditure or income basis.

The Green Paper then described a number of possible reforms to the rating system. These were: a levy on earning non-householders, allowing rates to be offset against income tax, restructuring domestic rate relief and capital valuation (as opposed to imputed rental value) to replace the existing method of assessing rateable values. The first two of these changes were likely to be difficult or expensive to administer, while reforming domestic rates would have the effect of shifting the existing burden without changing the basis of the system. Capital valuation, the Green Paper reminisced, had been proposed by the Layfield Committee and would be beneficial for two reasons; first, there was much more evidence about the capital value of property than about rental values, second, capital valuation would be more comprehensible to ratepayers. The burden would inevitably shift between householders, with the likelihood being of a movement of burden away from middle-priced properties and towards those with higher and lower values.

In conclusion, the Government made it clear that a reformed rating system (involving some of the reforms described above) was an acceptable possibility to be considered along with others. Some of the reforms suggested in the section on rates might also be thought of as transitional measures, rather than long-term alternatives of the existing system.

*(b)   Local sales tax*   The Green Paper then went on to examine a local sales tax and a local income tax (LIT). These chapters of the document were very similar to parts of those in the 1971 Green Paper, in particular those dealing with LIT. In considering a local sales tax, the Government ruled out the idea of a value added tax akin to the national VAT. It would be difficult to attribute a local VAT for a product which was made in several stages in different local authorities, where each stage was subject to the tax. VAT could not, according to European Community rules, be applied differentially from authority to authority.

Therefore, if local authorities were to be given a sales tax, it would probably have to be a single-stage levy. The Government considered two models:

(i)    A single-stage tax system administered and collected by HM Customs and Excise in conjunction with VAT; the tax would be applied to all goods and services currently subject to VAT, but authorities would be free to set the rate of tax, possibly within limits set by Parliament.

(ii)   A single-stage tax with a separate system of collection administered by the local authorities themselves, possibly with each authority having the power to decide which goods and services should be taxable.

There would, however, be a number of problems with such a tax. First, there would be difficulty in defining the transactions to which it applied, since it would be a replacement for domestic but not for non-domestic rates and should in theory be applied only to goods and services bought by households. This would be an impossible distinction to draw in practice. There would also be problems in the interaction of a local sales tax and VAT, which might require the Government seeking a derogation from European Community rules. Registration for tax purposes might also need to be changed. The level at which businesses had to register for VAT in 1981 was set at a higher turnover figure than in many other countries. If a local sales tax were introduced, it would have given a considerable advantage to retailers who were not registered to pay VAT. If, on the other hand, all retailers were to be included, there would have to be a much-increased bureaucracy to cope with the extra policing and administration of the system.

Cross-border shopping would also be a problem, the Green Paper explained. Whereas in 1971 this problem was barely mentioned, the 1981 document stressed the problem (as had Layfield) of shopping becoming concentrated in urban centres and of major shopping centres which served several authorities. Rural areas and those without major centres and stores would lose out because of this. Where an authority had a large amount of retail floor-space, a lower tax rate would provide the same income as that yielded by a higher tax rate in an area with little retail floor-space. Lower tax rates in some authorities might lead to trade being diverted, and thus the problem would become worse. This would inevitably lead to demands for equalization grants. In addition to these difficulties, a decision would have to be taken about where services were deemed to be supplied. It would be almost impossible to produce a combined VAT/local sales tax rate of a round figure; a tax rate set to several decimal points would be awkward for retailers and incomprehensible to consumers. Mail-order traders would be another problem; there would be a considerable incentive for them to set up national businesses in low-tax areas.

The cost of administering a sales tax could be lower than those of the domestic rates system, though if a more complex system were evolved (in particular, if it involved an individual authority-based system) the cost of administering domestic rates might be exceeded, with the possibility of extra costs for businesses. The Government did not think a local sales tax of any kind could be introduced before 1987–8 at the earliest.

Unless some new form of income support were introduced, those who were currently in receipt of rebates and supplementary benefit might lose out if a sales tax were introduced, though the number of people actually paying tax to an authority would be much increased. This would result from individuals who currently receive whole or partial rate rebates having to pay local sales tax on non-essential items. Perceptibility could be maintained only if retailers had to show the local sales tax separately on all items. Such a requirement would, however, add to retailers' costs.

The yield of a sales tax would not be easy for an authority to predict (and would thus make financial planning difficult) because retail sales change from year to year, and this would cause difficulties for local authorities. Rates, because of their stable base, can be predicted to within a very narrow range. In addition, the Government would not, according to the Green Paper, be likely to allow changes in the local tax rate of less than 1 per cent. That is, if an authority wished to increase its tax rate, it would have to increase it from, say, 7 per cent to 8 per cent. This would mean a large increase in yield from one year to the next; 1 per cent on 7 per cent would lead to a 14 per cent change in yield.

Therefore, the Government made it clear that a sales tax could be considered only as an additional source of revenue rather than as a sole source. Another more flexible source would have to be given to authorities, to allow 'fine-tuning'.

The Green Paper estimated that a combined VAT/local sales tax rate of about 22 per cent (i.e. a local sales tax of 6–7 per cent) would allow the abolition of domestic rates, though even a partial abolition of rates would add considerably to the combined rate. This, in turn, would affect retail sales and therefore income from VAT, reducing Government freedom to change VAT nationally. A formal constraint on local authorities would help the Government to retain this freedom. However, such a constraint would (especially if the sales tax were to be an important part of local authority income) threaten local independence and accountability.

Concluding, the Government stated that it envisaged a local sales tax, if feasible, being given only to the upper tier of local government: counties in England and Wales and regions and island authorities in Scotland. Local authorities would almost certainly have to retain another income source and there would be a range of difficulties to overcome. Many of the issues raised in the Green Paper would need much further consideration.

*(c) Local income tax*   Local income tax received more consideration than it had in the 1971 Green Paper, though many of the points raised in 1981 were similar to those made then and in Layfield. The 1981 document looked in most detail at LIT fully integrated with the existing tax system, which was the kind favoured by the Layfield Committee. It also examined how LIT might operate if the national system were radically changed so that an assessment was made of each taxpayer each year. Two systems involving collection of LIT by local authorities themselves were discussed.

LOCAL INCOME TAX INTEGRATED WITH THE EXISTING NATIONAL SYSTEM   LIT integrated with the national tax system would, the Government believed, be suitable only for the major spending authorities (largely because changes in the rate of tax could probably not be smaller than 0.25p in the £, which would be large amounts of money for many non-metropolitan districts). It could not be introduced until the 1990s. It would be charged on the same tax base as national income tax. But LIT would mean that taxpayers' places of residence would have to be recorded by the Inland Revenue. The existing income tax system operated (and still does) by taxing most people at their place of *work* rather than where they live. If LIT were to be a truly local tax, it would have to be paid by taxpayers in their home authorities, and therefore the Inland Revenue would have to find out where taxpayers lived. Although it would be a major task, once this was done it would be possible for each council to set its own tax rate.

Once the Inland Revenue had been informed of a particular council's tax rate, it could inform employers of changes in the tax coding of employees so as to allow a deduction of LIT at the appropriate rate. The Green Paper envisaged that authorities would not be able to alter the rate of LIT by less than 0.25p. It might be necessary to bring forward authorities' budgetary cycles in order to allow the Inland Revenue sufficient time to alter the system for the start of each financial year.

The costs of collecting a nationally run LIT would probably be much the same as the costs of domestic rates; if rates were abolished there could be savings in valuation staff at the Inland Revenue.

LOCAL INCOME TAX WITH YEAR-END ASSESSMENT    The Government also considered LIT linked to a new national system of year-end assessment for income tax. This would make introduction of LIT easier and would allow a much more flexible system, possibly involving lower-tier authorities. There would be no need for an earlier budget cycle. The costs of adding a local element to a year-end assessment system of this kind would probably be lower than those of changing the existing system.

LIT could also be administered locally on the basis of information provided by the Inland Revenue to local authorities. The local authority would then be responsible for assessing the local tax at its own rate, and collecting it direct from the taxpayer. Alternatively, each local authority could set up a separate system of income tax independently of the national system. Both these schemes would be more costly in terms of administration than either the 'national' system or the year-end assessment arrangements.

LOCAL INCOME TAX: CONCLUSION    The Government judged that, compared with domestic rates, a local income tax would be seen to spread the tax burden more widely, and an individual's tax liability would be related more closely to ability to pay. The most straightforward means of introducing LIT would be to integrate it closely with the existing national system. LIT would extend to about 25½ million (from 20 million) the number of people paying local taxation, though there would be a shift of incidence from those with low to those with higher incomes. An integrated LIT/national tax system would not be particularly perceptible, even if an annual statement of the income tax rate were sent out by each council.

LIT would increase the burden of direct taxation, which would run counter to the Government's stated policy of switching taxation away from income and on to expenditure. The Chancellor's decisions on personal allowances and tax reliefs would have a direct effect on an authority's LIT income, while local government's collective decisions on income tax would affect the Chancellor's freedom to manoeuvre. The Government might feel the need to limit local tax rates, which would reduce local independence and accountability. Like a sales tax,

LIT would provide local authorities with a less predictable income source than rates. In short, there were deemed to be very considerable obstacles to the introduction of LIT.

*(d) Poll tax*   Poll tax was the other new income source considered. The 1971 Green Paper mentioned such a possibility in only the briefest of considerations. In addition there had been some discussion of a straightforward per capita tax in the months prior to the publication of the 1981 document. The Green Paper in 1981 conceded that such a tax had not been given detailed consideration in previous examinations of possible local authority finance reforms.

A poll tax could be levied according to a number of different criteria. For example, it could be levied on every adult, every elector or every person with an income. The Green Paper stated that a poll tax of about £120 per head from each of the 40 million adults in Great Britain would bring in roughly the £4.8 billion required at that time to replace domestic rates. If there were exemptions from the tax (e.g. pensioners) the per capita tax would be higher. It would be most likely that a poll tax would be a supplement to another local tax, rather than local authorities' sole tax source.

But there would be considerable difficulties in assessing individuals for poll tax. If the electoral register were to be used in order to establish who should vote, there would be the danger that some people would fail to register. A separate roll could be created, though this would increase costs. There would also be costs if instalment schemes were introduced and if a rebate system were instituted for the less well off.

A poll tax would be highly perceptible, possibly more so than domestic rates. Like rates, it would produce a predictable yield and could be adjusted in small steps. The implications for the tax system as a whole were difficult for the Government to predict because it would be quite different from any existing tax. Finally, poll tax would be suitable for all tiers of local government, including parish councils.

*(e) Other taxes*   The Green Paper ruled out four other possible local taxes, each of which had been considered in earlier examinations of local government finance. These were: *local petrol, alcohol or tobacco duties*; *local vehicle excise duty*; charges for *licences for the sale of alcohol or petrol*; and *local payroll tax*. Each was briefly considered in an annexe to the Green Paper and each rejected because it was too expensive to collect, because it reduced Government control over the tax system, because the tax would fall unevenly or because (in the case of a payroll tax) the Government simply did not want any extra tax on business.

*Other options*
Having considered several tax alternatives to domestic rates, the

Green Paper went on to look at other ways of reducing rate burdens. '*Assigned revenues*' would give local authorities a share of the revenue from a national tax or taxes. There would be little difference in practice between assigned revenues and increased Exchequer grant; the total of each would be determined by the Government, as would its distribution. Local freedom could be substantially reduced if assigned revenues replaced domestic rates (especially because the removal of domestic rates would mean, according to the Green Paper, that the level of non-domestic rates might not then be left to individual authorities to decide).

The Green Paper effectively ruled out assigned revenues, on the grounds that they would break the link between local spending and tax-raising, that there would be an additional cost to national taxation and because there would be less flexibility for local authorities. The whole relationship between local and central government would be changed, because of the high increase in authorities' dependence on centrally controlled income sources.

'*Exchequer grants to local authorities*' were also examined, though not as an alternative to domestic rates. The purposes of grants were considered, including ensuring that certain services were provided to a particular level, general subsidy, equalization and central influence over local spending. New block grant arrangements could be used, the Green Paper proposed, to iron out some of the difficulties which might arise if a new tax or taxes were introduced. On the other hand, the Green Paper argued that if local authorities were to become dependent on more than one tax, the mechanics of the grant system might have to cope with equalizing more than one tax base.

The Green Paper also considered the arguments for and against extending charging for services. Although there might, it was stated, be limited scope for increasing *fees and charges*, there could be little hope that this would produce any significant increase in income. In some cases it would be impractical or inefficient to try to charge customers the economic cost of services. The Government felt that this applied to street lighting and cleaning, public open spaces, police and fire services. Other local services were deliberately organized so that the poor were shielded from the cost of their provision. In education, law and order, highways and social services there was thought to be little scope for increasing charges, though it was possible that some environmental services could extend charging.

One other part of the Green Paper deserves attention. Annex B looked at the possibility of introducing an '*education block grant*'; of removing education altogether from local government, or of making teachers' salaries 100 per cent centrally funded. The idea of having a separate block grant for education (run on lines similar to the existing block grant for all services) was most widely discussed during the search to find a way of cutting domestic rates in the months after the publication of the Green Paper.

An education block grant would operate with the Government running two parallel arrangements for giving grant aid to local authorities. One would deal solely with education. The Department of Education and Science would make an explicit assessment of what each authority should be spending on education each year: an education GRE. This, as was mentioned earlier in this chapter, was already done in the build-up of total GRE for the existing block grant. As with the overall block grant, grant received would have been influenced by the relationship between this GRE and an authority's budgeted spending level. Grant disincentives could have been imposed (although the Green Paper did not claim this) on authorities which over- or underspent the Government's figure of assessed spending need.

Such a system would have given the DES a clearer say in what each authority spent on education. Incentives could have been built into the system which would be designed to encourage spending closer to the assessed spending need figure, regardless of whether an authority was spending above or below it. The DES was known to favour this kind of grant, which would allow it to encourage higher spending in some of the lower-spending education authorities while discouraging spending elsewhere. An education block grant would not have required changes in the local administration of education, except that education funding would have to be kept separate from other services.

If the introduction of an education block grant were to lead to a reduction in domestic rates (which was the purpose of the Green Paper) there would have had to be an increase in the level of grant support within the new education grant. A figure of 75 per cent was widely assumed to be most likely during the discussion of education block grant which took place in 1982. These discussions faded out, as the Government let it be known that an education grant had no future well before the 1983 rates White Paper.

In its conclusions to the Green Paper, the Government stated that it was 'committed to the reform of the domestic rating system'.[47] But the difficulty of replacing some £5 billion of domestic rate income was recognized: 'The arguments for and against the rates are already well rehearsed. The system has become particularly controversial as spending has grown and in times of high inflation. This Paper examines and compares the options for reform. None of them is easy – no tax is popular.'[48]

Publication of the Green Paper was followed by a period of consultation which was formally ended with the publication of a White Paper in August 1983 about the *Rates*.[49] During this period the Select

Committee on the Environment undertook an investigation about the rates[50] in parallel to the consultation on the White Paper.

The Select Committee concluded in its report that rates should be retained, though on the basis of capital valuation. A local sales tax and poll tax were rejected. The committee favoured a detailed examination of a local income tax, though it had not received evidence suggesting that there would be widespread political support for its introduction. Assigned revenues and changes in the funding of education were rejected. Finally, the committee argued for a reduction in the level of RSG support if a local income tax were to be introduced.

In the conclusion to chapter 6 of the report, MPs sought to express a view on the subjects of central control and local accountability:

> The Committee recognises also the dilemma of any central government in balancing its determination to achieve overall economic targets with its desire to preserve a proper level of autonomy and independence for local authorities, but concludes that Government needs to devote more care and attention to the nature and extent of its controls than has been the case in recent years in order to secure greater consistency in its policies and the understanding and co-operation of the local authorities.[51]

*Commentary*
The Green Paper and the Select Committee's enquiry are interesting side-issues, being reactions to expressions of disquiet about much of local government finance and the relationship between local and central government. But neither advanced beyond the arguments which had been made by the 1971 Green Paper and Layfield. The problems which had become apparent as early as 1966 remained unsolved. The 1981 Green Paper made it clear that there was most unlikely to be significant change to the way in which local government was funded. The size of rate yield (about £5 billion from domestic rates alone) meant that the Treasury would not contemplate giving up such a successful income source (though it had, in the past, given up purchase tax when introducing VAT). Increases in income tax, sales tax by way of local supplements, or additions to central taxes to pay for grant increases appeared unrealistic steps for a government which was committed to reducing tax levels.

But ministers and others had spent some time nurturing grievances about the rates and encouraging people to regard the payment of rates as an unfair and unnecessary imposition. Having done so, they were forced to produce a Green Paper which suggested that the problems associated with other taxes were greater than any imagined difficulties with the rates.

Outside government, there was support for new forms of local taxation. The local authorities' associations were broadly in favour of introducing a local income tax, as were several academic commentators.[52] Rates were generally supported as a local tax by local government itself, though others (for example, ratepayers' groups) favoured abolition. The Government did not produce proposals following the Green Paper exercise. Only in the months before the publication of the Conservative Party manifesto in May 1983 (and in the manifesto itself) was it confirmed that domestic and non-domestic rates were to remain, and that as far as Mrs Thatcher was concerned all other possibilities were rejected.

The Green Paper had been used deliberately to put off the day when action had to be taken. Revaluation of the rate base and all other possible improvements had to wait until the end of a period of anticipation of the Green Paper and a further period of consultation after the Government had described its view of the alternatives to domestic rates. Supplementary rates had been abolished as a short-term measure prior to reform. Yet there was little expectation in or outside government that an alternative would or could be found. The Green Paper served its purpose by diffusing opposition to the rates for another two years, until a solution of a quite different kind was to be tried.

## (11)   INCREASING THE SQUEEZE ON LOCAL AUTHORITIES: TARGETS AND PENALTIES

The Local Government Finance Act allowed the Government to set targets – see the earlier discussion in section (7) of this chapter – and, if an authority decided to spend above its target, to impose grant penalties. The system operated in 1981–2 was the first of several different ones to be used in succeeding years. The method of setting targets and the penalties imposed on 'overspenders' were both different in 1981–2, 1982–3, 1983–4, 1984–5 and 1985–6. The extent of the Government's success in making local authorities spend (in total and individually) at target levels also varied from year to year. Targets and penalties were abandoned at the end of 1985–6.

Tables 8.3 and 8.4 describe how targets were set and penalties operated in each year from 1981–2 to 1985–6, as well as the timing of announcements in each year. In 1981–2 targets were set in terms of 'current' expenditure, in volume terms. From 1982–3 onwards, targets were set in cash out-turn prices in terms of 'total' expenditure – i.e. the same definition as was used for GREs and described in section (7) above. In 1982–3 targets started from each authority's minimum volume budget for 1981–2, revalued to 1982–3 prices. The resulting figure was then adjusted to take account of the relationship between:

(a)   1981–2 spending and 1981–2 target; and
(b)   1981–2 spending and 1982–3 GRE.

Table 8.3  Construction of Targets, 1981–2 to 1985–6 (England only)

| Characteristic | 1981–2 | 1982–3 | 1983–4 | 1984–5 | 1985–6 |
|---|---|---|---|---|---|
| (1) Price basis | Constant prices (November 1980) | Cash out-turn | Cash out-turn | Cash out-turn | Cash out-turn |
| (2) Expenditure base | 1978–9 out-turn current expenditure | 1981–2 minimum volume budget total expenditure (MUB) | 1982–3 budget, 1982–3 effective target, or 1981–2 MVB. All total expenditure | 1983–4 target, the higher of 1983–4 settlement and First Supplementary Report GRE or 1983–4 budget. All adjusted for the reduced rate of NIS. Total expenditure | 1984–5 GRE, 1984–5 target, and 1984–5 budget |
| (3) Method of construction | 1978–9 out-turn current expenditure less 5.6% | Minimum volume budget total expenditure, then two-stage process: <br><br>(i) Rescaling. MVBs rescaled to 1982–3 cash totals using class factors which reflect cash changes in GRE service totals between 1981–2 and 1982–3 <br>(ii) Skewing. Each authority's scaled MVB was adjusted to take account, first, of the relationship between its MVB estimate of current expenditure in 1981–2 and its 1981–2 current expenditure target (both at November 1980 prices) and, secondly, the relationship between its rescaled 1981–2 budgeted total expenditure and its 1982–3 GRE | Based on the extent of budgeted compliance with 1982–83 'effective targets'. <br><br>The rules were: <br><br>(i) Authorities budgeting in 1982–3 to spend up to 1% above 1982–3 'effective target'. 1983–4 target = 1982–3 budget + 4% <br>(ii) Authorities budgeting in 1982–3 to spend more than 1% above 1982–3 'effective target'. 1983–4 target = 1982–3 'effective target' + 5% | The basic rule is: 1984–5 target = higher of 1983–4 GRE and target + 2.5% | The basic rule is: 1985–6 target = either (a) 1984–5 GRE plus 3.75% or (b) 1984–5 target plus 3.75%. <br><br>(a) applies to authorities spending below GRE in 1984–5; (b) applies to those spending over GRE |

The above characteristics relate to the National Schedule. In practice the grant penalties are disaggregated (split between tiers)
*Source*: Local authorities' associations, *Rate Support Grant (England) 1984–5*, appendix F.3, modified to include 1985–6.

| | Cash out-turn 1981–2 repriced to November 1980 prices | Cash out-turn 1982–3 | Cash out-turn 1983–4 | Cash out-turn 1984–5 | Cash out-turn 1985–6 |
|---|---|---|---|---|---|
| (4) Constraints | | (a) No target to represent a real increase in expenditure<br>(b) Authorities which budgeted to spend below 1981–2 target and were projected to spend below 1982–3 GRE should not have a target which implied a real reduction of more than 1%<br>(c) The real reduction implied by a target should not exceed 7%<br>(d) Targets should sum to the cash total of GREs | (a) Where rule (i) would lead to a target less than 1981–2 MVB then the latter = 1983–4 target. Authorities in category (ii) are subject to two other constraints<br>(b) 1983–4 target to represent no more than a 1% cash reduction from 1982–3 budget<br>(c) No target is to increase more than 25% (cash) above 1981–2 MVB | (a) The maximum increase from 1983–4 NIS adjusted budget is 3%<br>(b) The maximum reduction from 1983–4 budgets is 6%<br>(c) The maximum increase from 1981–2 minimum volume budget is 24% for authorities spending above target and GRE in 1983–4 | (a) The maximum increase from 1984–5 NIS adjusted budget is 4.5% costs (4.625% for some authorities)<br>(b) The maximum reduction from 1984–5 NIS adjusted budget is 1.5% |
| (5) Expenditure to be assessed against target | Cash out-turn 1981–2 repriced to November 1980 prices | Cash out-turn 1982–3 | Cash out-turn 1983–4 | Cash out-turn 1984–5 | Cash out-turn 1985–6 |
| (6) Expenditure to be disregarded for assessment against target – section 8(4) of 1982 Act | Certain expenditure by certain authorities under the following headings:<br>(i) Urban Programme<br>(ii) Riot expenditure<br>(iii) Winter damage 1981–2<br>(iv) Section 138 of the Local Government Act 1972 and the additional cost of police pay award | (i) Certain expenditure consequent on the 1982 police pay award<br>(ii) Certain Urban Programme expenditure | (i) Certain Urban Programme expenditure<br>(ii) Additional cost of the 1983 police pay award | (i) Cash increases in Urban Programme expenditure<br>(ii) Cash increases in civil defence expenditure<br>(iii) Increased expenditure on community care schemes jointly financed | (i) Cash increases in Urban Programme expenditure<br>(ii) Cash increases in civil defence expenditure<br>(iii) Increased expenditure on community care schemes jointly financed |

*Notes*:
1 Disregards are to be used to give effect to GRE exemption in 1981–2 and 1982–3
2 'Minimum volume budget' in relation to 1981–2 was the lower of an authority's original and revised budgets for 1981–2, adjusted to take account of inflation and certain other factors.
3 The budget base line for authorities subject to the constraints in 1984–5 was modified for housing authorities with net budgeted transfers of funds from HRAs to General Rate Funds in 1983–4, for authorities budgeting to spend lower than 2% below target in 1983–4 and for authorities with high levels of interest receipts in 1983–4
4 NIS: National Insurance Surcharge.
*Source*: Local authorities' associations, *Rate Support Grant (England) 1984–5*, appendix F.2, modified to include 1985–6.

Table 8.4 *Penalties, 1981–2 to 1985–6 (England only)*

| | 1981–2 | 1982–3 | 1983–4 | 1984–5 | 1985–6 |
|---|---|---|---|---|---|
| (1) Timing of notification | June 1981 | December 1981 | December 1982 | December 1983 | December 1984 |
| (2) Spending level above which penalties are incurred | Higher of volume target or GRE | Higher of target or GRE = 'effective target' | Target, i.e. no GRE exemption | Target, i.e. no GRE exemption | Target, i.e. no GRE exemption |
| (3) Penalty scheme | Stepped – see method of implementation | Continuous. 3p for each percentage point above 'effective target' | Continuous. 1p for each of the first two percentage points above target. 5p for each % point thereafter | Continuous. 2p for the first percentage point; 4p for the second percentage point; 8p for the third percentage point. 9p for each percentage point thereafter | Continuous. 7p for the first percentage point; 8p for the second percentage point; 9p for each percentage point thereafter |
| (4) Maximum penalty | No maximum | 15p at 5% or more above 'effective target' | No maximum | No maximum | No maximum |
| (5) Method of implementation | Resetting of poundage schedule so as to increase the rate poundage cost of spending at GRE by 9.03p with steeper slope and taper. Full protection for authorities spending below the higher of GRE or target. Authorities not more than 2% above target protected from 75% of grant loss and authorities between 2% and 4% above target protected from 40% of grant loss – by means of multipliers less than 1 | Increased poundage schedule with full protection for authorities spending below 'effective target' and partial protection for those spending up to 5% above 'effective target' by means of multipliers less than 1 | Multipliers greater than 1 set for authorities exceeding target | Multipliers greater than 1 set for authorities exceeding target | Multipliers greater than 1 set for authorities exceeding target |

No target resulting from this process could result in a real-terms increase compared with 1981–2 spending or a reduction of more than 7 per cent. Any authority which had spent below 1981–2 target and was projected to spend below 1982–3 GRE could not have a target representing a real-terms cut of more than 1 per cent. Finally, targets were made to fit (in total) the same cash figure as GREs.

In 1983–4 targets were based on 1982–3 budgets or the higher of an authority's 1982–3 GRE and target. (For the purpose of calculating penalties in 1982–3 the higher of an authority's GRE and target had been used, and became known as its 'effective' target.) For authorities which had budgeted to spend in 1982–3 up to 1 per cent above their 1982–3 'effective' target, their 1983–4 target was their 1982–3 budget plus 4 per cent. In authorities where budgets in 1982–3 were more than 1 per cent above 1982–3 'effective' target, the 1983–4 target was 1982–3 effective target plus 5 per cent. Again there were constraints to limit the effect of targets.

In 1984–5 the starting-point for targets was either 1983–4 target, or 1983–4 GRE, or 1983–4 budget. The basic rule simply added 2.5 per cent to whichever of an authority's GRE or target were higher. No authority could have a target which led to a cash increase of more than 3 per cent nor a decrease of more than 6 per cent. As in 1982–3, authorities which had increased spending very much since 1981–2 (in particular the Greater London Council) were given a more severe target than other authorities.

The targets set for 1985–6 announced in July 1984 were related to each authority's 1984–5 GRE or target. For an authority which budgeted in 1984–5 to spend at or below its GRE, its 1985–6 target would be 3.75 per cent above its 1984–5 GRE. For all other authorities (i.e. those spending above GRE in 1984–5), 1985–6 target would be their 1984–5 target plus 3.75 per cent. Most authorities would not have a target more than 4.25 per cent above nor more than 1.5 per cent below their 1984–5 budget. Nevertheless, changes to the treatment of budgeted interest receipts and of budgeted transfers from authorities' Housing Revenue Account to their rate fund meant that some authorities had very considerable target increases (e.g. Wansdyke, 56.3 per cent) compared with 1984–5 budgets. In addition, a number of adjustments were made to targets to take account of the removal of the National Insurance surcharge, the inclusion of part of the transport supplementary grant within block grant, the transfer of part of non-advanced further education to the Manpower Services Commission and the transfer of London Transport to central government.

*Grant penalties*
In each year from 1981–2 to 1985–6 some items of expenditure were disregarded when calculating whether an authority was overspending its target or not. For example, spending generated by abnormally

severe weather, urban riots, increased civil defence provision, joint projects with the National Health Service and increased spending on Urban Programme projects have each been disregarded in one or more years. In some years adjustments were made to authorities' spending figures before targets were calculated, whilst in other years the adjustments were made during the financial year. Budgeted interest receipts in excess of 10 per cent of an authority's budgeted total spending (gross of budgeted interest receipts) for 1984–5 and budgeted transfers from an authority's Housing Revenue Account to its General Rate Fund in 1984–5 were left out of account when calculating 1985–6 targets.

The penalties imposed on authorities which decided to spend above target were stiffened from year to year. In 1981–2, as was shown earlier, penalties were progressive as spending increased above target. The penalties were imposed by resetting the schedule of rate poundages for spending in relation to GRE in such a way as to increase the rate poundage cost of spending at GRE by 9.03p and to steepen the increase in poundage for spending above GRE and threshold. Authorities which spent at or below target were exempt from penalties, as were those spending above target but below GRE. Those which spent not more than 2 per cent above target were protected from 75 per cent of the penalty, while those between 2 and 4 per cent above target were protected from 40 per cent of penalty.

In 1982–3 authorities which overspent target (or GRE, if it was higher than the target) lost grant at the rate of 3p for each percentage point of excess spending up to a maximum of a 15p grant loss. For 1983–4 authorities spending above target lost grant at the rate of 1p for each of the first two percentage points, followed by 5p for each percentage point thereafter. There was no maximum grant loss and no exemption for authorities spending over target though below GRE.

There was no exemption from penalty for authorities spending above target but at or below GRE in 1983–4, 1984–5, or 1985–6. In 1984–5 the grant loss for spending over target was equivalent to a 2p rate for the first percentage point, 4p for the second percentage point, 8p for the third and 9p for each percentage point thereafter, with no maximum. For 1985–6 the rate of penalty was proposed to be increased to 7p for the first percentage point, 8p for the second point and 9p for each additional percentage point. Table 8.5 shows the effect at ratepayer level (i.e. all tiers of local government in each area added together) of penalties in each year from 1982–3 to 1985–6 at various spending levels.

Table 8.5 shows that the effect of penalties became extremely severe, even for marginal overspend, by 1984–5 and 1985–6. The grant loss in 1985–6 for 2 per cent overspending was the same as it would have been in 1982–3 for any level of spending from 5 per cent upwards. Adjustments to operate penalties were brought about by changes in

Table 8.5

|        | 1%  | 2%  | 3%  | 4%  | 5%  | 10% | 20%  | 30%  |
|--------|-----|-----|-----|-----|-----|-----|------|------|
| 1982–3 | 3p  | 6p  | 9p  | 12p | 15p | 15p | 15p  | 15p  |
| 1983–4 | 1p  | 2p  | 7p  | 12p | 17p | 42p | 92p  | 142p |
| 1984–5 | 2p  | 6p  | 14p | 23p | 32p | 77p | 167p | 257p |
| 1985–6 | 7p  | 15p | 24p | 33p | 42p | 87p | 177p | 267p |

the block grant poundage schedule in 1981–2 and 1982–3, with multipliers being used to reduce the penalties of those authorities which the Government had decided to protect. In 1983–4, 1984–5 and 1985–6 penalties were imposed by a straightforward adjustment of the multipliers of those authorities to be penalized.

(12)  LOCAL AUTHORITY SPENDING 1981–2 TO 1984–5

Table App.11 shows the current, relevant and total expenditure of local authorities in England in the first four years after block grant was introduced. 'Relevant' expenditure is all revenue expenditure which has to be paid for out of rates and aggregate Exchequer grant, less a few very small items. 'Total' expenditure is relevant expenditure less specific and supplementary grants, *plus* a few small items. Total expenditure is thus all spending which has to be funded out of rates and block grant. 'Current' expenditure is that part of relevant expenditure which funds services (e.g. education, social services, transport, police, fire, environmental health). Items which are not part of direct service provision (e.g. debt charges) do not fall within current expenditure. Table 8.6 shows how the three figures were related at the time of the 1986–7 RSG settlement.

Table 8.6

|                                          | £m      |
|------------------------------------------|---------|
| Current expenditure                      | 22,254  |
| + Revenue contributions to capital outlay | 549     |
| + Loan charges (including leasing)       | 2,630   |
| + Rate fund contributions to Revenue Account | 366 |
| − Interest receipts                      | (470)   |
| Relevant expenditure                     | 25,329  |
| + Non-relevant expenditure               | 238     |
| − Specific and supplementary grants      | (2,776) |
| Total expenditure                        | 22,790  |

All three definitions are in common use, though others (i.e. 'total rate and grant borne' expenditure) may also be found. 'Relevant' expenditure is used when calculating the aggregate Exchequer grant percentage, while 'total' expenditure is used for setting targets and (except in 1981–2) GREs. 'Current' expenditure is, with some adjustments, the basis for Government planning taken from the Public Expenditure White Paper.

Taking the 'current' expenditure definition, Table App.11 shows that budgeted spending for 1981–2 was 8.4 per cent above the Government's planned level, compared with 7.0 per cent in 1982–3, 4.4 per cent in 1983–4 and 5.1 per cent above Government plans in 1984–5. At out-turn in 1981–2 and 1982–3 the excess of spending over the Government's expenditure plan was somewhat reduced. Variations between plans and budgets on a similar scale to those for 'current' spending are also shown by those for relevant and total expenditure.

To examine more closely what has taken place, Table App.12 shows the current expenditure in Table App.11 in constant prices for each year since 1981–2, while Table App.13 shows current expenditure in England in cash and in constant prices for years since 1979–80. Thus it is possible to see the movement in the volume of current expenditure in terms of the Government's plans, local authority budgets and, for the earlier years, as between out-turns. The volume of spending fell in 1980–1 and 1981–2 before rising in 1982–3, 1983–4 and 1984–5. Figure App.9 shows this point more clearly. The continuous line shows local authority spending falling marginally for two years before picking up for the next three, while the dotted line shows what the Government planned for current expenditure in 1981–2, 1982–3, 1983–4 and 1984–5. The gap between Government's plan and local authorities' spending closed to some extent, though this was largely because the Government lifted the planning figures in real terms rather than because authorities reduced their spending.

Because local authorities' budgeted and out-turn 'total' expenditure (the definition used for block grant calculation) exceeded that planned by the Government in each year from 1981–2 to 1984–5, a proportion of block grant was held back from those individual authorities which chose to exceed their targets. (Not all authorities lost grant for

Table 8.7    *Total of Hold-Back in Each Year 1981–2 to 1984–5*

|        |                  |
|--------|------------------|
| 1981–2 | £124m            |
| 1982–3 | £308m            |
| 1983–4 | £281m            |
| 1984–5 | £276m (estimate) |

*Sources*: Department of the Environment, unpublished.

overspending target; some received no grant while spending at or below target, because of the operation of the basic grant system. Others were exempted from penalties in 1981–2 and 1982–3 if spending above target though below GRE.) The total of hold-back for authorities in England in each year was as shown in Table 8.7.

This explains in part why the grant percentage announced by the Government at the time of the RSG settlement in each year was much higher than the level after budgets had been set or at out-turn: spending turned out higher than planned, while hold-back reduced grant. The percentage of expenditure met by grant consequently fell. The fall in the grant percentage taking hold-back into account was dramatic following the introduction of block grant. The England and Wales percentage was 58.0 per cent at 1980–1 out-turn, but fell to just over 47 per cent by 1985–6. Table App.9 gives settlement and out-turn grant levels for each year from 1967–8 to 1985–6.

The rapid fall in grant percentage is one of the reasons why rates rose rather more rapidly than prices generally in each year from 1979–80 to 1983–4, thus weakening the relationship between movements in rates and spending, though the rates rise of 5.4 per cent (England and Wales) in 1984–5 was very close to the prevailing inflation rate.

The relationship between changes in local authority spending and rates levied was also distorted in the years after block grant was introduced partly because of the build-up of rate fund balances and the increased use of special funds. In the years from 1981–2 onwards, local authorities as a whole built up considerable special funds in an attempt to manage the uncertainty which had arisen with year-to-year changes in block grant, targets and penalties. Authorities put money into such funds in the expectation that uncertainty would continue and that penalties would become increasingly severe. The advantage of special funds lay in the fact that their use allowed authorities to manipulate the incidence of spending as between years: putting money into them counted as expenditure, while taking such money out (in a later year) did not count as spending. This allowed authorities to build up a reserve of resources which could then be used in future years without any effect (in the later year) on spending (and therefore let authorities decide to incur penalties in a year when they were relatively less severe).[53] The use of special funds in this way, coupled with building up and running down rate fund balances at different times, helped authorities to maximize grant income. Such practices came to be known as 'creative accounting'.

(13) WALES

Until the end of 1980–1 England and Wales were treated together for purposes of RSG distribution; a single RSG settlement and order covered both countries. The needs and resources elements worked in precisely the same way in Wales as in England, though there was a higher rate of domestic element in Wales (36p, as opposed to 18.5p).* From 1981–2 onwards, RSG was operated separately in each country. This meant that block grant was developed separately (though under the same legislation) in Cardiff and in London. As a result, the Welsh system was significantly different from that in England. The use of targets and penalties has also been different. The control of capital spending was also operated separately in Wales from 1981–2 onwards.

The GREs used in block grant were developed separately for the Welsh system, and were much simpler than those used in England. There were eighteen factors used to calculate county council GREs and eleven for district councils, though some factors were weighted by secondary indicators to take account of such things as population density and 'composite social indicators'. As in England, GREs in Wales were largely calculated by attempting to relate the cost of providing a unit of service to an estimate of the 'clients' in need of provision. Unlike in England, it was not possible to work out service-by-service GREs for individual authorities.

A grant-related poundage (GRP) was set for authorities spending at GRE, along with a formula to calculate GRPs for variations in spending above and below GRE. As in England, a threshold was set 10 per cent above GRE. For all spending below this threshold, grant increased (or decreased) at a constant rate as spending increased (or decreased). The slope of the GRP schedule was made to increase above the threshold so that each extra increment of expenditure above threshold progressively accelerated the increase in GRP. The effect of such a relationship is shown in Figure 8.4. Three different relationships between changes in spending and movements in GRP are shown. The 'curved' schedule is the effect achieved by the Welsh block grant from 1981–2 to 1985–6, while the 'linear discontinuous' schedule is what has occurred in England. In 1986–7, Wales's block grant moved to the linear discontinuous schedule. The 'linear schedule' shows what would happen if authorities did not face a higher rate poundage cost for exceeding threshold. (In England, as shown by Figure 8.4, the slope of the GRP schedule above threshold was straight, and increased the GRP at a rate faster than for spending below threshold.) The effect of the Welsh *curved* schedule was slightly less penal than that in England for authorities marginally above threshold and rather more penal for those substantially above threshold.

Multipliers were used for similar purposes in Wales as in England: to limit changes in grant entitlements resulting from changes made to the grant system. However, the basis of equalization used in calculat-

---

* Domestic rate relief grant (as domestic element became known from 1981–2) was cut to 18.5p in Wales in 1982–3.

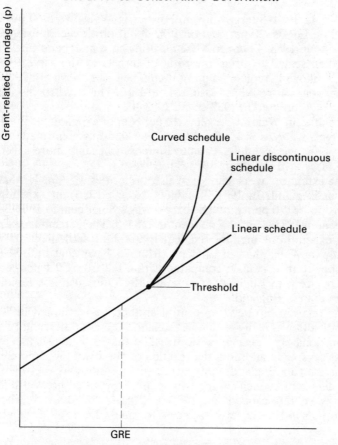

Figure 4. *Different relationships between spending and GRP.*

ing GRP changes for variations in spending from GRE was different from that used in England. Wales used variations expressed as percentage differences from GRE, whereas in England such variations were calculated as amounts per head of population. The choice of one basis of equalization rather than the other had implications for the distribution of grant between authorities.

Targets and penalties were used in Wales in each year from 1981–2 to 1985–6, although in 1981–2 they were not announced until after the end of the year. The methods used for setting targets and implementing penalties were different from those used in England. For example, in 1981–2, when authorities in England were faced with targets 5.6 per cent below their 1978–9 current expenditure out-turn, authorities in Wales faced reductions of 4.6 per cent compared with

1978–9. In 1984–5 targets for authorities in Wales were 60 per cent based on GREs, 30 per cent on 1982–3 out-turn expenditure and 10 per cent on 1983–4 budgets. The resulting current expenditure figure was then scaled to bring the total of targets to the same total as GREs, allowing targets no more than 6 per cent above nor less than 1.5 per cent above 1983–4 assumed out-turn. This was broadly similar to the method used in 1982–3 and 1983–4.

Penalties in Wales were set at 10 per cent of expenditure in excess of target, whereas in England there was an adjustment made to the rate poundage schedule. Penalties imposed became more severe in each successive year from 1982–3 to 1984–5.

The extent of 'overspend' by Welsh authorities was smaller than by that in England. In 1981–2 budgets exceeded current expenditure provision by 2.0 per cent. The excess was 4.8 per cent in 1982–3, 1.6 per cent in 1983–4 and 1.7 per cent in 1984–5. The percentage of relevant expenditure met by Exchequer grant at settlement fell less rapidly in Wales than in England (from 73.4 per cent in 1981–2 to 66.8 per cent in 1986–7, compared with a fall from 59.1 per cent to 46.9 per cent in England). Consequently, rates rose less rapidly in Wales than in England.

The relationship between central and local government in Wales did not suffer as badly as that in England. The grant percentage was, proportionately, not cut as much, while targets and penalties were not as severe. In addition, the reaction of authorities was more compliant than in England. A measure of the difference between the compliance of councils in the two countries was that no Welsh authority was rate-capped in 1985–6, 1986–7 or 1987–8 whereas authorities in England were selected for limitation in all three years.

### (14)  SCOTLAND

A different Rate Support Grant system operated in Scotland (under different legislation) from that used in England and Wales both before and after 1981–2. A system of needs and resources elements which to some extent resembled the England and Wales arrangements before 1 April 1981 continued in Scotland after that date. However, changes were made in the Scottish RSG which ensured that a system that already offered greater opportunities for central control than in England and Wales became even more centrally directed.

The Secretary of State for Scotland had powers under the Local Government (Scotland) Act 1966 to reduce retrospectively any element of RSG (after consultation with the authority or authorities concerned), in authorities which he felt had spent excessively or unreasonably, though these powers were not used before the 1979–83 Government. If the secretary of state laid a report before Parliament which was approved by a resolution of the House of Commons, he could reduce the element of grant accordingly.

The passing of the Local Government (Miscellaneous Provisions) (Scotland) Act 1981 marked a significant advance of central control. It allowed the Government to intervene selectively in the expenditure decisions of individual councils. It did this by giving the secretary of state the power to reduce grant during the course of a particular financial year and prohibited authorities from making up any lost grant by extra borrowing. Cuts in grant would thus have to be funded by reduced spending.

Selective action was announced in 1981–2 against seven councils, with seven selected in 1982–3 and five in 1983–4. After a process of negotiation, reductions were made in each of the authorities' budgets. Some of the authorities agreed cuts with the Government, whereas others made reductions only after the Government had passed an order approving the RSG reduction. Then the Government decided to take further legislative action in the Local Government and Planning (Scotland) Act 1982. This legislation supplemented the power to reduce RSG by allowing the secretary of state to decide whether to reduce an authority's grant or to require the authority to reduce its rate and to reimburse its ratepayers, or to combine a cut in RSG with a cut in rates.

The gap between the Government's plans and local government budgets became smaller between 1981–2 and 1983–4. In 1981–2 – when the Government first used its powers under the Local Government (Miscellaneous Provisions) Act – overspend was 14.0 per cent. In 1982–3 the excess was 8.3 per cent, and in 1983–4, 4.6 per cent.

The Government took more far-reaching powers in Scotland than in England, and did so in advance of moves towards toughening up targets and penalties and well before the introduction of rate-capping. These powers have been more fully discussed elsewhere.[54] Undoubtedly, the extent of change in Scotland and its constitutional implications for the rest of Britain were considerable.[55]

(15)  CAPITAL

*The system before the Local Government, Planning and Land Act 1980*

As well as introducing block grant, the Local Government, Planning and Land Act changed the Government's controls over local authority capital expenditure. Up till 1981–2 the Government had controlled authorities' powers to borrow money to fund capital expenditure. From 1981–2 onwards control was exercised over expenditure. This section briefly considers capital spending control. Although the bulk of political activity involving local government finance during the

1960s, 1970s and 1980s has involved current expenditure, some major changes have affected capital spending.

In the years up to 1971 a local authority had to obtain government permission to borrow money to finance capital spending (current expenditure could not and still may not be financed by borrowing, except in the short term against expected income during the year). Because sources of capital income other than borrowing (e.g. rates, capital receipts) offered little scope for extensive use, loan sanction was a powerful way of controlling capital expenditure.

The system was altered from 1 April 1971.[56] New arrangements categorized capital expenditure into three classes:

(a) *Key sector*, which, like the former system, still required specific approval and which included major capital items for services such as education, housing and police.

(b) *Subsidiary sector*, for which general consent to borrow was given by means of circulars. It included expenditure on land for key sector projects, expenditure on slum clearance and housing renovation grants.

(c) *Locally determined sector*, which included all capital schemes not falling within the other two sectors. To cover this sector a block borrowing approval was allocated to local authorities and all capital expenditure not financed by other means (e.g. from capital receipts, revenue contributions, capital funds, repairs and renewals funds or capital grants) had to be met from this allocation. In the non-metropolitan counties, the allocations between the individual county council and district councils were made by co-operation and agreement between the local authorities within each county. There was flexibility which meant that up to 10 per cent of allocations could be brought or carried forward from one year to another, and individual local authorities could transfer borrowing allocations to and from each other. Within this allocation each local authority was free to determine its own spending on individual schemes which fell within this sector.

The Government became unhappy about the operation of this method of control. First, it was not particularly precise, though it should be added that much capital expenditure cannot be controlled as precisely as current spending at the individual authority level because of difficulties in timing land transactions and because of the effect of the weather on programmes. Second, there were several ways of making capital spending which did not count against the loan sanction allocation. The most important of these were expenditure met out of revenue, capital funds, capital receipts, repairs and renewals funds, leasing and grants paid by one authority to another.

Table 8.8    *Local Government Capital Account Income[1], 1974–5 to 1981–2 (England)*

| | 1974–5 | 1975–6 | 1976–7 | 1977–8 | 1978–9 | 1979–80 | 1980–1 | 1981–2 |
|---|---|---|---|---|---|---|---|---|
| Sales of assets | 51 | 65 | 79 | 120 | 235 | 314 | 420 | 882 |
| Borrowing | 3,209 | 3,284 | 3,097 | 2,677 | 2,627 | 2,992 | 2,900 | 2,527 |
| Govt grants | 128 | 177 | 249 | 255 | 351 | 385 | 492 | 470 |
| RCCO[2] | 89 | 114 | 122 | 146 | 143 | 166 | 238 | 218 |
| Transfers from funds | 112 | 141 | 177 | 200 | 257 | 375 | 507 | 380 |
| Receipts from other LAs[3]) | 218 | 76 | 55 | 49 | 51 | 56 | 70 | 53 |
| Other capital receipts[4]) | | 225 | 322 | 419 | 391 | 351 | 478 | 441 |
| Total | 3,807 | 4,082 | 4,101 | 3,866 | 4,055 | 4,639 | 5,106 | 4,971 |
| Borrowing as % of total | 84.3 | 80.5 | 75.5 | 69.2 | 64.8 | 64.5 | 56.8 | 50.8 |

*Notes*:
[1] Total income of capital accounts is larger than gross expenditure because of changes in capital account balances, and some income is used to repay debt.
[2] Revenue contributions to capital outlay.
[3] Includes agency payments
[4] Includes repayment of housing advances.
[5] Figures may not add up due to rounding.
*Source*: Hansard, 25 April, 1983.

Table 8.8 shows how capital spending was increasingly funded from sources other than borrowing.

*The Local Government Planning and Land Bill*
Part VIII of the Local Government, Planning and Land Bill proposed a new form of control over local authorities' capital activities. Some of the features of the proposals had already been embodied in the system of Housing Strategies and Investment Programmes (HIPs) and Transport Policies and Programmes (TTPs).[57] Control was to be exercised over capital expenditure made by each local authority.

In the committee stage of the Bill, the then Minister for Local Government and Environmental Services, Tom King, explained:

The issue that is central to this amendment and to the understanding of this part of the Bill is the misunderstanding which arose at the very beginning in the speech of the right hon. Member for Widnes (Mr Oakes) when he said that local authorities will not be able to spend money from revenue. Right hon. and hon. Members then raised these points about capital funds, sinking funds, various proposals, and the implication seems to have come across that this expenditure is in some way forbidden. I illustrated the example over leasing as well whereby it is open to authorities, if they choose to use the leasing method, to continue to do so. Any method of funding is in no way precluded within the Bill.

All these things are within the overall total, and if the situation were that they sought to make such expenditure in excess of the allocations and the various concessions surrounding those allocations, yes indeed, such expenditure would be in excess and would be subject to the various procedures that follow in the Bill ... This question of the allocations themselves, as I have already mentioned, is qualified by the fact that although the allocations initially were made the five traditional blocks, in the hands of an individual authority those are then aggregated together to become a single block, and, albeit the allocation is given a certain amount of capital expenditure allocation maybe for education, if it is the judgement of a local authority that, for a planning reason or some difficulty over getting access, the school project might be delayed but that there is a higher priority for old people's homes, it will now be open to that authority to proceed with it. That gives it the discretion and freedom ... to go ahead, and there would not be the limitation or restriction within blocks.[58]

Mr King stressed the importance of extending local authorities' freedom within the new system: 'There must be an overall financial umbrella within which central government must control the economy. Within that limit we are determined to ensure the maximum freedom for local authorities to determine their priorities as they are best able to do.'[59]

Thus the Government's intention was to bring all capital expenditure, however funded, within the expenditure allocations made in each of five blocks. The freedom to aggregate the blocks or use part of one to fund spending in another block, coupled with the new control over expenditure, was seen as a way of giving individual authorities greater discretion within a system which offered the Government better aggregate control.

*How the New System Operated*
From 1 April 1981 the provisions of the Local Government, Planning and Land Act came into force, applying to all authorities in England and Wales. Controls over capital expenditure were introduced from this date, with minor differences in administrative procedures in England and in Wales. Capital expenditure was defined in paragraph 1 of schedule 12 of the Act, while paragraph 4 of the same schedule permitted the secretary of state to make regulations providing that certain types of expenditure shall not be prescribed as 'capital' (e.g. expenditure on the acquisition of vehicles, plant or machinery by

leasing where the asset does not become the property of the local authority).

There is, in reality, no precise distinction between capital and revenue expenditure. Many authorities which had previously (under the system of loan sanction) treated small items of expenditure as running expenses rather than capital were allowed to continue to do so under the new system.

The new legislation replaced the system of loan sanctions with annual expenditure allocations to each authority. These allocations limit the amount that may be spent on prescribed capital expenditure in each year. Thus the emphasis of control was switched from that of the starting time of a project ('starts' as they were known) and the borrowing power associated with such projects to a system of controlling the cash amount spent on capital within a particular financial year, however financed.

The allocations are made by the relevant central government departments in five blocks: education, personal social services, transport, housing and 'other services'. From 1 April 1984 a new Urban Aid block was introduced to cover spending on derelict land and the Urban Programme (formerly part of the 'other services' block).

The allocation process starts with the overall capital allocations for each service in local government. These are distributed to authorities according to a combination of bids, formulae and, partly, on the advice of the local authorities' associations.

Despite the fact that allocations are made in six blocks, local authorities are allowed considerable flexibility. First, they are allowed to vary allocations from block to block; any allocation made in one block may be used for capital spending in any of the other blocks. Thus it would be possible for an authority to spend the total of its allocations from each block on a single service. Second, authorities are allowed 10 per cent 'tolerance' about their limit. This means that an amount of capital allocation equivalent to 10 per cent of a year's total allocation may be carried forward from unused allocations in the previous year or taken from the next year's anticipated allocation.

In addition, net capital receipts (i.e. income from selling off capital assets) may be used – according to rules determined by the Government – to supplement the total allocation. Profits from trading undertakings may also be used in this way. Finally, authorities are allowed to transfer part of their allocation to other authorities.

An authority's prescribed expenditure limit is thus calculated from the following components:

(a) the six block allocations plus or minus up to 10 per cent between-year tolerance;
(b) allocations made directly to a local authority for individual projects;

(c)  plus or minus any allocation transferred from or to another authority;

(d)  a proportion of net capital receipts (prescribed by the Government); and

(e)  profits from trading undertakings.

The Government may reduce or withdraw an allocation, provided that the authority has not bound itself legally to proceed with spending that part of the allocation. In addition, individual central departments may require approval for some major items of spending within a block.

The limits put on the use of capital receipts have changed from year to year. In 1981–2 councils could use up to 100 per cent of capital receipts to augment their basic allocations. Subsequently limits were put on the proportion of a year's receipts which could be used within that year. In 1983–4, 50 per cent of housing and non-housing capital receipts (with small exceptions) could be used. By 1985–6 the proportion of housing capital receipts available was cut to 20 per cent. The proportion of an authority's receipts which could be used to increase their basic allocation has thus been severely cut back. This has probably affected authorities' enthusiasm to sell off more assets. Authorities have general borrowing consent to cover the amount of the total capital expenditure contained in the six blocks, plus or minus any adjustments made because of transfers of allocations from other authorities and because of the use of 'tolerance'. Borrowing consent also relies on compliance with any conditions applied by central departments to major schemes for which individual sanction is required.

The change from control over borrowing to expenditure control brought about by the Local Government, Planning and Land Act had the effect of bringing all capital spending within the scope of control. Previous use of revenue contributions, leasing (i.e. paying for capital items as part of year-to-year recurrent spending), or deferred payments were no longer ways for authorities circumventing control. On the other hand, the freedom to move spending from block to block within allocations has given authorities some additional freedom. The effects of the Government's control mechanisms will be considered next.

*Capital Expenditure*

Successive governments have used local authority capital expenditure as an accelerator or as a brake on total public spending. During the 1970s and early 1980s, as economic crises affected government policy, local authorities found that plans for any particular future year were unpredictable. Table 8.9 shows, for local authorities in Great Britain, the plans published in each year's Public Expenditure White Paper for future changes in the volume of capital expenditure.

Table 8.9   *Local Government Capital Expenditure Plans, 1970–1 to 1983–4*

| White Paper | (% Change in Volume terms) | | | | | | |
|---|---|---|---|---|---|---|---|
| | *1970–1* | *1971–2* | *1972–3* | *1973–4* | *1974–5* | *1975–6* | *1976–7* |
| Cmnd 4234 (Dec.'69) | +5.4 | +6.4 | | | | | |
| Cmnd 4578 (Jan.'71) | | +3.9 | +3.2 | | | | |
| Cmnd 4829 (Nov.'71) | | | +6.2 | +0.5 | +0.8 | +1.5 | |
| Cmnd 5178 (Dec.'72) | | | | +3.3 | −4.2 | −1.6 | +0.3 |

| | *1974–5* | *1975–6* | *1976–7* | *1977–8* | *1978–9* | *1979–80* | *1980–1* | *1981–2* |
|---|---|---|---|---|---|---|---|---|
| Cmnd 5519 (Dec.'73) | −12.2 | −3.5 | −0.3 | +1.1 | | | | |
| Cmnd 5879 (Jan.'75) | | −6.4 | −3.0 | −0.9 | −0.6 | | | |
| Cmnd 6393 (Feb.'76) | | | −12.4 | −6.0 | −4.6 | −2.5 | | |
| Cmnd 6721 (Jan.'77) | | | | −24.2 | −6.0 | | | |
| Cmnd 7049 (Jan.'78) | | | | | +6.6 | +2.8 | +1.0 | +0.4 |

| | *1979–80* | *1980–1* | *1981–2* | *1982–3* | *1983–4* | *1984–5* |
|---|---|---|---|---|---|---|
| Cmnd 7439 (Jan.'79) | +3.1 | +1.0 | +0.1 | −0.4 | | |
| Cmnd 7841 (Mar.'80) | | −15.7 | (−5.0) | (−6.0) | (−3.0) | |
| Cmnd 8175 (Mar.'81) | | | −12.6 | (−3.0) | (−4.0) | |

*Source*: Public Expenditure White Papers, Cmnd 4234 to Cmnd 8175.

These figures in Table 8.9 show that governments regularly planned for significant increases or decreases in capital expenditure in the year immediately after plans were published. In several years there were plans for a major increase or decrease in the next year, followed by more moderate changes in the next three years. Taking the successive plans for, say, 1977–8, it is possible to see how local authorities would have had to treat government plans with caution. For that year plans changed from a 1.1 per cent increase to a 24.2 per cent cut within four White Papers, despite the fact that local authority capital spending fell quickly between 1973 and 1977.

In fact, capital spending fell continuously during the mid- and late

1970s. Having risen (with government encouragement) in the 1960s and early 1970s, economic crises led governments to plan for contraction from the end of 1973 onwards. As Table App.1 shows, the proportion of GDP devoted to capital expenditure fell from 4.5 per cent to 1.1 per cent between 1973–4 and 1981–2. In cash, expenditure (see Table App.4, which shows gross spending) fell in 1976–7, 1977–8 and 1981–2, while real-terms capital expenditure fell very quickly. Table App.6 shows net capital expenditure from 1976–7 to 1985–6 (taken from Public Expenditure White Papers). Net expenditure is gross expenditure less any income to authorities from the sale of capital assets. Because authorities sold off capital assets at an increasing rate from the mid-1970s onwards, the fall in net spending is more dramatic than the gross figures in Table App.4.

The pressure to cut current spending at various times also meant that the extra revenue costs in future years arising from a new capital project became a discouragement to capital spending. Some capital items (e.g. roads) which had no immediate manpower requirements had lower revenue implications than others (e.g. an old people's home) where manpower and running costs would be higher. This factor helped to bring local authority capital spending on to a consistent downward path. In the year before the new capital controls were introduced by the Local Government, Planning and Land Act, local government capital spending was equivalent to 1.8 per cent of GDP, having been 4.5 per cent just seven years earlier.

Continuing pressure on current spending in the years following 1980 meant that capital spending continued to fall. By the end of 1982 the Government was so concerned at the low level of capital investment by authorities that the Prime Minister wrote to each local authority asking them to increase their capital expenditure. So great had been the decline during the previous decade that, although the Government had been content to allow the decline to continue between 1979 and 1981, the lack of stimulus to some basic industries (in particular to construction) had begun to concern ministers. The Secretary of State for the Environment wrote to authorities at this time encouraging them to redefine some items of current spending (e.g. repairs and maintenance) as capital spending.

The consequent pick-up of capital spending during 1983–4 and 1984–5 was sufficient to lead the Government to ask for voluntary restraint in signing new contracts for capital works during 1984. Local authority capital expenditure exceeded Government plans in 1983–4, 1984–5 and 1985–6, which led to new proposals (made during the early weeks of 1986) to move to controls over *gross* rather than net capital expenditure. Such a change would have brought much more of authorities' capital spending under control and would have led to reductions in future levels of capital spending. The possibility of a moratorium was discussed. The rapid cycles of expansion and contraction in capital expenditure during the 1970s continued in the 1980s.

### (16)   COMMENTARY: 1979 TO 1983

The years from 1979 to 1983 saw unprecedented interest and activity in the relationship between local and central government. The earlier sections of this chapter have detailed how the Government sought to encourage, threaten and force councils to cut their expenditure and how the authorities chose to respond. At different times the Government expressed different intentions and attempted (with differing degrees of success) to pass much new legislation. The relationship between central government and local authorities undoubtedly came under more continuous pressure than ever before. The result of the Government's struggle with the local authorities in this period has been described by a senior local authority officer as a 'dishonourable draw'.

In the early days of the administration the Government was concerned with reducing public expenditure. Later, interest turned to cutting the spending of particular 'overspenders' and then to protecting ratepayers. The stress at different times on hitting overall spending plans, on attacking a small number of 'overspenders' and on protecting ratepayers suggests either that the Government changed its mind, or (more likely) that it was trying to do several things at once. If the first hypothesis were correct, it would be unlikely that any of the things attempted would be achieved. If, on the other hand, an attempt was made simultaneously to achieve overall spending plans, to reduce individual councils' spending, to protect ratepayers (while at the same time reducing overall tax burdens), it is small wonder that the Government had difficulties.

If, for example, reducing overall spending had been the overriding objective, then a sustained, considerable and planned reduction in the grant percentage between 1979 and 1983 would have been an important instrument of policy. This would undoubtedly have increased rates ahead of inflation, but would also have exerted tremendous pressure on authorities to reduce spending, particularly had the Government's original spending plans been adhered to. As it was, the grant percentage was barely reduced (at settlement) until 1982–3, while spending plans were revised upwards in the light of 'overspend'. In addition, such changes were made to the grant system between 1979 and 1983 that the normal effects of a grant reduction (i.e. to reduce spending) might anyway have been obscured by authorities changing their behaviour to cope with the new arrangements.

A serious attempt to protect ratepayers could have been undertaken in a number of ways. Grant could have been increased within falling expenditure plans. This would not have exerted pressure on authorities to reduce their expenditure, though presumably a large number would have complied with Government exhortations in the opposite way that, in reality, many did not comply with targets, despite grant reductions. Alternatively the Government could have taken powers to cash-limit individual authorities and, in conjunction with its grant distribution powers, exercised close control over rate bills in that way. Eventually the Rates Act 1984 took direct powers over rates.

These possible policies are in many cases incompatible with each other. The author would certainly not wish to propose them. But the Government's objectives were incompatible; squeezing the grant paid to authorities between 1979 and 1983 actually transferred burdens from taxpayers to ratepayers. As individual councils chose to over-spend their targets, so their ratepayers were faced with extra burdens. Government policy between 1979 and 1983 ensured that for most ratepayers the rates burden increased faster than retail prices. In some places, block grant penalties made rates rise very quickly indeed.

During the period when the Government was extending its influence over spending and rates, much came to be said about the 'traditional relationship' between central and local government. Politicians disagreed about why it had changed, though there was widespread agreement that by 1983 the relationship was quite different from what it had been five or six years earlier.

Much of the change derived from realignments in politics, though the continued failure to reform local government finance encouraged both the Government and some councils to behave in new ways. Between 1979 and 1983 the internal difficulties of the Labour Party had a number of effects, including the setting up of the Social Democratic Party and its alliance with the Liberals. Many Labour councils became much more radical, often with commitments rather wider than the provision of local authority services. At the same time the Conservative Government prided itself on being different from previous administrations, claiming that it had a mandate for taking action against high-spending local authorities. The gap between the Conservatives in central government and many Labour authorities became a chasm.

The continued failure to reform rates and grants as part of a fundamental programme to restore the system of local government finance exacerbated the political differences. The Government increasingly claimed that local authorities were able to raise huge sums from an antiquated tax base which (because of rate rebates, domestic rate relief and non-domestic rates) did not bring home to many ratepayers the true cost of local spending. Yet at the same time it failed to reform the system. Some authorities, on the other hand, backed up by huge traditional majorities, pushed up rates and spending despite the fact that only a small part of their income came from ratepayers who were likely directly to express their views through the ballot box. A reform of local government finance which widened the number of local taxpayers and increased the amount of local income derived from such taxation would have made councillors more accountable and thus reduced the scope for central–local disagreement.

The years from 1979 to 1983 saw a succession of ill-thought-out policies which neither achieved the Government's objectives nor maintained a sound and healthy system of local government. Many of the government's policies towards local government were pursued with short-term vigour, though with no long-term vision. The Government appeared to pursue several conflicting ends at a time when politics in Britain was changing. No real attempt was made to reform the basis of finance. The scene was set for further moves towards central control after the 1983 general election.

NOTES: CHAPTER 8

1   *Control of Public Expenditure*, Cmnd 1432 (London: HMSO, 1961).
2   The Consultative Council in Local Government Finance was announced by the Chancellor of the Exchequer in his budget speech in April 1975. It is chaired by the Secretary of State for the Environment, and is attended by ministers and officials from all departments involved with local government (i.e. the Department of the Environment, the Department of Education and Science, the Home Office, the Department of Health and Social Security and the Treasury). Members and officers from the local authorities' associations (the Association of County Councils, the Association of Metropolitan Authorities, the Association of District Councils, the London Boroughs' Association, the Association of London Authorities and the Greater London Council) also attend meetings of the council. Between meetings officers of the Government and local authorities meet in an 'Official Steering Group' to draw up papers and consider requests for information from the Council.
3   See Department of the Environment Circular 84/76 (26 August 1976).
4   *The Government's Expenditure Plans*, Cmnd 6721-I (London: HMSO, January 1977).
5   Conservative party manifesto 1979, p. 8.
6   *The Government's Expenditure Plans*, Cmnd 7841 (London: HMSO, March 1980), p. 3.
7   'Public Expenditure 1980–1', statement by the Secretary of State for the Environment, tabled at a meeting of the Consultative Council on 31 July 1979.
8   Ibid.
9   'Rate Support Grant 1980–1', statement taken from Parliamentary Written Answer to William Shelton MP (16 November 1979).
10   Ibid.
11   Statement by Michael Heseltine on publication of the Local Government, Planning and Land Bill (4 December 1979).
12   'Rate Support Grant 1980–1', op. cit.
13   Secretary of state's statement to the Consultative Council on Local Government Finance (16 December 1979).
14   See Committee of Inquiry into Local Government Finance Report, Cmnd 6453 (London: HMSO, May 1976), appendix 7.
15   *Local Government Finance*, Cmnd 6813 (London: HMSO, May 1977).
16   House of Commons, Official Report, Standing Committee D, on the Local Government, Planning and Land Bill (25 March 1980), col. 756.

17  House of Lords, Official Report, Committee on the Local Government, Planning and Land Bill (9 October 1980), col. 642.
18  House of Commons, Official Report, Standing Committee D, op. cit. (1 April 1980), col. 1009.
19  Ibid. (27 March 1980), col. 840.
20  House of Lords, Official Report, Committee on the Local Government, Planning and Land Bill, (9 October 1980), col. 632.
21  Ibid. (9 October 1980), cols. 594–5.
22  House of Commons, Official Report, Standing Committee D, op. cit. (27 March 1980), cols. 840–1.
23  Statement by the Association of County Councils (February 1980).
24  'Local Authorities' Proposals for Block Grant', joint local authorities' press release (19 February 1980).
25  Letter from Michael Heseltine to Sir Gervas Walker (10 March 1980).
26  'Rate Support Grant', joint local authorities' press release (11 March 1980).
27  *Financial Times* (5 August 1980).
28  Local Government, Planning and Land (No. 2) Bill, clause 39.
29  Local Government, Planning and Land Act 1980, clause 58 (2).
30  Statement by Michael Heseltine (18 September 1980).
31  Statement by Michael Heseltine to Consultative Council on Local Government Finance (16 December 1980).
32  Rate Support Grant Report (England) 1980, House of Commons Paper 56 (16 December 1980), para. 25.
33  Statement by Michael Heseltine to Consultative Council on Local Government Finance (2 June 1981).
34  Statement by Tom King to Consultative Council on Local Government Finance (4 August 1981).
35  Parliamentary Written Answer No. 148 (19 November 1981).
36  See, for example, a speech by the Rt Hon. Leon Brittan QC MP, Chief Secretary to the Treasury, to the Society of Local Authority Chief Executives, at York, on 16 July 1982, and a speech by Jock Bruce-Gardyne MP, Economic Secretary to the Treasury, to the annual regional seminar of the Chartered Institute of Public Finance and Accountancy, at Torquay, on 30 September 1982.
37  *Alternatives to Domestic Rates*, Cmnd 8449 (London: HMSO, December 1981).
38  House of Commons, Official Report, Standing Committee D, op. cit. (28 January 1982) col. 44.
39  Ibid. (2 February 1982), col. 73.
40  Ibid.
41  In the Conservative Party's October 1974 general election manifesto there was a commitment to abolish domestic rates. In May 1979 the Conservative manifesto stated: 'cutting income tax must take priority for the time being over abolition of the domestic rating system' (p. 14).
42  Rating System (Abolition) Bill. Introduced by Sir Hugh Fraser, supported by Richard Shepherd, Peter Temple-Morris, Sir Derek Walker-Smith, Tony Durant, Patrick Cormack, Sydney Chapman, Christopher Murphy, Teddy Taylor, James Pawsey, Anthony Beaumont-Dark and John Heddle.
43  *Alternatives to Domestic Rates*, op. cit.
44  Ibid., p. 1.
45  Ibid., p. 3, para. 10.
46  Ibid., p. 3, para. 14.
47  Ibid., p. 64, para. 14.1.
48  Ibid., p. 64, para. 14.3.
49  Department of the Environment, Welsh Office, *Rates: Proposals for Rate Limitation and Reform of the Rating System*, Cmnd 9008 (August 1983).
50  House of Commons Select Committee on the Environment, Second Report, session 1981–2, *Enquiry into Methods of Financing Local Government in the*

Context of the Government's Green Paper (Cmnd 8449), House of Commons Papers 217-L, 217 i–viii.

51  Ibid., ch. 6, para. 78.

52  See, for example, George Jones and John Stewart, *The Case for Local Government* (London: Allen & Unwin, 1983).

53  See Audit Commission for Local Authorities in England and Wales, *The Impact on Local Authorities' Economy, Efficiency and Effectiveness of the Block Grant Distribution System* (London: HMSO, August 1984), pt I.

54  A full examination of developments in Scotland is contained in Arthur Midwintor, *The Politics of Local Spending* (Edinburgh: Mainstream Publishing, 1984).

55  See George Jones and John Stewart, *The Case for Local Government*, op. cit., ch. 5.

56  Reform followed Department of the Environment Circular 2/70, and was modified to some extent by Circular 86/74.

57  See Department of the Environment Circulars 104/73, 60/74, 18/77.

58  House of Commons, Official Report, Standing Committee D, op. cit. (15 April 1980), cols. 1160–1.

59  House of Commons, Official Report (5 February 1980), Vol. 978, p. 244.

*Chapter 9*

# 1983 AND BEYOND:
# RATE LIMITATION AND ABOLITION

## (1) THE 1983 GENERAL ELECTION

The political parties approached the 1983 general election with local government finance unreformed. The failure to find an acceptable alternative to domestic rates, coupled with continuing rate rises ahead of the rate of inflation (largely because of grant cuts), meant that both the Conservatives and opposition parties put proposals for changes to local authority funding into their manifestos. Structural changes were also promised.

For Mrs Thatcher, the problem was acute. After years of promising to 'do something' about rates, it had become clear that all the alternatives (and, more importantly, the period of transition from one tax to another) were fraught with difficulties. The Government had not formally replied to the Environment Select Committee's *Enquiry into Methods of Financing Local Government in the Context of the Government's Green Paper (Cmnd 8449)*,[1] which meant that the Conservative manifesto was seen as, in effect, the Government's response to the Select Committee and to the representations which had been made following the publication of the Green Paper on *Alternatives to Domestic Rates*.[2]

The manifesto contained two major proposals. The first was to limit the rate increases of several or all local authorities, while the second was to abolish the Greater London Council and the six metropolitan counties. The manifesto briefly explained the Conservative Government's achievements and why further steps were to be taken:

We have checked the relentless growth of local government spending, and manpower is now back down to the level of 1974. The achievement of many Conservative authorities in saving ratepayers' money by putting services out to tender has played a major part in getting better value for money and significantly reducing the level of rate increases. We shall encourage every possible saving by this policy.

There are, however, a number of grossly extravagant Labour authorities whose exorbitant rate demands have caused great distress both to businesses and domestic ratepayers. We shall legislate to curb excessive and irresponsible rate increases by high-spending councils, and to provide a general scheme for limitation of rate increases for all local authorities to be used if necessary...

The Metropolitan Councils and the Greater London Council have been shown to be a wasteful and unnecessary tier of government. We shall abolish them and return most of their functions to the boroughs and districts. Services which need to be administered over a wider area – such as police and fire, and education in inner London – will be run by joint boards of borough or district representatives.[3]

Labour, on the other hand, proposed to give local authorities greater powers. Most dramatically, it was proposed to repeal the *ultra vires* rule, so that authorities would be able to do anything which was not expressly forbidden by statute. The Labour manifesto continued: 'We shall also seek to define the relationship between central and local government – as part of our consideration of the universal application of realistic minimum standards – so that basic provision of key services is available in all parts of the Country.'[4] The possibility of structural reform was also raised:

> We are examining how best to reform local government. We believe that services such as health, water and sewerage should become answerable to a much greater extent to elected members; and we aim to end, if we can, the present confusing division of services between two tiers of authority. Unitary district authorities, in England and Wales, could be responsible for all of the functions in this area that they could sensibly undertake.[5]

Expansion of the economy as a whole would be reflected in local government by way of more RSG. Grant would be directed, in particular, into urban areas. Finally, the Conservative Government's recent legislation would be repealed: 'We will therefore repeal the Tory legislation which allows the government to impose penalties on local authority spending, and to impose penalties on local authorities whose spending exceeds those ceiling. We shall repeal the ban on supplementary rates'.[6] The manifesto also proposed removing the threat of surcharge from councillors and restricting the duties of auditors.

The programmes of the two major parties were vastly different. Both promised structural and financial reform. But the Conservatives were outlining a programme of increased central involvement in local government, while Labour was apparently offering a massive increase in local authority power. It is worth noting that two major Labour commitments (those to apply minimum standards and to give greater freedom) did appear to conflict.

The Environment Secretary, Tom King, explained during the election campaign why the Conservatives proposed to restrict authorities' powers: 'there are an increasing number of Labour Councils where the extreme left have taken over, where they are set on doing the maximum damage in the shortest possible time. They spend more and more on all sorts of irresponsible schemes, and place intolerable burdens on their domestic ratepayers, and the business in their area.'[7] In notes prepared for Tory election candidates, and signed by Mr King, it was made clear that the Conservative Party was now a supporter of rates:

> Of course there are many anomolies in the rating system, but it would be irresponsible to change to a new tax with serious, if different, flaws. Whatever its failings the rating system is cheap to administer, easy to collect, difficult to avoid and certain to yield. In any case some of the unfairness of rates are met by rebates and grant paid out of other taxes. The incorporation of rate rebates in the new housing benefit means that more people will be eligible for help with their rate bills.[8]

After almost a decade of opposition to rates (since the October 1974 election), the Conservative party officially accepted that 'there is no alternative'.

Abolition of the metropolitan counties and the GLC was seen partly as a financial matter and partly as a reform which would lead to better government. Tom King explained: 'It is now abundantly clear that these are an unnecessary tier of government. This is the first consideration in reaching our decision. It is also true that under the present Labour control they have become extremely wasteful and expensive bodies who have imposed heavy additional burdens on their ratepayers.'[9]

Local government did not, in fact, feature prominently in the election campaign. Either the local government issues raised by the major parties were deemed less important than employment, defence and others which dominated the campaign, or they involved issues which traditionally fail to arouse the electorate.

## (2)   THE *RATES* WHITE PAPER

Following the Conservatives' overwhelming election victory (in terms of seats), in June 1983 the new administration set about the lengthy and complex process of implementing (in the first instance) rate-capping and (secondly) abolition. A White Paper entitled *Rates*[10] was published in August 1983. This set out the Government's proposals for reform of the rating system. It also contained the Government's official views on the future detailed operation of the rating system following discussion of the Green Paper *Alternatives to Domestic Rates* and the Environment Select Committee's report.

The White Paper started by discussing the financial relationship between central and local government. Acknowledging the importance of local government in maintaining the well-being of the public and private sectors, the Government immediately stressed that local authorities were only creatures of Parliament: 'we believe in a unitary and not a federal state. Although local authorities are responsible to their electorates, they derive their powers from Parliament. Their structure, duties and functions have been subject to frequent modification by Parliament as the needs of the country have changed.'[11]

Three reasons were given by the Government for why local ratepayers should not alone decide how much their local authority should spend. These were: first, that ministers were accountable to Parliament for the broad conduct of the economy; second, rates formed a heavy burden on business and commerce; and third, rates were part of the Retail Prices Index. In addition, it was agreed that the Government had a major interest in local government services and that the Layfield Committee had accepted that the Government should have a major role in relation to local government expenditure.

Having considered the financial relationship between central and local government in these terms, the White Paper traced the growth in local government spending and manpower in the 1960s and 1970s, and also the attempts to reverse the growth of local government services since 1979.

The White Paper showed how local government had failed to achieve Government spending plans in 1979–80 to 1983–4: 'Whilst local government as a whole continues to spend more than the Government believe the country can afford, the problem has been greatly aggravated by the behaviour of a small number of large authorities'.[12] Current expenditure had, according to the Government, risen by 4 per cent between 1978–9 and 1983–4, which was 12 per cent higher than the planned total first proposed for 1983–4 in the March 1980 Public Expenditure White Paper.

Chapter 1 of the White Paper concluded by stating that the Government had decided to take further measures to restrain local government spending:

> some of the discontent with rates stems from the sheer weight of the burden placed upon them, which the rating system was never intended to bear. The Government therefore think it essential to put further restraints of the amount of expenditure financed by the rates. One way forward would have been to increase the accountability of local councils to their electorates by requiring a referendum or local poll by authorities proposing exceptionally high levels of spending and rates. This proposal did not however meet

with the approval of Parliament, and was dropped. The Government have therefore reluctantly concluded that direct action must be taken. Chapter 3 describes a selective scheme of rare limitation, applicable to the minority of authorities whose spending and rating is clearly excessive.[13]

A general rate limitation scheme, for all authorities, was proposed as a fall-back scheme, should the selective scheme fail to achieve results.

Chapter 2 examined the arguments which had been put forward about alternative approaches to local taxation. There had been no consensus about an alternative to domestic rates, with retention and abolition of rates equally supported. Of those who supported abolition, some favoured assigned revenues as a replacement, other local income tax (LIT) and others a poll tax. Most of those who wanted to keep rates wanted them reformed.

The arguments against sales tax, poll tax and LIT which had been rehearsed in earlier reports and White Papers were then repeated. Further work on LIT was explicitly ruled out on the grounds that there was not widespread support for it and because additional direct taxation would conflict with the Government's objective to reduce direct taxation. Assigned revenues were rejected, as was the transfer of education from local to central funding, 'because central finance of local services would effectively eliminate the responsibility of local authorities for their spending decisions'.[14] A separate education block grant and all other taxes which had from time to time been mentioned were also dismissed.

Thus, as had been clear at the general election, rates were to remain the local tax. Their advantages, as listed by the Conservatives during the election, were repeated. Instead of reforming the local tax base, restrictions were to be placed on its use.

Chapter 3 of the White Paper outlined a selective limitation scheme for rates, while chapter 4 described a similar scheme for general application to all authorities. As with block grant, separate schemes would operate for England and for Wales. The selective scheme would operate in stages, starting with the designation of a number of authorities and the setting of a spending level for each. The spending level (which would be assumed in setting the rate cap) might be the subject of negotiations between an authority and the Government. At the time of the Rate Support Grant Settlement, each authority's spending level would be used to calculate a rate limit. If an authority agreed with its rate cap, then such a rate would become the maximum that could be charged in that authority. If an authority did not agree, the Government could lay an order before Parliament specifying the maximum rate.

Councils spending less than £10 million or below GRE would be excluded from selective rate-capping. The general scheme would operate in a way similar to the selective scheme, except that all authorities would be involved. There would still be a power to exclude small authorities. Both the selective and general schemes will be considered further in the section dealing with the Rates Bill.

The White Paper also proposed a non-domestic rating revaluation on the grounds that there had not been a revaluation since 1973. A revaluation would be set in train on the basis of rental values. Domestic rates, on the other hand, would be the subject of a consultation document. It would not, it was stated, be possible for a domestic revaluation to take place until the end of the 1980s.

Although the reintroduction of the business rate was rejected, the Government proposed to legislate to give local authorities the duty to consult representatives of business before fixing their rates or precepts. Information would have to be provided as the basis of this consultation. There were also a number of minor rating amendments proposed, the most important of which was the removal of authorities' discretion to rate empty industrial property.

### (3)  REACTIONS TO THE WHITE PAPER

The White Paper on rates added little to what was already known about the Government's intentions. Rate limitation (or 'rate-capping' as it was known) had been outlined in the Conservatives' manifesto, while it had long been known that the search for an alternative to domestic rates had proved hopeless.

The arguments used in the White Paper were widely condemned from inside and outside of local government. The Association of County Councils, for example, which was strongly Conservative-controlled, claimed:

> the implementation of the Government's proposals appears to be based on expediency and would result in an unacceptable centralisation of power, in practice in the hands of the Executive rather than of Parliament, and the further weakening of local democratic control. The price to be paid is too high, for a problem which is over-stated and can be reduced by further improvements to the system of local taxation.[15]

The Association of District Councils (also Conservative-controlled) was less polite: 'the proposals for rate limitation in the White Paper on *Rates* ... are totally unacceptable in that they represent a major constitutional change that would be a fundamental breach of local democracy and accountability and be wholly unworkable in practice'.[16]

The Labour-controlled Association of Metropolitan Authorities also protested about the proposals:

> The main proposals of the Government's Rates White Paper (Cmnd 9008) would, if enacted, represent perhaps the most fundamental constitutional change in modern times. They would transform the basic relationship between central government and local authorities by circumscribing the powers of local government to determine its own taxation and expenditure. Since the introduction of rates in 1601, every local authority has had the right to levy the rate it considers necessary to meet its statutory and discretionary functions. The new powers would end that right.[17]

Business and commerce generally welcomed the proposals in the White Paper. The CBI and Institute of Directors supported the idea of rate limitation, though the Association of British Chambers of Commerce entered the caveat that the constitutional nature of the general scheme made it possible that it might be threatened by parliamentary opposition. If this happened, the ABCC was prepared to see the general scheme dropped in order to ensure the selective scheme passed into law.[18]

The newspapers, however, were largely hostile to rate limitation. Editorials in the *Guardian* and *Financial Times* were particularly concerned about the constitutional consequences of rate limitation and, indeed, about whether the schemes would work. The local government press, in particular the *Local Government Chronicle*, was virulent in its opposition to the measures.

### (4)   ARGUMENTS FOR AND AGAINST RATE LIMITATION

Apart from the chorus of concern about the proposals themselves, there was much argument with the Government's justification (in the White Paper) for the proposals. As set out in chapter 1, these were:

(a)   Economic regeneration of the country could not take place if local government were to be too great a burden for the private sector (para. 1.3):

(b)   The Government could not ignore the sense of grievance felt by ratepayers, within a system of limited accountability, about excessive rate and spending increases (para. 1.3):

(c)   Local government, being heavily dependent on government grants, should be subject to central direction (para. 1.5):

(d)   The Government should have an interest in services which were national in character or of national importance (para. 1.9):

(e)   The Government, being responsible for the national economy, must control local authorities as part of that economy (paras. 1.10 and 1.11).

Opposition to the White Paper claimed[19] that each of these justifications was incorrect or not proven. For example, it was pointed out that there was no evidence in the White Paper that the cost of local government was too great a burden for the private sector to bear. The Government *did* say that local rates were comparatively heavier than national taxes and that they were the single heaviest tax on business, but this was not itself an argument that they were necessarily too heavy. A survey carried out during 1983[20] by the London Chamber of Commerce showed that rates were only a marginal concern to businesses in the capital.

The argument about ratepayers' grievances was given little more than an extension of the idea that people did not like paying taxes. In fact, there had been repeated opinion poll evidence in 1980 to 1983 that many people were prepared to pay taxes for services. Some commentators pointed out that value added tax had doubled only three years before and that taxpayers could always express their opinion about changes in taxes at the ballot box.

The use of the level of grant support to justify central intervention appeared odd because it was successive governments that had increased the proportion of local spending funded in this way. There had long been a choice between supporting the constitutional position of local government, by seeking additional independent sources of finance (as the Conservative Government had proposed in its 1957 White Paper) and undermining it through increased grants (as Labour had done in its 1966 White Paper). In the past the 'general grant' principle had left authorities free to treat grant as their own revenue and to take decisions upon expenditure. The White Paper was, it was argued, wrong to imply a long-standing policy to the contrary.

Government interest in local services had hitherto been expressed in legislation governing each service. There had been no evidence that laws for individual services were deficient in this regard, and, more importantly, the suggestion that financial legislation should be used to secure particular service interests went well beyond the normal uses of financial controls. Much was said by the local authorities' associations and others about the weakness of the government's economic case.[21] It was argued that local government spending had risen less quickly than that of central government; that the rapid increase in rates had been due to RSG cuts and that local government's share of the gross domestic product (GDP) had increased only because the GDP had itself fallen from 1979 to 1981.

The stated object of a reduction in local government spending was hoped to lead to a consequent fall in public sector borrowing and taxation. Yet it was widely pointed out that the local authority current spending funded out of increased rates had no effect on public sector borrowing. Taxation by local authorities, the AMA stated, had lagged behind the increase in the general rise in prices between 1974–5 and 1981–2. The tendency for rates to increase more quickly than general inflation had taken place only since the RSG percentage had been cut back severely.[22] Anyway, it was argued, local authority rates made up less than 4 per cent of the inputs to the Retail Prices Index, and were far less important than items like alcohol, eating out or consumer durables.[23]

Critics of the White Paper were united in condemnation of the lack of evidence in support of the justification for rate limitation. At no point did the Government make a convincing case for claiming that the extent of the influence of local government spending, borrowing and taxation on national economic policy was such as to require the government to take rate limitation powers.

(5)  THE RATES BILL

Despite the widespread disapproval expressed with the arguments and proposals in the *Rates* White Paper, the Government went ahead with its plans for rate limitation. A Rates Bill was published on 20 December 1983, which included the selective and general schemes for limiting rates that had been put forward both in the Conservatives' election manifesto and in the White Paper. It also contained provisions for ensuring consultation between local authorities and businesses about annual rate precept and expenditure decisions.

Compared with the Local Government, Planning and Land Bill, the Rates Bill was very short (it consisted of eighteen clauses and two schedules). Part I contained a selective rate limitation scheme, while part II consisted of a similar scheme to apply to all local authorities (the schemes became known colloquially as 'rate-capping').

The reaction of the local authorities was immediately hostile. Sir Jack Smart, then chairman of the Association of Metropolitan Authorities, said of the Government's decision to go ahead with the Bill: 'If . . . the Government really believes in democracy it should be looking for ways of enhancing local accountability. The rates legislation would do the opposite. It would deal a deadly blow at local democracy.'[24]

The selective scheme was to work in a number of stages:

(a)  The Government would, each year, decide whether it wanted to operate selective rate limitation.
(b)  If it was decided to operate the scheme, a number of authorities would be designated using a one or more principles to decide which authorities would be chosen. Such principles would have

to apply to all authorities in a class (e.g. to all non-metropolitan counties).

(c) Having selected authorities, the secretary of state would give each a spending figure for the following year which would be used as the basis for a rate limit.

(d) Between the setting of the spending figure and the RSG settlement for the following year, it would be open to an authority involved to apply to the secretary of state for a higher spending limit (though, if granted, such an increased figure might have conditions attached to it – e.g. it might be deemed that council-house rents were increased). It would also be possible for the secretary of state to *reduce* the figure.

(e) After the announcement of the RSG settlement, the secretary of state would notify each authority concerned of a proposed rate limit for the following year. In doing this, he would have to take account of the spending limit determined – as in (c) above – or redetermined as in (d) above – of the block grant which the authority was likely to receive at that spending figure, of any grant receipts or contributions affected by the London Rate Equalization scheme and of the authority's financial reserves.

(f) If the authority agreed with a maximum rate, the secretary of state would serve a notice on the authority specifying the rate as its final maximum for the next year.

(g) If the authority did not agree a maximum rate with the Government, the secretary of state would have the power to notify the authority of a maximum rate equal to or greater than that originally notified.

(h) The maximum rate for each authority involved – in (g) above – would be specified in a single order which would require the approval of the House of Commons.

(i) Where no maximum has been set for an authority – in (g) or (h) above – before a specified date, the secretary of state would be able to notify the authority of an interim maximum until a final maximum rate could be set.

Authorities spending less than £10 million or below their grant-related expenditure would be excluded from selective rate-capping.

Before and during the parliamentary stages of the Bill, ministers repeatedly claimed that the selective scheme would be used for only between twelve and twenty authorities. Nevertheless the Bill did not specify a maximum, which meant that the selective scheme could be widened to take in any number of local authorities. Attempts to pass an amendment to the Bill specifying a maximum mumber of authorities were defeated.

The general scheme (part II of the Bill) was very similar to the selective, except that all authorities in England (or in Wales) could be included. The Bill proposed that the secretary of state could activate the general scheme by introducing an order which would require the approval of both Houses of Parliament.

The Bill was given a second reading on 17 January 1984. During the debate, it became clear that a number of government back-benchers were unhappy with parts or all of rate limitation and that some would abstain or vote against the Government. Patrick Jenkin, the Environment Secretary, defended his measure thus:

> when one has councils whose spending has risen nearly twice as fast as the average, councils whose spending exceeds GRE by as much as 20, 30 per cent or even 50 per cent, councils whose rates have risen three or four times as fast as the cost of living, councils where the small proportion of domestic ratepayers who pay full rates are powerless to curb that headlong rush to profligacy then I say that it is the duty of the House to act. We have a duty to protect ratepayers from blatant exploitation. We have a duty to ensure that all parts of the public sector work within national economic policies. Other efforts to make these few authorities see reason have failed. This is why we seek the powers in the Bill.[25]

The opposition to the Bill in the Commons came from all sides. For the Labour Party, shadow Environment Secretary Dr John Cunningham led the attack: 'No one in the House interested in democratic freedoms, local choice or local decision taking, no one interested in the decentralisation of power, no one who opposes bureaucratic central control – Whitehall domination – could espouse the case embodied in this most sinister measure to control freedom proposed by any British Government this century.[26]

Dr Cunningham was first of a large number of MPs, including several senior Conservatives, to attack the Bill. The former Prime Minister, Edward Heath, made a wide-ranging attack on both the principles underlying the Bill and the consequences for accountability. On the former issue, he argued of the two rate limitation schemes: 'Those are draconian powers in both the selective section of the Bill and in the general powers section. They are powers such as we have never taken before, even in two world wars. This is why I regard the conferment of the powers as a matter of principle of the utmost importance'.[27] Later Mr Heath considered the question of accountability: 'The complexity of the Bill will lead to an enormous growth of bureaucracy. Ministers themselves will not have the time to go into the details of each local authority and it will have to be left to civil servants.'[28]

Another senior Conservative (and an ex-Environment Secretary), Geoffrey Rippon, was scathing in attacking his own Government:

I am sorry to have to say that I believe that this is one of the most deplorable Bills that has been brought before the House in all the time that I have been a Member . . . its nature is undemocratic and contrary to the spirit of our unwritten constitution. Its purpose is to create the illusion of rate reform and rate reduction while avoiding the fundamental changes in the structure of local government finance that are needed.[29]

Reg Prentice and William Benyon were among other Conservative back-benchers to express concern at the provisions contained in the Rates Bill.

The Rates Bill was given a second reading by a majority of 100 votes. This meant that the Government's majority of over 140 had been reduced to 100 by abstention and opposition on the part of its own back-benchers. The committee stage of the Bill started on 26 January 1984. Only one 'rebel' (Anthony Beaumont-Dark) featured among the seventeen Conservative members of the committee, which ensured that the Government encountered little opposition at this stage.

Mr Beaumont-Dark voted against the Government (or abstained) on a number of occasions. But the Government never came close to losing divisions on amendments. During the course of the committee stage Mr Jenkin suggested that, had eighteen high-spending authorities been rate-capped in 1983–4, then there might have been savings of the order of £300 million.[30] The secretary of state also published a list showing the kind of factors which might be taken into account in determining which authorities would have their rates limited.

Despite intensive efforts by the local authorities' associations – in particular the AMA, which provided a considerable amount of the Opposition's briefing – the committee made no changes to the rate limitation proposals in the Bill. In order to complete the committee stage quickly, the Government 'guillotined' the proceedings. The report and third reading stages took place on 27 and 28 March.

In a statement published imnmediately prior to the final Commons stages of the Bill, the ACC, ADC and AMA reiterated their combined opposition to the Bill:

The selective scheme will deliver only very limited reductions in total local authority expenditure. Despite repeated assurances that the general scheme is only a reserve power which the Secretary of State hopes will never be used, the Associations believe that disappointment over the limited results from the selective scheme will lead to pressure to introduce the general scheme. This would set the scene for central intervention on such a massive scale that any marginal gains in reducing expenditure which might ensue could not possibly justify the administration effort involved. The Secretary of

State has already freely acknowledged that the introduction of the general scheme 'would be a major centralisation of power as against local autonomy' (Conservative Newsline, January 1984).'[31]

During the final Commons stages of the Bill, the Government said that there would be a concession which would be introduced in the House of Lords. This would exempt authorities from the general rate limitation scheme if they had spent below GRE or target over a period immediately prior to the use of the selective scheme. The ACC responded without enthusiasm: 'any exemptions based on GREs or expenditure guidance are of limited value when decisions on GREs rest entirely with Ministers who can change them for grant distribution purposes and thus change the base for assessing the "performance" of local authorities in meeting spending targets'.[32]

The opposition to the Bill, both inside and outside Parliament, encouraged the House of Lords to take an unusual step. Normally the upper House would give a Bill an unopposed second reading. But the Opposition in the Lords decided on this occasion to put down a 'reasoned amendment' to the motion which would give the Bill a second reading. The reasoned amendment did not seek to throw out the Bill, but to pass it with a comment attached. The amendment, put down by Lady Birk, Labour's Environment Spokesman in the Lords, added to the motion: 'But this House believes that it will result in damaging constitutional changes in the relationship between central and local government, will undermine the authority and responsibility of local councillors and will gravely weaken local democracy and accordingly calls upon Her Majesty's Government to embark on a thorough reform of local government finance'.[33]

Lord Bellwin, the Minister of State at the Department of the Environment, encapsulated the Government's arguments by stating:

What we have seen over the last few years is a fight by the Government to re-establish the economic position of the country. Local Government has had to play its part in that, and the majority of local authorities ... have done their best to help. It is the small minority which have not, and it is they who have put unreasonable burdens on their ratepayers. The Bill's principle purpose is to put that right, and it is to restore accountability in those areas where it has all but disappeared from view.[34]

The Government defeated the amendment by 235 votes to 153, despite speeches expressing reservation or opposition from its own side. Two Conservatives (Lords Alport and Sandford, the latter being president of the ADC) voted against the Government, as did a number of cross-benchers and bishops. Nevertheless during the committee stage the Government was able to defeat Opposition amendments (albeit with small majorities on some occasions) except where it wanted to introduce changes of its own. There were two significant amendments of this kind.

First, an amendment was introduced to fulfil the commitment given in the Commons to restrict the use of the general scheme. The amendment would exempt from general rate limitation an authority which:

> was not designated under the selective limitation scheme during the three previous years or is likely to be so in the current year; and which (a) did not appear likely to exceed its GRE in the current year and had not done so in the three previous years; or (b) did not appear likely to exceed its expenditure target in the current year and had not done so in the three previous years.

This meant, in effect, that an authority would have to spend under GRE or target for four successive years and have avoided the selective rate-capping scheme in order to be exempt from general rate limitation. Because of the length of time over which an authority had to spend at or below GRE or target, the local authorities' associations did not feel that this concession had significantly reduced their objections to the Bill. The second major amendment to those parts of the Bill introducing rate limitation was seen by the local authorities as another example of increasing central control.

This second amendment had the effect of giving the Government the power to subdivide each class of authorities to which it applied principles when determining which authorities should be designated for selective rate-capping. The purpose of this change was to give the Government the opportunity to treat authorities which were subject to selective rate-capping in a particular year in a different way from authorities which had *not* been capped in that year when it came to designating authorities for selective limitation in the following year. In effect, the secretary of state would be able to use different principles within each class depending upon whether or not an authority was designated in the previous year. This offered the possibility of keeping particular authorities on the selective rate-capping list for several years.

Lady Birk opened consideration of the introduction of this change by claiming: 'The Government seem more and more to be approaching the Bill in the manner of somebody who, with one lock on a door, then puts a bolt on the door, then puts on another lock and another bolt, and then a screw lock in order to get double security. It really is an extension of the braces and belt principle.'[35]

The Government accepted an amendment tabled by Lord Sandford which had the effect of linking – to the Government's planned level of current spending – the limit of £10 million whereby authorities were automatically excluded from the selective scheme of limitation. This meant that as planned current spending rose with inflation, so would the exemption limit.

Apart from the above amendments and a minor concession to several peers who had pressed for the exemption of spending on voluntary organizations from falling within rate-capping, there were a number of small amendments to rating law. But in total the changes made in Parliament failed to reduce the opposition to rate limitation.

Having faced considerable criticism from senior Conservatives in the Commons, coupled with effective advocacy of the Labour Party's case from Dr John Cunningham and the unusual challenge of a vote at second reading in the Lords, the Government must have been well pleased with the shape of the Rates Act. Only two very limited amendments were accepted to restrict the use of rate-capping. The operation of both the selective and general rate limitation schemes was now possible (though the latter would require an affirmative resolution of both Houses of Parliament to activate it).

The failure of the Opposition to inflict any significant changes to the legislation was largely due to the Government's large Commons majority and because there had been a clear manifesto commitment to introduce rate-capping. Although the local authorities' associations had exerted considerable pressure on members of both Houses of Parliament to oppose the Bill, Conservative Party ties inevitably toned down the extent to which the ACC and ADC could actively assist Labour and Alliance Politicians.

The passing of the Rates Act was similar in many ways to that of the Local Government, Planning and Land Act. On both occasions the Government was accused of destroying local government democracy by local authorities' associations which were largely Tory-controlled. On both occasions it was anticipated that the Lords would considerably amend the legislation. On both occasions the major grant or spending provisions passed almost unscathed.

(6)   RATE LIMITATION IN 1985–6 AND 1986–7

The Government announced on 24 July 1984 that it intended to use the selective rate limitation scheme. The Rate Limitation Report 1984[36] listed eighteen local authorities in England which were to be subject to rate limitation (under the selective scheme) in 1985–6. The principles used in designating, which were applied to all authorities, were that the authority's 1984–5 budget:

(a)   exceeds its grant-related expenditure as determined in the Rate Support Grant Report (England) 1984 by at least 20 per cent; and

(b)   exceeded the expenditure guidance issued to the authority for that year by at least 4 per cent.

An authority which spent less than £10 million of its GRE (whichever was the greater) was excluded from the selective scheme by section 2 of the Rates Act.

The Government also published the 1985–6 expenditure level which would be taken into account when setting each authority's rate limit. The eighteen authorities, the percentage of their excess over GRE and target in 1984 and their 1985–6 expenditure levels were as shown in Table 9.1.

The Government sent a letter to each authority to be rate-limited, stating that any application to have its expenditure level increased would have to reach the Department of Environment by 1 October 1984, to give the Government time to decide whether to change the spending level (and notify any conditions attached to such a revised figure) and to feed all the expenditure levels into final RSG calculations. Notification of the proposed rate limit would then be announced at the same time as, or within days of, the RSG settlement. Authorities were requested to respond to the rate limit within three weeks of its announcement.

The selected authorities reacted by making a number of announcements, some of which hinted at likely responses to having their rates limited. Meetings were held of sixteen of the eighteen

Table 9.1

| Designated authority | % excess of budget over GRE in 1984–5 | % excess of budget over target in 1984–5 | 1985–6 expenditure level |
|---|---|---|---|
| | | | £m |
| Basildon | 70.62 | 17.23 | 13.662 |
| Brent | 21.05 | 5.11 | 140.021 |
| Camden | 86.44 | 16.36 | 117.429 |
| GLC | 80.90 | 66.65 | 785.233 |
| Greenwich | 79.16 | 16.20 | 66.584 |
| Hackney | 40.79 | 4.92 | 82.315 |
| Haringey | 34.15 | 6.10 | 128.658 |
| ILEA | 73.17 | 15.62 | 900.366 |
| Islington | 49.86 | 22.21 | 85.564 |
| Lambeth | 46.89 | 12.83 | 113.558 |
| Leicester | 27.72 | 4.94 | 24.392 |
| Lewisham | 60.70 | 6.99 | 79.301 |
| Merseyside | 23.78 | 8.72 | 205.180 |
| Portsmouth | 34.57 | 5.26 | 16.751 |
| Sheffield | 21.13 | 4.68 | 216.573 |
| Southwark | 51.91 | 16.79 | 108.437 |
| South Yorkshire | 66.72 | 6.31 | 178.291 |
| Thamesdown | 90.26 | 5.05 | 14.199 |

authorities (all except Conservative-controlled Portsmouth, and Brent, where no party was in control). Although no final approach to limitation was immediately determined, it was decided soon after the announcement of the authorities to be selected that none of the sixteen Labour-controlled authorities would apply for a higher spending limit and that any discussions with the government would include all the authorities involved.

The authorities made it clear in the press that the expenditure levels set for 1985–6 were for technical reasons much less attainable than might appear. The government had set the spending levels for 1985–6 at precisely the same cash figures as 1984–5 budgets; that is, savings would have to be found to offset the effect of inflation. The GLC, the ILEA and Greenwich, which had increased their current expenditure by more than 30 per cent since 1981–2, were given 1985–6 expenditure levels 1.5 per cent below their 1984–5 budgets (in cash).

These levels were not attainable, it was argued, because most of the selected authorities had financed expenditure in 1984–5 budgets out of special funds. This expenditure did not show up in 'total' expenditure for block grant purposes. Yet 'total' expenditure at budget was being used as the basis for setting 1985–6 spending levels.

The decision not to apply for a higher spending level arose from a fear that the Government might attach conditions to any higher spending figures, which might be only fractionally higher, or that the Government would set a lower figure.

For the medium term the Labour-controlled authorities, or their individual leaders, discussed several options for non-compliance with the Government. Among them were: (a) setting a rate in the usual way without any reference to the rate limit; (b) setting a rate within the legal limit, though proposing to spend higher than the level implied by the rate (i.e. deficit budgeting); (c) setting a rate within the legal limit, while proposing to spend higher than the level implied by the rate, as in (b), though with a single negative item in the budget for 'unallocated savings', which would bring the budget back into balance; (d) failing to make repayments on outstanding debt; and (e) making no rate at all.

Of these possible forms of non-compliance, (a), (b) and (d) would be illegal. Setting a rate within the legal limit, while proposing to spend higher than the level implied by the rate, but with a negative balancing item, the 'fudged budget' option, was thought to be less likely to be judged improper or illegal than most other options. However, the idea of not setting a rate gained widest support.

The confusion created by Liverpool's failure to set a rate during the spring and summer of 1984 was cited as justification for the 'no rate' option. Several leading councillors publicly asserted that this option might bring pressure to bear on the Government. There was speculation in the press that the Government would take further legislataion to deal with the problems created if one or more authorities were to refuse to set a rate.

The RSG settlement for 1985–6 confirmed (although there was no legal reason to do so) the spending levels which had been set in July 1984 for the eighteen authorities selected for rate limitation. The full details of the grant system for 1985–6 allowed the Government to estimate the grant payment to each of the selected authorities, assuming each spent at the set spending level. Once the Government could calculate the grant entitlement for a particular level of expenditure, it was also possible to estimate the amount which the authority would have to raise from its own rates to fund the gap between spending and grant. The Government set the rate cap by reference to the implied rate-borne spending, though an assumption was made by officials about the likely need to add to, or the possibility of taking money from, reserves.

The rates which the Government set in December 1984 are shown in Table 9.2, compared with each authority's actual 1984–5 rate or precept and the percentage change from one to the other.

The different effect of rate limitation on rate poundages from authority to authority is clear; some faced significant rate increases, while one would find its rates falling by as much as half. In some cases the rate reductions were largely because of grant increases, which were in turn due to changes in the target-setting rules, while in

Table 9.2

|  | Local rate/precept 1984–5 | Rate limit 1985–6 | Rate change implied by limit |
|---|---|---|---|
| Basildon | 42.80p | 50.33p | +17.59% |
| Brent | 193.42p | 196.42p | + 1.55% |
| Camden | 91.94p | 92.02p | + 0.09% |
| GLC | 36.55p | 36.52p | − 0.08% |
| Greenwich | 118.91p | 96.42p | −18.91% |
| Hackney | 119.30p | 114.09p | − 4.37% |
| Haringey | 229.16p | 222.17p | − 3.05% |
| ILEA | 80.00p | 74.19p | − 7.26% |
| Islington | 122.74p | 111.21p | − 9.39% |
| Lambeth | 122.34p | 107.57p | −12.07% |
| Leicester | 37.50p | 16.27p | −56.61% |
| Lewisham | 115.74p | 87.49p | −24.41% |
| Merseyside | 65.00p | 82.86p | +27.48% |
| Portsmouth | 27.20p | 26.88p | − 1.18% |
| Sheffield | 208.24p | 207.07p | − 0.56% |
| Southwark | 149.74p | 112.69p | − 4.74% |
| South Yorkshire | 83.30p | 81.32p | − 2.38% |
| Thamesdown | 54.19p | 57.22p | + 5.59% |

Leicester the huge rate reduction arose largely from the Government's assumption that the council would use a large proportion of its accumulated reserves to cut the rate.

In announcing the rate limits Mr Jenkin said:

> The proposed rate and precept limits I am announcing today will be warmly welcomed by ratepayers in the areas concerned. For 13 of the 18 authorities I have set rate or precept limits which are lower than the rates or precepts being charged this year. In the 5 remaining cases the rate or precept is lower than it would have been without rate-capping.[37]

The Government set a deadline of 15 January 1985 by which authorities could appeal to the secretary of state for higher rate limits than those set in December 1984. Unlike the procedure for appealing against the spending limits set in July 1984, appeal against the rate limit was expected to be more acceptable to the authorities concerned. If an authority appealed against its rate cap, the secretary of state could revise the cap only upwards or leave it unchanged. If a higher cap were granted, the Government could not impose any conditions on the authority.

Although the rate-capped authorities remained opposed to the principle of limitation, there was now some support for a joint approach to the Government. Indeed, there was a meeting on 4 February 1985 between the Government and the rate-capped authorities, which also involved Labour front-bench spokesmen. However, no authority applied explicitly and directly for a higher rate cap, although some sought to make clear to the Government by indirect means (e.g. public statements about the use of special funds and assessments of anticipated deficits in 1984–5) that a higher cap was needed than what had originally been set.

The Government had to be very careful that the rate caps set were not so tight as to force one or more councils into a position where a court might decide (if there were a legal challenge) that, to stay within the rate cap, spending would have to fall below the level where services complied with other legislation. For example, an authority's rate cap could be so low that it was no longer able to provide education to a standard judged by a court to be sufficient to comply with the Education Act.

Thus the final rate caps that were approved by Parliament in February 1985 included a number of upwards revisions to the caps which had been set earlier. The revised precepts are shown in Table 9.3, along with those originally set in December 1984.

Compared with the original limits, Hackney, Haringey, Leicester and Lewisham each had a significantly higher final rate cap. In the cases of Hackney and Haringey, the change meant that instead of a

Table 9.3

|  | Original rate limit 1985–6 | Final rate limit 1985–6 | Rate change (compared with 1984–5) |
|---|---|---|---|
| Hackney | 114.09p | 147.18p | +23.4p |
| Haringey | 222.17p | 268.50p | +16.7p |
| ILEA | 74.19p | 77.25p | − 3.4p |
| Islington | 111.21p | 112.07p | − 8.7p |
| Leicester | 16.27p | 25.22p | −32.7p |
| Lewisham | 87.49p | 99.66p | −13.9p |

rate cut there was to be a large rate increase.

After the rate caps were approved by Parliament, the 'phoney war' that had taken place in the months following the original publication of the names of the authorities to be limited came to an end. In this time the sixteen Labour-controlled councils, all except Brent and Portsmouth, had severally and individually made the case that rate-capping would lead to massive cuts in services and large numbers of redundancies, while the Government was insisting publicly and privately both that the rate caps were reasonable and that there would be a considerable reduction in spending by the authorities compared with what it otherwise would have been.

Once the final rate limits were approved, there were only a few weeks before the start of the new financial year. By this time the mood among the sixteen Labour-controlled rate-capped councils had altered. There was now support for a meeting with the Environment Secretary to discuss such matters as higher grant payments for inner-city authorities. The Government refused to change the grant distribution, arguing that it was impossible to do so once Parliament had approved a particular pattern of block grant.

The Labour-controlled authorities were now thrown back on their various strategies for non-compliance with the Rates Act. The most significant move was a joint agreement to refuse to set a rate for 1985–6, which, it was hoped, would put pressure on the Government to negotiate and compromise over rate-capping and higher grant payments. It also allowed Labour councillors to convince local activists that the fight against rate-capping was being continued. At first all the Labour authorities agreed with this strategy.

However, as the start of the new financial year approached, members in several authorities decided that failure to set a rate was not a sustainable policy. There were thus a split between what the representatives of the Labour-controlled rate-capped authorities decided – i.e. a 'no rate' strategy – and what could be delivered in votes in individual councils. This split was particularly acute in the four precepting authorities and the three Labour-run non-metropolitan districts.

The precepting authorities – the GLC, the ILEA, Merseyside and South Yorkshire – faced a different legal position from that in the fourteen rating authorities. Precepting authorities have a legal obligation to issue their precept within twenty one days of the start of the financial year. Failure to do so would have been a clear branch of statutory duty, and there was some doubt as to whether an authority would have any power to issue a precept during the financial year if it failed to meet the deadline. There would inevitably have been legal proceedings against councillors responsible for any failure to set the precept on time.

No comparable clear or statutory deadline existed for the rating authorities, though there were several factors which put pressure on councillors to set a rate in time. Councillors would, it was assumed, have to set a rate in time to pay precepts to their county authority and to allow ratepayers to exercise their rights to pay rates by instalments. Councillors in all authorities had to take account of the law which forbids them deliberately to make a loss. Failure to set a rate could mean that an authority had to borrow money and pay interest on the borrowing until the rate income came in. Any such interest, and possibly any interest forgone on rate income which might have been expected to build up in an authority at the start of the financial year, could be judged to be a loss incurred by 'wilful misconduct'. Councillors who are judged guilty of wilful misconduct face personal financial surcharge and possible disqualification from office.

The fear of failure to comply with the twenty one-day deadline encouraged a majority of politicians in all four of the precepting authorities to set a precept by 10 March 1985. In the GLC the decision to set the precept did not come until the middle of the evening of Sunday 10 March, after a meeting which had continued over several days.

Of the fourteen rating authorities, Brent, Portsmouth, Basildon, Thamesdown and Leicester each set their rate before or soon after the start of the 1985–6 financial year. The remaining nine councils – Camden, Greenwich, Hackney, Haringey, Islington, Lambeth, Lewisham, Sheffield and Southwark – continued to fail to set a rate beyond the end of April. Liverpool, which had not been rate-capped in 1985–6, also refused to set a rate, on the grounds that it would have either to make spending cuts in order to keep the rate to an acceptable increase or to put up the rate massively in order to maintain expenditure.

Gradually during May 1985 most of the remaining authorities set legal rates. The Metropolitan District Auditor wrote to councillors in those London authorities which had failed to set a rate before the last

week in April, warning that there were increasing dangers of surcharge and disqualification as delay in setting a lawful rate continued.
These dangers arose from the losses incurred because of the failure to
set a rate. On 9 May the Metropolitan District Auditor wrote to all
members of councils then maintaining resistance to the Rates Act,
promising action against councillors unless a lawful rate were made by
the end of May. The auditor (Brian Skinner) explained that if the total
loss incurred by the authority was more than £2,000 he would go to
court to seek recompense from the councillors responsible. Such
action would lead to the councillors being disqualified from office.

By 31 May all authorities in England had set a legal rate with the
exception of Camden, Lambeth and Liverpool. Camden set a rate on
5 June, leaving only Lambeth and Liverpool, which finally set their
rates by early July. The District Auditors served notices on councillors
in Lambeth and Liverpool, on the grounds that their failure to set a
rate had incurred losses for local ratepayers. The councillors pledged
themselves to oppose the auditor's claim.

The councillors' appeal against the auditors' judgement was lost.
The Divisional Court found, on 5 March 1986, that the councillors
from both Liverpool and Lambeth had been guilty of wilful misconduct which had resulted in losses for ratepayers. Lambeth councillors, who did not appeal against the judgement, were disqualified as
councillors at the end of March 1986. The District Auditor for Greater
London then went on to consider the possibility of action against other
councillors who had delayed setting rates at the start of 1985–6.

Thus did the first round of rate limitation finish. The Labour
authorities' commitment to non-compliance was broken by existing
statutes which demanded that precepting authorities issue their precepts within a deadline, that councillors avoid financial losses and that
authorities' expenditure and income must balance. The Government
had done little apart from refuse to talk further with the authorities,
(on the grounds that such negotiations might give the impression that
there was still a possibility of Government concessions), and to express
its view that the authorities would gradually come into line.

The policy of non-compliance failed because moderate, and some
radical, councillors in the rate-capped authorities were not willing to
risk illegality. While the leaders of authorities like Lambeth and
Sheffield promised that no rate would be set, there was no way of
carrying the votes of their fellow councillors. How far such leaders
pursued their non-compliance policy in the knowledge that in most
cases they would be saved from illegality by the votes of moderates is
difficult to assess. However, it was clear to many observers that the
majority of councillors in the original sixteen Labour-controlled
authorities would not deliberately break the law. Perhaps what was
surprising was that at least two councils (Lambeth and non-capped
Liverpool) found themselves in a position where the auditor could

take action against them, while some others (e.g. Merseyside, Leicester and Sheffield) appeared to risk legal challenge by running a deficit budget.

For the authorities which duly set rates there was much reliance on switching from a policy of 'no rate' to a reserve policy of 'no cuts'. By creative accounting and budgets which might not be precisely met by income, the rate-capped authorities moved to a policy of making no reductions in services. This switch made it possible to placate some local Labour Parties on the grounds that a form of resistance was continuing to the Rates Act. Proof as to the final outcome of the first year of limitation would come only with manpower and out-turn expenditure figures, which would be published during or at the end of the financial year.

Budgets for 1985–6 suggested that rate-capping had not been as effective in holding down expenditure as the government had hoped. Table 9.4 shows for each authority its rate limitation spending level, as set in July 1984, its 1984–5 budget and its 1985–6 budget. In a number of authorities 1985–6 budgets were well above the Government's rate-capping spending level, and in some cases above 1984–5 spending as well. However, the figures must be treated with some caution, as some authorities may actually have budgeted to spend higher than the figures returned to the Department of the Environment.

Overall, spending rose less in the rate-capped authorities than in the country as a whole; according to the Department of the Environment, cash spending rose by 2.9 per cent in the rate-capped authorities, compared with a 4.2 per cent increase in England as a whole. However, individual authorities managed to exceed the rate-cap spending levels by a wide margin. For example, the ILEA budgeted almost £45 million above the spending levels, Brent over £8 million, Hackney almost £15 million, Haringey over £7 million and Merseyside almost £8 million. The GLC, on the other hand, budgeted over £40 million below the spending level.

The gap between the original spending levels and 1985–6 budgets in the authorities which managed to spend in excess of the Government's figures can be explained by the Department of the Environment's lack of information about each authority's individual financial position. The DoE had little certain information about authorities' reserves, particularly about the build-up and use of special funds. For example, Hackney and Haringey had both supported spending in 1984–5 out of special funds. This spending did not show up in the 1984–5 figures upon which the DoE originally based rate limitation spending levels. Consequently the DoE raised the rate caps of some authorities to take account of spending from special funds in 1984–5. On the other hand, some authorities were probably able to support expenditure in 1985–6 out of special funds and rate fund balances, of which the DoE was not

Table 9.4

|  | 1984–5 budget | 1984–5 adjusted budget | 1985–6 rate-cap spending level | 1985–6 budget |
|---|---|---|---|---|
|  | £m | £m | £m | £m |
| Basildon | 13.754 | 13.662 | 13.662 | 13.662 |
| Brent | 141.433 | 140.021 | 140.021 | 148.356 |
| Camden | 118.217 | 117.429 | 117.429 | (117.429) |
| GLC | 935.798 | 799.176 | 785.233 | 744.995 |
| Greenwich | 68.052 | 67.598 | 66.584 | 66.584 |
| Hackney | 82.868 | 82.315 | 82.315 | 97.150 |
| Haringey | 129.919 | 128.658 | 128.658 | 136.048 |
| ILEA | 923.293 | 914.123 | 900.366 | 945.057 |
| Islington | 86.138 | 85.564 | 85.564 | 85.723 |
| Lambeth | 114.320 | 113.558 | 113.558 | 116.212 |
| Leicester | 24.556 | 24.392 | 24.392 | (24.392) |
| Lewisham | 79.883 | 79.301 | 79.301 | 81.682 |
| Merseyside | 179.750 | 205.180 | 205.180 | 213.000 |
| Portsmouth | 16.863 | 16.751 | 16.751 | 16.511 |
| Sheffield | 218.854 | 216.573 | 216.573 | 218.631 |
| Southwark | 109.165 | 108.437 | 108.437 | 108.437 |
| South Yorkshire | 172.025 | 178.291 | 178.291 | 178.674 |
| Thamesdown | 14.294 | 14.199 | 14.199 | 14.199 |

*Notes*:
1 '1984–5 budget' means the figures returned to the Department of the Environment at the start of 1984–5;
2 '1984–5 adjusted budget' means the 1984–5 budget figures adjusted to take account of changes in National Insurance surcharge, changes in the funding of non-advanced further education, the move to a capital-only transport supplementary grant and because of the transfer of London Transport from the GLC to central government.
3 '1985–6 budget' figures shown in the final column are the figures returned to the Department of the Environment at the start of 1985–6. Figures in brackets indicate that the authority had not returned figures by July 1985, and it is assumed here that such councils spent at their rate-capping spending level.

fully aware when setting the original spending levels. Other forms of creative accountancy explained authorities' ability to fund spending above the rate-capping spending levels.

Manpower changes during the whole of 1985–6 will probably give the best guide to the real stringency applied by the first round of rate limitation. Manpower figures for the first part of 1985–6 suggested that no significant inroads were made into the spending of the councils. Claims by council leaders about the effects of the Rates Act were therefore much exaggerated. The threat of huge cuts in services was used in an attempt to generate opposition to the government.

Equally, the apparent flabbiness of the rate caps set for 1985–6 suggests that the first year of rate limitation did not produce the effect on spending which the Government wanted.

The Government probably emerged in better condition at the end of the first year of rate limitation, notwithstanding the merits of the policy, than the rate-capped councils. Many of the authorities promised outright non-compliance, which in the event simply could not be delivered. While some radical councillors were able to vote against a legal rate at all points, other Labour members, generally, carried the vote. The Government's policy of sitting back and waiting was effective, as one by one the authorities set legal rates. The final result of the District Auditors' moves against councillors would be uncertain for some time after the end of the 1985–6 financial year.

A few weeks after Lambeth and Liverpool set their 1985–6 rates, the Environment Secretary announced the details of rate limitation for 1986–7. Twelve authorities would be subject to selective rate limitation, including ten which had been limited in 1985–6 and two new authorities. In addition, twenty authorities would be subject to limitation under the terms of the Local Government Act 1985.

There were three ways in which authorities were selected for capping in 1986–7. First, there were the principles used to select authorities from among those which were capped in 1985–6; second, there were principles used to select from among authorities which were not capped in 1985–6; and third, there were the authorities which were automatically selected as a result of the legislation abolishing the GLC and the metropolitan counties.

The principles used to select from among those authorities which had been capped in 1985–6 would choose an authority for limitation in 1986–7 if its 1985–6 budget was more than 20 per cent above its grant-related expenditure and either more than 1 per cent above target or more than 30 per cent above its spending level in 1981–2. The principles used to select from among those authorities which were not limited in 1985–6 would rate-cap an authority in 1986–7 if its 1985–6 budget were more than 20 per cent above its grant-related expenditure and more than 4 per cent above target. The latter principles were the same as those used in 1985–6 to select authorities in the first round of rate-capping. The Local Government Act 1985 stated that all the new joint boards (of which there were nineteen) and the new Inner London Education Authority would be subject to selective rate limitation for the first three years of their existence.

Basildon, Camden, Greenwich, Hackney, Haringey, Islington, Lambeth, Lewisham, Southwark and Thamesdown were the ten authorities which were carried forward from rate-capping in 1985–6 to 1986–7. Newcastle-upon-Tyne and Liverpool were the two new authorities selected for the first time. The fire, police and transport joint boards in each metropolitan county, plus the London Fire Board and the Inner London Education Authority, were the authorities selected under the Local Government Act 1985. Thirty-two authorities were thus involved in the second round of rate limitation. By 1987–8, forty authorities were rate capped.

Of the original eighteen rate-capped authorities, four were dropped from limitation in 1986–7, while four ceased to exist at the end of 1985–6. Sheffield, Brent, Portsmouth and Leicester were not selected by the principles applied to those authorities which had been capped in 1985–6. The GLC, Merseyside and South Yorkshire were all to be abolished at the end of 1985–6, while the ILEA would become a new, elected authority.

Of the twelve authorities subject to rate limitation under the Rates Act 1984 – i.e. not those involved because of the Local Government Act 1985 – nine were set spending levels for 1986–7 which were precisely the same as their 1985–6 budgets. Their rate caps would be set on the assumption that they spent at these levels. Liverpool, Hackney and Lewisham were each set a spending level for 1986–7 which was equivalent to their 1984–5 budget plus 10 per cent – a tighter constraint than a cash freeze on their 1985–6 budget would have imposed. Spending levels for the fire and police joint boards were set by the Home Secretary, while those for transport boards were set by the Transport Secretary. The Secretary of State for Education set the spending level for the ILEA.

In an attempt to make it easier for authorities to apply for higher expenditure levels, the Environment Secretary gave an undertaking that he would not reduce the spending level or impose any conditions on a council which appealed for a redetermination principally on the grounds that its spending level made inadequate allowance for the costs of abolition or where 1985–6 spending had been artificially depressed by use of special funds or other accounting devices.

In fact, some authorities did apply for higher spending levels for 1986–7. Of the twelve authorities capped under the Rates Act (as opposed to the joint boards and the newly elected Inner London Education Authority, which were capped under the terms of the Local Government Act 1985), seven applied for and received redetermined spending levels. Table 9.5 shows, for each of the authorities selected under the Rates Act, their 1986–7 original spending level, their redetermined spending level and their original rate limit for 1986–7. Because of the transfer of services from the GLC and the metropolitan counties to London boroughs and metropolitan districts, spending levels for these authorities cannot readily be compared with those for 1985–6.

Some of the original rate limits for 1986–7 were raised following

Table 9.5

| | 1986–7 Rate-cap spending level | 1986–6 Rate-cap spending level (revised) | 1986–7 Rate limit |
|---|---|---|---|
| | £m | £m | p |
| Basildon | 13.662 | — | 52.75 |
| Camden | 133.669 | 136.919 | 118.35 |
| Greenwich | 88.629 | 95.228 | 124.21 |
| Hackney | 119.422 | 128.572 | 141.96 |
| Haringey | 152.813 | — | 254.59 |
| Islington | 106.113 | — | 93.20 |
| Lambeth | 144.068 | 152.309 | 126.11 |
| Lewisham | 112.062 | 115.594 | 141.86 |
| Liverpool | 265.070 | 274.550 | 232.09 |
| Newcastle-upon-Tyne | 151.252 | 154.652 | 321.23 |
| Southwark | 134.190 | — | 121.16 |
| Thamesdown | 14.199 | — | 54.68 |

appeals from authorities. Budgets for 1986–7 showed that a number of authorities had managed to spend considerably above their revised spending levels. Considerable 'creative accounting' was undertaken in the attempt to preserve spending levels. This meant that both in 1985–6 and in 1986–7 authorities had increased their spending *within* the rate limits. Thus rate caps appeared once again to be relatively generous in 1986–7, with no authority having to make real reductions in spending.

Politically, the second year of rate limitation seemed unlikely to be as bumpy as the first. Although local authorities remained implacably opposed to the Rates Act, the experience of opposition to the first year of the Act proved salutary. No concessions had been wrought from the Government in 1985–6, and yet councillors had been disqualified for their actions in attempting non-compliance. Moreover, the Government passed legislation (the Local Government Act 1986) during the early months of 1986 which forced authorities to set their rates by 1 April each year. This put rating authorities in a similar position to that of precepting authorities; i.e. they had to fix their rates by a particular date.

On the other hand, the Government was also interested in avoiding trouble in 1986–7. The abolition of the GLC and the metropolitan counties had to be achieved with as little disturbance as possible, which meant that rate-capped councils (many of which were picking up services from the abolished authorities) had to be treated with leniency. It appears that capped authorities were indeed able to fund many or all of the services they inherited within their rate limit. This issue is dealt with in more detail later. Nevertheless, the continuing existence of rate limitation and such instruments as block grant seemed likely to ensure that the relationship between many local authorities and central government would remain difficult.

## (7)  ABOLITION

The abolition of the GLC and the six metropolitan counties had, along with rate limitation, been part of the Conservatives' manifesto. Soon after the *Rates* White Paper, a second White Paper was published entitled *Streamlining the Cities*,[38] which outlined the Government's case for abolition. No figure was put on likely savings either in the White Paper or in the several consultation papers which were produced by individual service departments on such topics as the arts, transport and planning.

*Streamlining the Cities* proposed that the metropolitan counties be abolished and that their functions should be passed to joint boards constituted from district council members for fire, police and transport, and in most other cases to the district councils. In London the GLC would go, and fire services would be provided by a joint board constituted of borough nominees. The Metropolitan Police would continue to be the responsibility of the Home Secretary; London Transport would pass from the GLC to central government control, though this change was to take place in 1984, well before abolition. In inner London, education was to continue to be provided by a single authority, an Inner London Education Authority nominated by the constituent boroughs. In the GLC and in the six metropolitan counties, some provision which was intended to become a borough or district function, e.g. waste disposal and debt charges, might have to continue to be provided though some kind of joint arrangement. All other services would pass to district or borough councils.

There were two consultation papers which dealt specifically with the financial difficulties of abolishing the GLC and metropolitan counties.[39] The first examined the consequences for block grant, while the second considered the difficulties brought about by the disappearance of the GLC precept.

Block grant would have to be changed because the GREs, poundage schedules, multipliers and other features of the system would have to be redistributed from the existing upper-tier councils to the boroughs and districts. Targets would similarly have to be reallocated. Because the upper-tier authorities were in many cases spending well above GRE and target, the Government would have to decide whether simply to redistribute the existing figures or to set new, higher GREs and targets.

The reason was simple. The GLC, for example, planned to spend £824 million in 1983–4, compared with a target of £566 million and a

GRE of £480 million. If the £566 million target were somehow allocated to the thirty two boroughs and the City, while the GLC's spending of £824 million could not immediately be reduced, the boroughs and joint boards would find themselves 'inheriting' overspend. This burden might fall even on lower-spending authorities. Overspend would lead to grant penalties for the boroughs, which the GLC did not suffer because all its grant had already disappeared under the basic block grant distribution arrangements. It was thus possible that abolishing the GLC could actually put up rates because of extra grant penalties suffered by the boroughs, or by new joint authorities. Similarly it would be awkward for the Government, with its commitment to increase spending on law and order, if, for example, the six new police boards outside London were penalized for 'overspending' GRE or target.

Thus there were not only the technical problems of redesigning the grant system, but also difficulties caused by the difference between the GLC's and metropolitan counties' targets, GREs and spending.

The second consultative paper dealt with the disappearance of the GLC precept. Here the difficulty created by abolition was the loss of automatic equalization of rateable resources achieved by the GLC. The GLC, like all other upper-tier authorities, levied a precept on all the ratepayers in its area and spent the income on services within the same area. But as rateable value and expenditure need were not necessarily in the same place, there tended to be a redistribution of resources from areas with high rateable resources and low spending needs to those with low rateable resources and high spending needs.

The loss of such automatic equalization in the six metropolitan counties outside London could, in principle, be dealt with by the block grant, which would automatically take account of changes in the relationship between spending need and rateable resources in each district – provided that the grant system was aptly redesigned. But in London block grant could not cope. The vast difference in rateable values between the central boroughs and the rest meant that very great equalization was taking place because of the GLC precept. The Cities of London and Westminster and the borough of Camden received no block grant because of their high rateable resources. They were the authorities which would gain most from abolition of the GLC precept, yet there was no way of reducing their block grant to compensate for their reduced payments towards GLC-wide services. Other boroughs, with lower rateable values, would, on the other hand, receive extra grant to compensate for the loss of their net benefit from the GLC precept and spending.

The solution proposed to the loss of the automatic equalization achieved by the GLC was to extend the London Rate Equalization scheme. This scheme had existed for a number of years to allow a small redistribution of resources from the central boroughs to some or all of the rest. The LRES operated in addition to the other RSG arrangements and could, it was argued in the consultation paper, be used to redistribute a relatively large pool of money from central London to the other boroughs.

The problems created by abolition for the operation of block grant and London equalization would be immense. Other financial consequences were to be dealt with by more direct means. The White Paper *Streamlining the Cities* proposed that all the joint boards would have Government-imposed restrictions on their precept and manpower levels for at least three years after abolition. In exercising these new controls, the Government would wish 'to be satisfied that the joint boards' proposed administrative structures will result in the economical operation of services, and that, where appropriate, arrangements have been made for the sharing of administrative and other staff and for the contracting out of specialist services'.[40]

Abolition, which appeared to be little more than limited structural change, would therefore have considered financial consequences. If block grant and the London equalization arrangements could not be satisfactorily reformed, there was a possibility of huge grant shifts from authority to authority. The increase of control over local authority rates and precepts given to the Government by rate-capping was to be extended to the new joint boards and supplemented with manpower limits even before the authorities first set a precept.

The Government would not commit itself to achieving any particular level of savings after abolition: 'it is not possible to put a figure on the savings arising from abolition, or the transitional costs. These will depend largely on the way in which the transfer of functions is achieved, and on decisions to be taken by the authorities concerned'.[41] The prospects for reduced spending and greater efficiency were therefore incalculable. Despite continuous pressure from local authorities and the press for an estimate of the likely savings, the Government steadfastly refused to give one until after the Bill to abolish the councils was published. Abolition was justified on the grounds that the upper tier of local government in the cities was redundant and that its abolition would inevitably lead to savings.

Abolition was timed to take place in 1986–7, a year after rate limitation had been used for the first time. To pave the way for abolition, the Government planned, during 1984, the pass legislation abolishing the elections to the GLC and metropolitan counties due in May 1985. The Local Government (Interim Provisions) Bill proposed to cancel the elections and hand over control of the seven councils to joint boards for the eleven months from May 1985 to April 1986. Such boards would be constituted from members appointed by constituent boroughs and districts. The Inner London Education Authority would also be run by a joint board.

During the Bill's passage through Parliament the House of Lords passed an amendment to the Bill which would not allow elections to be cancelled until *after* the main legislation implementing abolition was passed. This forced the Government to a fall-back position of extending the life of the existing councils until April 1986 while imposing limits on their spending powers for their last year in office.

The GLC, led by Ken Livingstone, and metropolitan counties mounted an expensive and effective campaign both against the Interim Provisions Bill and in preparation for the main abolition legislation. Considerable public sympathy built up for the threatened councils, which, coupled with opposition from powerful Conservative politicians at the GLC and in Parliament, put massive pressure on the Government to modify or drop the abolition proposals.

The legislation to abolish the councils was introduced into Parliament on 22 November 1984. The proposals put forward in the White Paper *Streamlining the Cities* appeared in the Bill largely unchanged, though the original proposal that the Inner London Education Authority should be a nominated joint board was replaced by a directly elected ILEA because of concerns within the Government that the House of Lords would oppose a board for the ILEA. The manpower, spending and organization of the new joint boards would be subject to Government control for the first three years following abolition.

Other financial provisions in the Bill included the application of block grant and other existing local government legislation to the new authorities. Targets for those authorities affected by the reform would for the first year after abolition be set judgementally by the secretary of state as opposed to the usual practice of setting targets according to principles applied to all councils. Any additional equalization required in London (i.e. on top of that achieved by block grant) would be achieved under the London Government Act 1963. Section 66 of the 1963 Act was already used for operation of the London Rate Equalization scheme.

The Financial Memorandum to the Bill included the Government's estimates of savings to be brought about by abolition. After months of refusing to make such estimates, these figures were the first given by the Environment Department about the expected savings. The Financial Memorandum was, nevertheless, cautious:

> The government's current estimate . . . is that, subject to decisions yet to be taken by successor authorities, a saving of the order of £100 million annually will be achievable by removing a tier of government and eliminating duplication of functions. There will be some transitional costs falling most heavily in 1986/7 and reducing sharply thereafter.[42]

The memorandum explained that central government would have to take over the funding of £51 million worth of services, mainly support for the arts. It was also hoped that reductions in spending might arise from successor bodies operating more efficiently. Finally, it was estimated that 8,000 jobs would disappear from local government, while some 900 extra jobs would be created in other public-sector institutions.

The local authorities to be abolished challenged the claimed savings and alleged that the Bill contained massive new central controls over local government. The provisions to give the Government the power to control the manpower, spending and organization of the new joint boards were seen as particularly dangerous. The number of ministerial reserve powers was also criticized.

During the second reading of the Bill the Government came under pressure from its own back-benchers. The pattern which had been set by the passage of the Rates Bill and the Local Government (Interim Provisions) Bill through Parliament looked likely to be repeated. For example, Edward Heath launched into the Government with a scathing attack: 'The Bill contains proposals for a major constitutional change and it comes without precedent because no public inquiry has been carried out as a basis for it. What is more, the case against the GLC or the metropolitan counties remains unproven ... There is no logic in the Government's approach to local government.[43] Later Mr Heath stated: 'We are witnessing the complete fragmentation of local government for one reason ... so that the Government can have more power over local authorities to deny them the money that their electors want them to have to carry out the services that are needed'.[44]

Other Government back-benchers joined in the attack on the Government both during the second reading and at later stages of the the Bill. Much concern centred on the lack of a London-wide elected authority after the abolition of the GLC. The passing of the early stages of the Bill was to take place at precisely the time that the first round of rate limitation approached the point when authorities would normally set their rates and precepts, which had the effect of splitting press and public attention between the two subjects.

The committee stage of the Bill lasted from 12 December 1984 to 7 March 1985. Clause 1 of the Bill was considered by a committee of the whole House of Commons since the issue raised in the clause, the principle of whether or not the GLC and the metropolitan counties should be abolished, was of constitutional importance. The remainder of the Bill was considered by a large standing committee (forty seven members and two chairmen). Despite the Government's huge parliamentary majority, which was reflected in the political balance of members of the standing committee, there were a number of votes in committee when the Government's majority became embarrassingly small.

For example, during the debate on the floor of the House on clause 1, there was a vote on an amendment put down by the Conservative member for Staffordshire South (Patrick Cormack), which proposed the setting up of a new London-wide elected authority – covering the same area as the GLC – which would have functions and powers determined by Parliament following an inquiry by a select committee of the House of Commons. The Government defeated the amendment by just 23 votes, with a large number of Conservatives either abstaining or voting against their own front bench. This majority compares with the Government's overall majority of some 140. A vote on whether clause 2 should stand part of the Bill, considered by the standing committee, saw the Government's majority cut from 13 to 2. However, the Bill emerged from the Commons committee stage without significant changes.

Some changes were introduced by the Government itself during the report stage of the Bill. These amendments were financial. One sought to stop the GLC and metropolitan counties undertaking contractual obligations which would not be wholly discharged before the abolition date, unless the secretary of state consented to such contracts. A second amendment sought to stop the councils disposing of assets and to reduce the size of contract which could be signed by the GLC and metropolitan counties without the approval of the secretary of state.

The Local Government (Interim Provisions) Act 1984 had forbidden the councils from entering into contracts worth more than £250,000 for building and engineering works or more than £100,000 for other items. The amendment to the Local Government Bill reduced both figures to £15,000. In introducing and passing these amendments the Government was hoping to stop the GLC and metropolitan counties from entering into contracts which would commit successor bodies to expenditure or from spending money rapidly during the last year of their operation.

The Government introduced an amendment to allow the funding of voluntary organizations by county-wide arrangements after abolition. The National Council for Voluntary Organizations and individual charities and bodies had lobbied hard because of the fear that the abolition of the GLC and metropolitan counties would lead to a reduction in the funding of voluntary organizations. In particular, it would be impossible for organizations which provided services over more than one district or borough to apply for grants. The Government's amendment allowed one borough to act as a lead borough for a county-wide scheme, provided at least half of the districts or boroughs agreed with setting up such a scheme. At least two-thirds of the constituent would have to approve the grants. Payment towards the cost of the grants would be made by boroughs and districts in proportion to their populations.

Once the Bill had passed its remaining Commons stages, it moved to the House of Lords. Here the Bill's opponents hoped to secure their greatest successes. In fact, the Lords made some amendments to clauses dealing with planning, waste disposal, highways and the Inner London Education Authority. Waste disposal, the Lords decided, should be run by a county-wide joint board in each area, while highways and traffic management should be run by the transport joint board in the six metropolitan county areas, and by the 'residuary body' in London. This 'residuary body' was set up under the legislation to run the debt management, pension funds and other functions of the councils which could not with ease be broken up or given to a joint board.

The commons overturned the Lords amendments dealing with waste disposal and highways, which meant that the Act that finally emerged was close to the original Bill. On financial matters, the only significant changes concerned the size of contracts, the disposal of assets and voluntary organizations.

As the start of the 1986–7 financial year approached, civil servants at the Department of the Environment were thus faced with operating rate-capping after abolition, as well as disentangling block grant and redistribution resources from upper-tier authorities to the boroughs and districts. Within London, retaining a balance of resources between the rateably wealthy central boroughs and the rest added a further difficulty. Careful reallocation of the system of finance would be required – possibly accompanied by more block grant – if abolition were not to become politically awkward for the Government.

The 1986–7 RSG Settlement in December 1985 showed how the Government had chosen to cope with the financial consequences of abolition. As expected, grant-related expenditure assessments and other aspects of block grant were recast so as to take account of the new structure of local government. A second London Rate Equalization Scheme was introduced so as to maintain the balance of resources between central London (Westminster, Camden and the City) and the rest of the capital. Further changes were made so as to maintain the balance of resources between London as a whole and the rest of England. 'Safety nets' were to be used to limit the shift of resources from one authority to another because of abolition (safety nets were also to be used to limit shifts in grant because of the removal of targets and penalties, and for certain other reasons).

The overall effect of the 1986–7 RSG settlement was to shift resources from the non-metropolitan areas into London. The Department of the Environment's early estimates suggested that over £200 million of block grant would move out of the shire areas and into London. As authorities set their budgets for 1986–7, it became clear that a significant shift of grant had indeed occurred. Many London boroughs – including those which were not rate-capped – managed to cut their rates, some by up to 30 per cent. In the non-metropolitan areas, rate rises were much above the rate of inflation, with some up by more than 30 per cent. Metropolitan district rate rises were generally higher than those in London, but lower than those in many non-metropolitan areas.

The low or negative rate rises in London were largely because of grant movements. Whether or not the Government deliberately intended this to happen cannot be certain, though it should be observed that full council elections were due in London in May 1986, as were elections to the new ILEA. It was at the very least convenient for the Government that the huge grant shift took place.

The costs or savings because of abolition were not fully clear in the period immediately after the reorganization took place. First, the budgets of the GLC and the metropolitan counties may have been artificially high or low in their last year, as unusual accounting devices were used and final spending decisions were made. Second, any unused balances from the abolished authorities were in some cases used to reduce the rates of successor authorities in the year after abolition. Third, there were so many successor authorities, particularly in London, that it was difficult to find out how much each one was spending on services inherited from the abolished authorities.

One financial consequence of the grant arrangements in 1986–7 was, as it has been stated, to shift grant from the non-metropolitan areas to London. Whether or not this was deliberately to assist the process of abolition, many authorities outside London saw it as such. As a result, Birmingham City Council started legal action against the Government about the use of multipliers to limit year-on-year grant losses. The Government announced in April 1986 that it intended to bring forward legislation during the 1985–6 parliamentary session to remove the possibility of successful legal challenge to the use of multipliers within block grant. This was done because the Government feared that Birmingham and other authorities would have been able, by legal challenge, to undermine the operation of multipliers for 1986–7 and for each previous year since 1981–2.

## (8)  TARGETS AND PENALTIES ARE ABOLISHED

In July 1985 the Government announced that targets and penalties were to be abandoned. After five years of mounting controversy and dislike, the Government bowed to pressure from such sources as the Audit Commission and the Comptroller and Auditor General. The Audit Commission had produced a report[45] in August 1984 which criticized the existing block grant arrangements on the grounds that they caused higher than necessary rates; that targets and penalties distorted a potentially sound grant system; that accountability was blurred and that there were no positive incentives to reduce costs. The commission's chief officer (the 'Controller of Audit'), John

Banham, made it clear in a number of public statements that he considered the existing block grant to be badly flawed.

In April 1985 the Comptroller and Auditor General (Sir Gordon Downey) published a report[46] which, although using less direct language than the Audit Commission's report, was also critical of block grant. The operation of targets and penalties was singled out for specific criticism:

> The addition of a regime of targets and penalties unrelated to objectively assessed spending needs, but designed to restrain spending, has detracted still further from the original purposes of the system, to the point of making its sophistication worthless. Nor has this regime had the result intended in every case because some authorities have judged it expedient not to restrain expenditure in the short term in order to maximise grant over a longer period.[47]

With the Government's own watch-dogs attacking block grant, the Environment Secretary finally had to abandon targets and penalties. Both the Audit Commission and the Comptroller and Auditor General concluded that targets and penalties actually discouraged lower spending. This criticism made it clear that the Government's main weapon in the battle to hold down local authority current spending had been counter-productive. Targets and penalties had also badly damaged central–local relations. The Government's use of this system appears to have led to the worst of all possible worlds.

Earlier chapters have described the reaction of local authorities of all parties to the imposition of expenditure targets and grant penalties. The removal of such a distortion of the original block grant was bound to be welcomed by local authorities. But for the Government there was a need to ensure that individual authorities (particularly high-spending ones) did not benefit massively from the reform because grant which had previously been taken away in penalties would now be returned. By increasing the rate poundage cost to ratepayers of spending above grant-related expenditure, the Government could ensure to some extent that higher-spending councils were not grossly advantaged.

At the same time as it was announced that targets and penalties would not be used in 1986–7 the Government outlined its plans to toughen up the basic block grant mechanisms. This would be achieved by sharpening the rate poundage effect of spending above grant-related expenditure. In the 1985–6 basic block grant arrangements, i.e. before the operation of targets and penalties, each £ per head of spending above GRE meant that an authority was expected to increase its grant-related poundage by 0.6p. If an authority exceeded a threshold which was set 10 per cent, on average, above GRE, the additional rate poundage was 0.8625p for each extra £ per head of spending. Under the 1986–7 arrangements each £ per head of spending above GRE would add 1.1p to the assumed rate poundage up to 10 per cent above GRE, while for each £ per head of spending more than 10 per cent over GRE 1.5p would be added to the rate poundage.

This meant that spending above GRE would lead to reduced grant receipts in most authorities in England. Similarly, as spending moved below GRE, grant would increase for most councils as spending fell. The Government hoped that the reductions in grant for overspending GRE, coupled with the grant increases in most authorities for spending under GRE, would encourage spending to fall.

Because of the inevitabloe big grant shifts that would result from the move from the 1985–6 grant system to the new, tougher block grant arrangements for 1986–7, the Government decided to limit, by use of multipliers, grant losses and gains.

The abolition of targets and penalties in 1986–7 was accompanied by a significant increase in Rate Support Grant. Following a number of years in which the aggregate Exchequer grant had either fallen or only risen marginally, the 1986–7 total of £11,764 million represented an increase of almost 5 per cent over the amount paid out in 1985–6. Because there would be no penalties in 1986–7, the total originally announced, i.e. £11,764 million, would almost certainly be paid in full.

The relative generosity of the 1986–7 grant settlement was to be helpful to the Government when it came to ensuring that the removal of targets, the abolition of the GLC and metropolitan counties and the second year of rate-capping did not lead to difficulties for individual authorities. Nevertheless the 1986–7 grant total was still very much below the level paid out in the late 1970s, and average rate rises were very high (11–12 per cent) compared with inflation.


(9)  FURTHER REFORMS ARE DISCUSSED

At the 1984 Conservative Party Conference ministers announced that there was to be another review of local government finance. The review would be conducted internally by DoE ministers and civil servants, though a number of external assessors would be appointed. The Government wished to undertake the work within the department so as to avoid being presented with conclusions, for example, by a Royal Commission, which it would see as politically impossible to implement. The original idea was to produce work within the DoE which would be used as the basis of a consultative document. In the light of public response to the consultative document, the Conservative Party's manifesto for the next general election would contain the Government's final plans for reform.

Although no papers were published, the Government made it clear that officials had been appointed to a special unit within the DoE and that all options were open. No evidence was sought from outsiders at this stage, though it was expected that responses would be invited to the consultative document. Then, during the spring of 1985, something happened which upset the Government's original plans.

Despite the failure to undertake a rating revaluation in England and Wales, the Government had gone ahead with a revaluation in Scotland. The 1985–6 financial year was the first in which the new values were used. Because of changes to the Scottish economy since the previous revaluation in 1978, there were considerable shifts in burden in 1985. In particular, domestic properties found that their share of the total rateable value rose from 37 per cent in 1978 to 42 per cent in 1985. For many individual ratepayers including some small businesses, the rise in rates from 1984–5 to 1985–6 proved dramatic. It led to a wave of discontent with the rating system and with the Government, culminating in the Government losing a very safe Conservative seat in a council by-election.

The Government reacted rapidly. The Scottish Secretary announced that relief was to be made available to any ratepayer whose value rose particularly steeply. This special relief ran contrary to the policy adopted by successive governments to reduce the real value of domestic subsidy and the policy to cut the overall level of Rate Support Grant.

In addition to the short-term relief for Scottish ratepayers, the Government changed the direction of the internal review of finance. Instead of aiming for a consultative document which would be used as the basis of Conservative policy at the next election, it was decided to bring forward legislation before the general election. Proposals would be enacted during the 1986–7 parliamentary session and would thus be on the statute book, though not in operation, at the time of an election in late 1987 or early 1988. If the Conservatives won this election – which would be fought in part on the issue of local government financial reform – the legislation would be brought into effect.

At hastily summoned meetings the Cabinet considered possible reforms. Before one such meeting in May 1985 the newspapers were told that the favoured package included central government control of non-domestic rates, the introduction of a poll tax and, possibly, the transfer of education to central funding. Ministers made it clear that rates, at least in their present form, could not be kept.

But as more work was undertaken by officials it became clear that such options as a poll tax were fraught with difficulties. If a poll tax were to be levied on *all* adults, many individuals who paid little or no rates – e.g. pensioners, the unemployed and students – would find themselves faced with a new poll tax bill. On the other hand, if some groups were exempted or relieved of the burden, the increased accountability which the Government desired would be lost. As the weeks went on, it was suggested, again, in the newspapers, that some form of graduated poll tax, i.e. with different levels of tax for people in different income groups, might be the best solution. The Government's supporters and critics were quick to point out that such a graduated tax resembled a local income tax.

Other, related issues were being considered during 1985. The Government had appointed a second inquiry, under the chairmanship of David Widdicombe QC, to review the practices and procedures of local authorities, including political advertising and officer–member relations. Legislation had been promised, for the 1985–6 parliamentary session, in which the Government would extend the range of local authority services where council staff had to compete with private contractors to win contracts to provide services.

In January 1986 the Government published a Green Paper which included proposals for a radical reform of local government finance in Britain. The Government had felt under pressure to find an alternative to domestic rates ever since Mrs Thatcher (then Opposition environment spokesman) promised to abolish household rates in the October 1974 general election campaign. Latterly, the shifts in the rates burden in Scotland in 1985–6 – resulting from the revaluation of the rate base – had led to considerable unpopularity for the Government, which encouraged the early publication of proposals for an alternative to the rates.

The Green Paper made the following major proposals:

- *Domestic rates* would be replaced by a *community charge* (previously called a 'poll tax') which would be a tax whose total yield would be determined by each authority and would be collected as an equal amount from every adult in the authority. A new register would have to be set up in order to establish residence.
- *Non-domestic rates* would be set by central government, following a revaluation of non-domestic properties. The Government favoured a single, uniform, non-domestic rate poundage to be levied on all businesses. The total yield of business rates would then be handed back to local government as an amount per adult. Authorities would have discretion to set small, additional non-domestic rate whose yield could be retained locally.
- *Grants* would be simplified. Block grant, with its equalization of spending needs and rateable resources, would go. In its place would be: (a) a needs grant, which would equalize for variations in spending need on the basis of a simplified grant-related expenditure assessment; and (b) a standard grant, which would be paid out as a simple amount per adult. Each of these would be at the start of the year and would not vary with expenditure.

There would be a transition period both for the introduction of the community charge/abolition of domestic rates and for the move to a uniform business rate. Domestic rates and the community charge would coexist for a decade or more in some authorities. The move from the old to the new system would be extensively 'safety-netted' to avoid huge shifts of tax burden in the short term. Some form of rebate system would continue to support the tax payments of the least well off.

In addition, the Green Paper proposed changes to controls over capital expenditure. The system of controls over net capital expenditure which had existed since 1981–2 was, as was shown earlier, concerned with limiting capital spending other than that funded out of sales of assets. The new system suggested in the Green Paper (and in a subsequent consultative paper) would have extended Government control to take in *all* capital spending. The purpose of this extension of control was to bring down the total of local authority capital expenditure.

Although the political reaction to the Green Paper proposals was muted, the possibility that changes would be made soon could not be ruled out. The Government intended to introduce legislation to implement the introduction of the community charge in Scotland during the 1986–7 parliamentary session. Domestic rates would start to be phased out in Scotland on 1 April 1989. England and Wales would follow within a year or two.

If the whole package were to be introduced, there would be large redistribution of tax burdens from authority to authority and from individual to individual. Businesses in authorities which currently have high rate poundages would be better off, while those in low-poundage authorities would be worse off. Individual taxpayers would be generally worse off in authorities which were spending radically above their spending need assessment and better off where spending was low relative to needs assessment. Many pensioners and the better off would gain by the introduction of community charge, whereas young single people would generally be worse off. No full measurement of these effects was made by the Government.

Thus another government document on local government finance was produced. Although the 1986 document went further than its predecessors in suggesting a new tax and grant system, there remained widespread suspicion that the introduction of the full new system would take so long (with the transition period and safety nets) that no Government could stay in power long enough to introduce the full package. It was even suggested that some members of the Government did not want to introduce a flat-rate per capita tax. Consultation on the Green Paper was set to end on 31 October 1986.

NOTES: CHAPTER 9

1 House of Commons Select Committee on the Environment, Second Report, Session 1981–2, House of Commons papers 217–I–III (July 1982).
2 *Alternatives to Domestic Rates*, Cmnd 8449 (London: HMSO, December 1981).

3   Conservative Party manifesto 1983, pp. 36–7.
4   Labour Party manifesto 1983, *The New Hope for Britain*, p. 30.
5   Ibid., p. 30.
6   Ibid., p. 31.
7   Extract from a speech by Tom King, Secretary of State for the Environment, at Bridgwater (20 May 1983).
8   Conservative Research Department, 'Questions of Policy 131', note to Conservative election candidates (18 May 1983).
9   Extract from a speech by Tom King at Bridgwater, op. cit.
10  *Rates*, Cmnd 9008 (London: HMSO, August 1983).
11  Ibid., para. 1.2.
12  Ibid., para. 1.24.
13  Ibid., para. 1.31.
14  Ibid., para. 2.12.
15  Association of County Councils, *Rates: The Way Ahead, response to the White Paper on rate limitation and reform of the rating system* (October 1983), p. 1.
16  From a resolution passed at a meeting of Association of District Council Branches and Leaders (14 September 1983).
17  Association of Metropolitan Authorities, *Rate Limitation: Summary of the AMA Response* (21 September 1983).
18  Association of British Chambers of Commerce, *Commentary on the Rates White Paper (Cmnd 9008)*, p. 7.
19  See, for example, the response of the local authorities' associations to the White Paper; or Tony Travers and Tyrrell Burgess, *Rates: A Response to the Government's Proposals for Rate Limitation and Reform* (North East London Polytechnic, September 1983).
20  London Chamber of Commerce and Industry, *Economic Report and Surveys* (June 1983).
21  See, for example, Association of Metropolitan Authorities, *Rate Limitation: The AMA Response*, (21 September 1983), ch. 4.
22  Ibid., paras. 4.18, 4.19.
23  Tony Travers and Tyrrell Burgess, *Rates: A Response to the Government's Proposals for Rate Limitation and Reform*, op. cit., p. 15.
24  Statement by Sir Jack Smart (16 December 1983).
25  House of Commons, Official Report (17 January 1984), col. 175.
26  Ibid.
27  Ibid., col. 185.
28  Ibid., col. 188.
29  Ibid., col. 193.
30  House of Commons, Official Report, Standing Committee G (14 February 1984), col. 442.
31  Statement by the secretaries of the Association of County Councils, Association of District Councils and Association of Metropolitan Authorities, published to coincide with the report and third reading stages of the Rates Bill (27–8 March 1984).
32  Statement by John Lovill, chairman of the Association of County Councils (29 March 1984).
33  House of Lords, Official Report (9 April 1984), col. 907.
34  Ibid., col. 1016.
35  Ibid., 5 June 1984, cols. 514–15.
36  *Local Government: The Rate Limitation Report 1984*, House of Commons Paper 589 (24 July 1984).
37  Department of the Environment press notice (11 December 1984).
38  *Streamlining the Cities*, Cmnd 9063 (London: HMSO, October 1983).
39  The consultation papers were: (a) *Streamlining the Cities: Implications for the Block Grant System* and (b) *Streamlining the Cities: The Disappearance of the*

*Greater London Council Precept*, both published by the Department of the Environment (26 October 1983).
40   *Streamlining the Cities* Cmnd 9063 (London: HMSO, October 1983), para. 6.6.
41   Ibid., para. 6.1.
42   Local Government Bill 1984, pp. iv–v.
43   House of Commons, Official Report (4 December 1984), cols. 190–1.
44   Ibid., cols. 192–3.
45   Audit Commission, *The Impact on Local Authorities' Economy, Efficiency and Effectiveness of the Block Grant Distribution System* (London: HMSO, August 1984).
46   Report by the Comptroller and Auditor General, *Department of the Environment: Operation of the Rate Support Grant System* (London HMSO, 2 April 1985).
47   Ibid., p. 8, para. 38.

# CONCLUSION

This book has shown that there has been a recognition of a problem with local authority finance for many years. Rates have become increasingly criticized as the single government tax, while the grant system has moved towards increasing complexity and political manipulation. Since the mid-1970s these problems have been compounded by a shift from a policy of growth to an attempt by central government to cut back local spending. Changes in the national political scene have exaggerated problems with finance. By 1986 almost everyone involved in local government finance, including ratepayers, had proposals for change.

Problems with the rates have existed throughout the twentieth century. From the early 1960s these problems have been regularly considered. The Committee of Inquiry into the Impact of Rates on Households (the Allen Committee), which was set up by the Conservatives in 1963, concluded that rates were regressive. The committee noted that, while rates represented a smaller proportion of local authority income, of personal incomes, or of total taxation than they had before the start of the Second World War, these proportions had been growing in recent years, i.e. up to 1965.

The Labour Government responded to the Allen Committee with a White Paper in 1966, which proposed a system of rate rebates to alleviate the hardship suffered by the poorest ratepayers. The Government considered alternatives to rates but concluded that no new tax could be introduced until after the structure of local government had been reformed. Upward presure on rates would be relieved, it was proposed, by increasing government grants. The result of the White Paper was legislation which, first, introduced rate rebates and, second, a new subsidy for domestic ratepayers and, third, led to an increase in the general level of central support to local government.

Structural reform followed the Royal Commission on Local Government in England 1966–9. Reform took place in Scotland, where there was a separate Royal Commission, and in Wales, where there was no commission. Although the English commission's terms of reference did not include finance, its report observed that the new, larger local authorities proposed would allow the Government to widen the local tax base and thus allow a reduction in the proportion of local authority income derived from grants. The commission proposed that rates should be retained, though kept up to date.

The 1970–4 Conservative Government enacted a reform of local government structure which took place in 1974. A Green Paper on finance had been published in 1971 examining a range of possible new taxes for local government. The Government explained that extra income was needed to fill the ever-widening gap between spending and rates, which had recently been filled by increasing grants. Increased rates, transfers of services to central government and higher charges were ruled out as ways of increasing local income. A new tax was the only answer.

Although no significant reforms took place following the 1971 Green Paper, the document is interesting as the first major discussion by a government of possible reforms to the rating system. Apart from new taxes, different bases for rating were considered. The importance of general grants, as opposed to those tied to specific services, was stressed.

The economic crises of the mid-1970s coincided with structural reform. Huge rate rises in 1974 prompted the then Labour Government to set up a Committee of Inquiry, the Layfield Committee, to examine local government finance. The committee concluded that the Government should choose between a system of local government with extensive central control or else move to a system with considerable local independence. The committee agreed that there were indeed problems with the rating system, though it was proposed that rates should be kept and reformed. Grants should be reduced as a proportion of local income, should be paid to each tier of local government and should be stable from year to year. If local autonomy was to be increased, as the majority of the committee wished, a local income tax should be introduced.

The committee recognized that local government expenditure was being used increasingly as a short-term economic regulator by central government. During the early 1970s Public Expenditure White Papers planned for considerable growth in the national economy. This growth would be encouraged by expansion in public spending. For example, local government current spending was planned to grow by 5 per cent a year in real terms between 1971–2 and 1976–7 in the Conservative Government's December 1972 Public Expenditure White Paper. Yet by 1976, when the Layfield Committee was writing its Report, Labour's February 1976 White Paper was planning real cuts in local authority current spending in 1977–8 and 1978–9.

This increased use of local government spending as an economic regulator was apparent in the Labour Government's 1977 Green Paper. The Government rejected Layfield's view that a decision had to be taken about whether control over local government activity should be placed firmly with central or with local government. From this decision it would have been possible, according to Layfield, to choose an appropriate system of finance. The Government did not think it necessary to decide between a 'centralist' or a 'localist' approach.

The 1977 Green Paper proposed that rates should be retained, though on the basis of capital values. Layfield had also proposed this change. But all new taxes were ruled out. Local income tax was not accepted because the Government did not believe that taxpayers would be aware of the incidence of such a tax, because there would need to be new equalization arrangements and because authorities could not be given complete freedom to set their own income tax rate.

It was also proposed to introduce a 'unitary grant', which would take the place of two existing grants. These grants, known as the 'needs' and 'resources' elements, equalized between authorities' social and economic circumstances. Layfield had discussed such a change, though the committee had pointed out that it would naturally be part of a more centralist system. Unitary grant, the Government argued, would allow greater equalization of spending needs and rateable resources while giving central government more influence over local spending.

Because the Government had no parliamentary majority, it proved impossible to gain enough support to bring forward legislation to introduce either unitary grant or capital valuation for rates. By the time of the 1979 general election the much-discussed problems with rates and grants remained unsolved. Just after the election a further economic recession began, intensifying the need for change.

The new Conservative Government was committed to abolishing domestic rates, but only after other direct taxes had been cut, although an unqualified promise to abolish domestic rates had been included in the Conservatives' October 1974 manifesto. The 1979 Government was also committed to reduce public spending. During the first months of the new government, local authorities were asked to cut their expenditure. At the end of 1979 new legislation was published that, among other things, would introduce a new grant, known as 'block grant', which was precisely the same as the previous Government's 'unitary grant'.

Block grant was designed to allow the Government to taper off additional grant to authorities which chose to spend more than a percentage above a centrally calculated assessment of spending need. A new measurement of spending need, known as 'GRE', would replace the much-criticized method used in the previous grant arrangements. But before the new grant system was used for the first time, in 1981–2, the Government superimposed a further mechanism. Each authority was set a spending 'target'. Unlike GRE, which was set by reference to factors deemed plausibly to generate a need to spend and to the cost of providing units of service, targets were set by reference to recent past spending. The Government then announced that if an authority chose to spend above its target, its block grant would be reduced. In addition, a one-off system of grant penalties for 'overspenders' was introduced for 1980–1 only.

Block grant, with annual changes to targets and penalties, operated from 1981–2 to 1985–6. Nevertheless local authority current spending in England and Wales exceeded Government plans in each year. For this reason, the Conservatives promised in their 1983 manifesto to take action to limit rate rises. The Rates Act 1984 introduced two schemes of rate limitation: a 'selective' scheme which would allow the Government to limit the rates of a number of councils, and a 'general' scheme which might include all local authorities. Rate limitation was used for the first time in July 1984, when the Government announced that eighteen authorities would have their rates capped in 1985–6. In the autumn of 1984 it was announced that a ministerial review was to be undertaken into local government finance and functions. A Green Paper on the future of Local Government finance was published in January 1986.

After six years of Conservative Government the rating system was still unreformed. A rating revaluation, due in 1983, had been cancelled. A Green Paper on *Alternatives to Domestic Rates* in 1981 described, as had the 1971 Green Paper, possible new local taxes. A White Paper in 1983 ruled out any new income sources. Instead of rating reform, grants were increasingly used in an attempt to influence spending. Finally, the Government simply took power to limit rate rises. Like their predecessors the Conservatives preferred to tinker with the existing system than to reform it. The last reform which can be said to have improved the system of local government finance, in the sense that it made local councillors more responsible for the money they collected and spent, took place after the White Paper of 1957. This reform led to a widening of the local tax base and a reduction in the number of specific grants.

Despite the mounting criticism of rates, Labour and Conservative Governments have transferred the burden of local spending from taxpayers to ratepayers since 1976–7 by cutting the percentage of authorities' income met by grants, which has meant that rates have tended to rise more quickly than prices, and has added to criticisms of the rating system. The 1974 Conservative commitment to abolish domestic rates, echoed to some extent in 1979, encouraged back-bench MPs and ratepayers' organizations to step up their efforts to discredit the rates. The possibility of reform, following the 1981 Green Paper, meant that the 1983 revaluation was cancelled. Although a Green Paper in 1986 promised the abolition of domestic rates, this would not take place in England and Wales until the early 1990s. Having encouraged the opponents of rates, the Government was forced to keep them at least into the medium term. The discrediting of a tax which in the event could not easily be removed was the worst of all worlds.

In the years up to the mid-1970s local government became increasingly dependent on central government support. As has been shown, the increase in grants was partly because of the Government increasing its contribution to pay for expanded services demanded centrally and partly to reduce criticism of the rates. The increased dependence on grants encouraged governments to feel that they should have greater control over what was spent. Once this idea had grown (i.e. that high grant percentages should lead to greater central control) there was no evidence that central influence abated when grant percentages were cut following 1975–6. In addition, block grant calculations involve an explicit measure of a centrally approved standard of spending for each authority. The fact that grant has been much reduced between 1976–7 and 1985–6 has not led to a reduction in central influence. In reality, the lower the grant percentage has fallen, the greater have been the Government's efforts to influence spending using the grant system.

Grant, which used primarily to be paid in an attempt to equalize spending needs and rateable resources while offering a level of general subsidy, is now used for social and economic policy. The 1974–9 Labour Government used the needs element of RSG to shift resources into the cities so as to support its inner-cities initiative. The Labour administration also used grant to encourage and then to discourage current spending. The 1979 Conservative administration built on this changing use of the grant system by introducing block grant, targets and penalties. The move from grant being relatively non-political to its current intensely political position was rapid. The increasing politicization of the grant system has been accompanied by far greater complexity. The rapid change in the needs element between 1974 and 1980 led to a phenomenally complex system by the time that block grant was introduced in 1981–2. Although the new 'grant-related expenditure assessments' (GREs) used in block grant are to some extent more open and logical than the methods used in the old needs element, it would be difficult to argue that they are less complex than in the old system. The increasing complexity has allowed central government to hide behind the computer output and decimal points, arguing that somehow the process is, because of its complexity, objective. Nothing could be further from the truth; the GREs, like the methods which preceded them, are no more than statistically dressed-up 'guesstimates'. The local authorities, which annually argue for minor changes in the needs assessment methodology, have to some extent given such needs measurement a greater credibility than it has ever deserved.

Why have the rating and grant systems continued to degenerate, damaging the relationship between central and local government at the same time? As has been shown, official documents have explained again and again what is wrong. The documents have rehearsed what might be done and often suggested why no change is ever possible. One of the most important changes to affect local government finance in recent years – block grant – was introduced without any consultation document. Rate limitation was introduced in the form spelled out in a White Paper, taking no heed of criticisms. It now looks as though Governments make the changes they want to without taking notice of the rest of the political system, while issuing consultative documents in order to *avoid* action.

Even such inquiries as there have been have occurred in a way which was unlikely to produce a workable solution. Examinations of finance (in 1957, 1966, 1971, 1974–6, 1977, 1981, 1983 and 1986) have taken place at different times from actual or potential structural reform. London government was reformed in 1965, local government in the rest of England and Wales in 1974, while a further reform of metropolitan government took place in 1986. Neither the structural reforms nor any prior examination of the subject took place alongside an examination of finance.

Although all governments since the early 1960s can be said to share the blame for the current state of local government finance, some are more culpable than others. The 1966–70 Labour administration was particularly bad. Having recognized the problems with the system of finance in the 1966 White Paper, the problem was solved in the short term by throwing grant at it. A Royal Commission was then set up to examine structure and functions. Finance was omitted from the terms of reference, although the commission discussed the subject at some length. The Royal Commission should have examined all aspects of local government including finance. As it was, the system proposed by the commission could only accidentally have provided an improved basis for local government finance.

The Conservative Government which implemented structural reform could also have done better. Despite the publication of a relatively detailed consideration of finance in 1971, at much the same time that the new structure was being decided, the 1974 reform of structure was not accompanied by any significant financial changes. To some extent the Conservatives were dealing with a more difficult issue by 1974 because of the effects of the oil crisis and inflation.

There can be no doubt that the period from 1966 to 1973 offered a far better environment for reform than has existed since. The economy was still growing relatively quickly, major institutional reform was fashionable and there was still considerable consensus about the relationship between central and local government. Sadly, neither Labour nor Conservative Governments managed to reform the tax or grant system in such a way as to allow local government to prosper in the more difficult years from 1974 onwards.

This failure to reform cannot excuse the follies of the Governments of the late 1970s and early 1980s. These latter Governments, largely peopled by the same ministers who had failed local government so recently, have moved into a new phase of the central–local relationship. Reform is more difficult during economic recession, which has undoubtedly made the possibility of, say, introducing a new local tax more unlikely than it would have been in 1970 or 1974. But to use the failures of the earlier years as an excuse to extend central control over local government has been wrong.

Changes in the treatment of local government in the years since 1979, i.e. those reforms brought about by the most recent Conservative administrations, may yet lead to a number of consequences that were not intended. For example, the use of targets and penalties against authorities, including many lower-spending ones loyal to the Government, has led to disenchantment among some Conservative councillors. The earlier chapters of this book have quoted senior Tory councillors opposed to much of the legislation passed between 1980 and 1985. Their aggravation with the Government has undoubtedly reduced the desire of able individuals to stay in local government. The calibre of Conservatives in local government may consequently be expected to be reduced, leading to less successful electoral challenges in future. Indeed, the 1985 county council election results led to the Conservatives losing control of a number of previously safe councils. Conversely, opposition parties were able to find powerful reasons to unite together against the Government.

The introduction of targets and rate-capping could undoubtedly be quoted as a precedent by a future government if it wanted to introduce minimum spending levels in authorities or in particular services. The Conservative Government quoted its manifesto commitment to cut public spending as evidence of the need for various new initiatives to reduce local authority expenditure. Another government, possibly committed to expansion of the economy, might point to its manifesto as it legislated to force Conservative-controlled councils to put up the rates and to pay for spending increases.

A future government could also point to the precedent of London Regional Transport, set up in 1984 as a Government-appointed quango to replace the GLC in running London Transport, or the 'residuary bodies', set up in 1985 as Government-appointed quangos to run some ex-GLC and metropolitan county services in the years after abolition, as an interesting new way of providing local services. Local quangos might be seen as a useful mechanism for making quick changes to the provision of major council services.

The abolition of the GLC will also require the Government to make much greater use of the London Rate Equalization scheme, whereby money is to be collected from the central London boroughs and redistributed to the rest of the capital. The Secretary of State for the Environment will have the responsibility for deciding how much shall be distributed and by what means. Although a limited LRES has operated in the past, the considerable expansion of such a mechanism will again offer a future government a useful precedent if it should want to shift resources from, say, the Cities of London and Westminster to other, poorer, London authorities.

There are a number of possible non-financial consequences of abolition. For example, the popularly felt desire for a London-wide authority might lead a future government to set up a new London authority with greater powers than the GLC, possibly covering a greater area. The removal of one tier of government in the cities might be taken as a reason for doing the same in the rest of the country; why not abolish the non-metropolitan counties, if the metropolitan counties can be removed? Equally, the setting up of the single-service, elected Inner London Education Authority may lead to pressure for more single-service authorities, especially to run education in the shire counties. The position of the City of London will surely have been made less secure by the abolition of the GLC. The existence of a top-tier authority to some extent reduced the arguments for abolishing the City which have often been made in the past. Once the City is, in effect, an all-purpose authority, its position will be much more exposed.

Finally, the Conservative Government's reliance on its manifesto commitments about public spending and local government reform will probably pave the way for other parties to use their manifestos similarly in future. In passing the Local Government, Planning and Land Act 1980, the Local Government Finance Act 1982, the Rates Act 1984 and the Local Government Act 1985, the Government pointed to its manifesto commitments when seeking to justify its policies. The House of Lords was told that legislation based on manifesto commitments could not constitutionally be rejected. There must be a real chance that parties will construct their manifestos with some thought about the strength that some commitments would give them when it came to pass legislation through the Lords.

We are now seeing the consequences of past failures compounded by changes in British politics. The Conservative Government and many Labour local authorities now claim to be more radical than their predecessors. This change has meant that the increasingly inadequate system of local authority finance has been put under further strain by central government manipulation of the grant system and by some local authorities' apparent carelessness about the rates. The media have fed on this conflict between the Government and local authorities, often giving the impression that the worst features of the conflict represent the norm for central–local relations.

The inadequacy of the system of finance has also been exacerbated by the changed recognition of local government's part in national economic life. As was described above, Governments have become preoccupied with measures of public spending and borrowing; local authorities' contribution to such measures have also become important. The Treasury's description of local government finance as the Achilles' heel of Treasury control over aggregate public spending in 1976, quoted by Professor Alan Day in his Note of Reservation to the Layfield Report, suggested that the Government would like more direct control over all local authority spending. Full control over capital spending was taken in the Local Government, Planning and Land Act 1980. The Government's failure to influence total current spending down to planned levels in each year from 1980–1 to 1984–5 led to the move to rate limitation. The Rates Act 1984 gives the Treasury the control over local authority finance which it has wanted for so long.

Control over individual authorities' rates will be a useful weapon for central government. Reductions can be sought in spending by particular councils without the Government having to take responsibility for the effect on services. Local authorities, it will be argued, remain free to spend their (albeit reduced) budgets as they wish. Thus the Treasury will have acheived the control over local government finance which it wanted without the rest of central government having to take the responsibility for any consequences.

The weakness of the financial base has been accompanied by shifts of services and finance from local to central control. Water and health services were transferred out of Local Government in 1974; London Transport became a nationalized industry in 1984; the Manpower Services Commission has started to increase its influence over the education system, leading to the transfer of a quarter of non-advanced further education to MSC control from 1985–6. Extra specific grants have been introduced in education, while there has been a consistent increase in the proportion of total grant made up by specific and supplementary grants (see Table App. 10). Rate limitation and the consequences of abolishing the Greater London Council and metropolitan counties will lead to further central controls over local authority spending and manpower.

The decay of local authorities' financial base and shifts of control to the centre have changed the relationship between central and local government. The previous conventional relationship, depending upon the law and practice, has given way to uncertainty. New law affecting local government finance has been passed regularly in recent years. Authorities controlled by both Labour and Conservative parties have complained that the grant system is grossly unfair. Government objectives are unclear or contradictory – is the purpose to reduce spending, to protect ratepayers, to increase fairness, or to increase central control? – while the grant system is altered constantly. There is now evidence that some of the information passing between local and central government has become misleading. Despite authorities' appeals for financial reform, no significant positive changes have taken place. In all, the relationship between the Government and local authorities has degenerated badly.

This analysis leads finally to consideration of what, if anything, might save local government. The most important factor must be the need for a Government which is genuinely committed to maintaining healthy and democratic local authorities. Such a Government would have to pass legislation that would give local government a local tax base compatible with the structure and functions given to authorities. The framing of such legislation would require consideration of structure, functions and finance together. There might well need to be a commitment to additional short-term expenditure to fund any reforms.

The financial arrangements would have to ensure that all local authorities have an adequate base. Rates would almost certainly be retained because of the difficulty of replacing such a large amount of taxation. In addition, rates have a number of well-rehearsed merits as a tax. But if authorities were to have an adequate base from which to fund the large range of services that are currently provided, a new tax would be inevitable. Local income tax would give authorities a buoyant new income source. New forms of assessment and payments could ensure that taxpayers were aware of how much was being paid to the local authority. Awareness of what was being paid to which taxing authority would be essential in any new local tax system.

Extra local tax income should mean that no authority would be heavily dependent on grants from central government; i.e. grants ought never to make up so much of an authority's income that Governments could argue that there was justification for involvement in the detail of policy. If this meant that grants were insufficient to achieve 100 per cent 'equalization' of the kind conventionally sought, then the failure to achieve full equalization would be a price worth paying for achieving a system where the Government could be kept at a distance, and where councillors were responsible locally for the bulk of their income.

There is another argument against the search for the perfect grant system. No such thing exists. The best that can be hoped for is an admittedly rough system which most authorities regard as broadly fair. Such acceptance would be easier to achieve if local authorities depended less heavily on grant as an income source. A relatively simple grant system with broad objectives must be better for local government than a so-called objective system swathed in complexity.

Whatever grant system is proposed, its distribution should be predictable and stable from year to year, to allow local ratepayers a much better sense of how far changes in rates reflected changes in spending. Grants would remain an overall instrument with which the government could influence local authorities. However, only that part of local government spending funded by grants should remain part of the public spending planning process. Grant would appear as a single item of central government expenditure. All local spending borne out of local taxation should, like private-sector expenditure, not be included in what is central government's own planning process.

Within the financial arrangements proposed, fees and charges would continue to offer authorities a small source of income. As such, they are useful both as a support to local independence and because charging is likely to encourage business-like attitudes. A review of local authority finance ought to examine whether local authorities should be given greater freedom to charge for services. The possibility of encouraging local authorities to find new and creative ways of provision, e.g. franchising or joint arrangements with voluntary bodies, should be examined; certainly authorities should not be stopped from adopting alternative methods of provision.

As the principles outlined above suggest, these ideas involve greater local autonomy coupled with greater local accountability to local taxpayers. It is inconceivable in a country with as many people and with such developed public services as Britain that any central government could properly control the whole of public spending from Whitehall.

This argument is not simply for aggrandizing the existing local authorities. One of the most unappealing consequences of the legislative activity of recent years is that it has allowed much of what is going on in local government to remain unconsidered. Many local authorities need the injection of new responsibilities and greater accountability to their local taxpayers to galvanize them into a move towards more open and locally democratic activity. This improvement could well require Government encouragement, though not legislation, for local authorities to transfer power from town halls to schools, housing estates and other local service centres. Access to information about council decision-making would also be essential.

If local government is to remain genuinely local and to involve local power and accountability, a reform of the system is essential. This book has shown how years of inaction and ill-considered action have produced the present unsatisfactory arrangements. Few people will agree about what precisely is needed. But unless a Government is prepared to look for a reform which commands reasonable support and then implement it, the decay of local government will continue. Each new difficulty with the existing system will be used as an excuse to take more control to the centre. The additional central control will then weaken local government finance and so on.

This picture is bleak indeed. Despite the proposals published in early 1986. British governments appear so conservative that the short steps towards the end of effective local government always seem easier to take than the longer stride towards a new and effective system of local authority finance. We are now in the last short period when it is still possible to save local government. Government should act radically and soon.

# APPENDIX: TABLES AND FIGURES

Table App. 1   *Local and Central Government as a Percentage of Gross Domestic Product (United Kingdom)*

| | Local authorities | | | | Central government | | | |
| | Current expenditure | Of which final consumption | Capital* expenditure | Of which* capital investment | Current expenditure | Of which final consumption | Capital expenditure | Of which capital investment |
|---|---|---|---|---|---|---|---|---|
| 1966–7 | 8.5 | 6.4 | 3.7 | 3.6 | 26.7 | 11.0 | 1.7 | 1.0 |
| 1967–8 | 8.9 | 6.7 | 4.0 | 4.0 | 28.4 | 11.2 | 2.7 | 1.1 |
| 1968–9 | 9.0 | 6.6 | 3.9 | 3.8 | 28.1 | 10.7 | 3.0 | 1.1 |
| 1969–70 | 9.3 | 6.7 | 3.7 | 3.7 | 27.7 | 10.4 | 3.1 | 1.1 |
| 1970–1 | 9.6 | 7.0 | 3.8 | 3.7 | 27.9 | 10.7 | 3.1 | 1.2 |
| 1971–2 | 9.5 | 7.1 | 3.5 | 3.4 | 28.5 | 10.9 | 2.8 | 1.1 |
| 1972–3 | 9.7 | 7.4 | 3.6 | 3.5 | 28.9 | 10.7 | 2.5 | 1.1 |
| 1973–4 | 10.5 | 7.7 | 4.5 | 4.2 | 30.4 | 10.9 | 2.6 | 1.2 |
| 1974–5 | 11.6 | 8.5 | 4.1 | 3.9 | 33.8 | 12.2 | 2.6 | 1.2 |
| 1975–6 | 11.8 | 8.7 | 3.7 | 3.5 | 35.7 | 12.8 | 2.4 | 1.3 |
| 1976–7 | 11.5 | 8.5 | 3.1 | 3.0 | 35.4 | 12.6 | 2.3 | 1.1 |
| 1977–8 | 10.8 | 8.0 | 2.4 | 2.3 | 34.3 | 12.1 | 2.1 | 0.9 |
| 1978–9 | 10.6 | 8.0 | 2.1 | 2.0 | 34.6 | 11.9 | 1.9 | 0.8 |
| 1979–80 | 10.6 | 8.0 | 2.0 | 1.9 | 34.5 | 11.9 | 1.8 | 0.8 |
| 1980–1 | 11.2 | 8.4 | 1.8 | 1.6 | 36.7 | 13.1 | 1.8 | 0.8 |
| 1981–2 | 11.2 | 8.5 | 1.1 | 1.0 | 38.4 | 13.4 | 1.7 | 0.7 |
| 1982–3 | 11.0 | 8.5 | 1.1 | 0.9 | 38.2 | 13.3 | 1.9 | 0.9 |

*Notes*:
(1) 'Final consumption' is expenditure on services; other expenditure within 'current' is on transfer payments.
(2) 'Capital expenditure' is expenditure on capital assets; other expenditure within 'capital' is on capital grants and subsidies.
(3) Columns marked with an asterisk (*) have had the proceeds from council-house sales netted off (i.e. the *gross* proportion of GDP would be higher). The value of these sales were (as % of GDP): 1977–8, 0.1%; 1978–9, 0.2%; 1979–80, 0.3%; 1980–1, 0.3%; 1981–2, 0.6%; 1982–3, 0.7%.
(4) Local authorities lost certain functions in 1974–5. Health services were transferred to central government. Water and sewerage in England and Wales, and public trust ports were transferred to public corporations. On 1 October 1973 responsibility for many local authority services in Northern Ireland (including police, fire and education) was transferred to central government. Broadly, these transfers reduced local authorities' current final consumption by about 0.5% of GDP, and capital investment of 0.4% of GDP. They increased central government final consumption by 0.3% of GDP.

*Sources*: (i) *Financial Statistics* (London: HMSO), (ii) *Economic Trends*, (London: HMSO).

Table App. 2 *Local Authority Revenue Expenditure, 1923–4 to 1984–5 (£ million)*

|  |  | General expenditure | Debt charges | Revenue contributions to capital outlay | All expenditure |
|---|---|---|---|---|---|
| (a) | England and Wales | | | | |
|  | 1923–4 | 283.5 | 59.8 | — | 343.3 |
|  | 1933–4 | 327.2 | 100.5 | 5.5 | 433.2 |
|  | 1943–4 | 575.8 | 116.1 | 6.1 | 698.0 |
|  | 1948–9 | 759.6 | 95.9 | 10.7 | 866.2 |
|  | 1953–4 | 940.0 | 172.3 | 15.2 | 1,127.5 |
|  | 1958–9 | 1,381.7 | 314.2 | 35.4 | 1,731.3 |
| (b) | England | | | | |
|  | 1958–9 | 1,301.0 | 296.4 | 33.8 | 1.631.2 |
|  | 1959–60 | 1,402.1 | 317.5 | 39.7 | 1,759.3 |
|  | 1960–1 | 1,504.1 | 353.3 | 46.4 | 1,903.8 |
|  | 1961–2 | 1,652.6 | 398.0 | 51.3 | 2,101.9 |
|  | 1962–3 | 1,821.4 | 427.1 | 58.8 | 2,307.3 |
|  | 1963–4 | 1,973.3 | 464.3 | 77.0 | 2,514.6 |
|  | 1964–5 | 2,129.3 | 531.4 | 75.4 | 2.736.1 |
|  | 1965–6 | 2,412.4 | 615.5 | 89.8 | 3,117.1 |
|  | 1966–7 | 2,634.4 | 687.5 | 94.0 | 3,415.9 |
|  | 1967–8 | 2,894.8 | 763.0 | 103.3 | 3,761.1 |
|  | 1968–9 | 3,095.4 | 877.6 | 107.3 | 4,080.3 |
|  | 1969–70 | 4,027.5 | 1,025.2 | 59.6 | 5,112.5 |
|  | 1970–1 | 4,631.2 | 1,145.6 | 64.3 | 5,841.1 |
|  | 1971–2 | 5,411.4 | 1,203.1 | 76.7 | 6,691.2 |
|  | 1972–3 | 6,165.7 | 1,326.9 | 70.0 | 7,562.6 |
|  | 1973–4 | 7,362.1 | 1,742.8 | 84.5 | 9,189.4 |
|  | 1974–5 | 9,449.3 | 2,031.2 | 89.5 | 11,570.0 |
|  | 1975–6 | 11,711.3 | 2,463.3 | 214.7 | 14,389.3 |
|  | 1976–7 | 13,311.5 | 2,846.3 | 227.5 | 16,485.3 |
|  | 1977–8 | 14,714.9 | 3,032.7 | 303.1 | 18,050.7 |
|  | 1978–9 | 17,052.9 | 3,456.5 | 308.1 | 20,817.5 |
|  | 1979–80 | 19,972.3 | 4,209.9 | 272.5 | 24,454.7 |
|  | 1980–1 | 24,164.2 | 4,882.0 | 330.0 | 29,376.2 |
|  | 1981–2 | 26,821.7 | 5,097.2 | 450.6 | 32,369.5 |
|  | 1982–3 | 29,246.5 | 4,988.9 | 753.0 | 34,988.4 |
|  | 1983–4 | 31,822.3 | 4,870.6 | 659.7 | 37,352.6 |
|  | 1984–5 | 34,034.8 | 5,266.2 | 315.0 | 39,616.0 |

*Notes*:
(a) From 1969–70 onwards data were collected by a revised system of returns and do not necessarily bear a direct comparison with earlier years.
(b) Reorganization of local government in April 1974 transferred responsibility for various services to regional health and regional water authorities.
*Source: Local Government Financial Statistics England and Wales 1984/5* (London: HMSO).

Table App. 3    *Local Authority Revenue Income, 1923–4 to 1984–5 (£ million)*

|  | Rates | Government grants | Mis-cellaneous | All income |
|---|---|---|---|---|
| *(a)* **England and Wales** | | | | |
| 1923–4 | 143.3 | 175.2 | 122.8 | 341.3 |
| 1933–4 | 148.6 | 121.6 | 176.4 | 446.6 |
| 1943–4 | 204.1 | 228.4 | 306.5 | 739.0 |
| 1948–9 | 284.4 | 284.8 | 308.8 | 878.1 |
| 1953–4 | 392.5 | 414.2 | 369.6 | 1,176.3 |
| 1958–9 | 579.3 | 658.8 | 550.3 | 1,788.4 |
| | | | | |
| *(b)* **England** | | | | |
| 1958–9 | 551.9 | 608.2 | 525.2 | 1,685.2 |
| 1959–60 | 618.2 | 652.3 | 566.4 | 1,836.9 |
| 1960–1 | 662.9 | 699.6 | 609.5 | 1,972.0 |
| 1961–2 | 711.6 | 768.8 | 658.5 | 2,138.9 |
| 1962–3 | 791.8 | 839.3 | 718.6 | 2,349.7 |
| 1963–4 | 879.3 | 946.3 | 788.0 | 2,613.6 |
| 1964–5 | 944.6 | 1,020.5 | 857.9 | 2,823.0 |
| 1965–6 | 1,077.0 | 1,168.2 | 954.9 | 3,200.1 |
| 1966–7 | 1,207.0 | 1,287.8 | 1,035.6 | 3,530.4 |
| 1967–8 | 1,262.9 | 1,475.8 | 1,128.3 | 3,867.0 |
| 1968–9 | 1,332.8 | 1,590.8 | 1,265.3 | 4,188.9 |
| 1969–70 | 1,446.7 | 1,820.6 | 2,061.9 | 5,329.2 |
| 1970–1 | 1,564.4 | 2,128.1 | 2,211.6 | 5,904.1 |
| 1971–2 | 1,821.2 | 2,474.1 | 2,488.2 | 6,883.5 |
| 1972–3 | 2,081.7 | 2,927.2 | 2,753.1 | 7,762.0 |
| 1973–4 | 2,310.6 | 3,632.0 | 3,338.7 | 9,281.3 |
| 1974–5 | 2,807.7 | 5,256.6 | 3,707.3 | 11,771.6 |
| 1975–6 | 3,655.2 | 7,172.3 | 4,484.8 | 15,312.3 |
| 1976–7 | 3,968.4 | 8,054.4 | 5,229.8 | 17,252.6 |
| 1977–8 | 4,505.1 | 8,508.2 | 5,944.3 | 18,957.6 |
| 1978–9 | 4,966.2 | 9,433.8 | 7,031.1 | 21,431.1 |
| 1979–80 | 5,868.0 | 10,743.2 | 5,544.2 | 22,155.4 |
| 1980–1 | 7,443.7 | 12,923.7 | 9,837.0 | 30,204.4 |
| 1981–2 | 9,071.1 | 13,029.5 | 11,817.7 | 33,918.3 |
| 1982–3 | 10,279.9 | 13,242.0 | 13,360.5 | 36,882.4 |
| 1983–4 | 10,465.6 | 15,566.0 | 13,147.7 | 39,179.3 |
| 1984–5 | 11,273.8 | 16,375.2 | 14,132.9 | 41,781.9 |

*Notes*:
(a) From 1969–70 onwards data were collected by a revised system of returns and do not necessarily bear a direct comparison with earlier years.
(b) Reorganization of local government in April 1974 transferred responsibility for various serives to regional health and regional water authorities.
*Source: Local Government Financial Statistics England and Wales 1984/5* (London: HMSO).

Table App. 4 *Local Authority Capital Expenditure, 1924–5 to 1984–5 (£ million)*

| | Expenditure on land works, etc. | Capital assigned to repayment of debt | All expend- iture | Gross debt at end of year |
|---|---|---|---|---|
| *(i)* **England and Wales** | | | | |
| 1923–4 | 50.0 | — | 50.0 | 820.3 |
| 1933–4 | 70.7 | 18.6 | 89.3 | 1,404.4 |
| 1943–4 | 19.2 | 6.2 | 25.4 | 1.513.2 |
| 1948–9 | 323.4 | 6.1 | 329.5 | 1,748.0 |
| 1953–4 | 531.5 | 12.2 | 543.7 | 3,414.2 |
| 1958–9 | 480.6 | 31.3 | 511.9 | 5,294.1 |
| *(ii)* **England** | | | | |
| 1958–9 | 453.6 | 29.4 | 483.0 | 4,998.8 |
| 1958–60 | 500.9 | 37.9 | 538.8 | 5,339.3 |
| 1960–1 | 543.3 | 40.5 | 583.8 | 5,678.4 |
| 1961–2 | 652.7 | 43.9 | 696.6 | 6,119.7 |
| 1962–3 | 689.0 | 55.9 | 744.9 | 6,585.6 |
| 1963–4 | 852.4 | 69.0 | 921.4 | 7,155.3 |
| 1964–5 | 1,076.2 | 83.3 | 1,159.5 | 7,922.3 |
| 1965–6 | 1,137.0 | 87.9 | 1,224.9 | 8,768.7 |
| 1966–7 | 1,236.0 | 103.1 | 1,339.1 | 9,636.4 |
| 1967–8 | 1,360.3 | 125.9 | 1,486.2 | 10,557.0 |
| 1968–9 | 1,383.5 | 129.9 | 1,513.4 | 11,484.7 |
| 1969–70(a) | 1,491.8 | 121.7 | 1,613.5 | 12,246.9 |
| 1970–1 | 1,792.2 | 149.5 | 1,941.7 | 13,384.3 |
| 1971–2 | 1,938.2 | 170.3 | 2,108.5 | 14,449.8 |
| 1972–3 | 2,417.8 | 212.8 | 2,630.6 | 16,104.6 |
| 1973–4 | 3,285.6 | 225.3 | 3,510.9 | 18,300.0 |
| 1974–5(b) | 3,711.5 | 127.1 | 3,838.6 | 18,884.4 |
| 1975–6 | 3,916.7 | 197.9 | 4,114.7 | 21,929.8 |
| 1976–7 | 3,782.7 | 311.9 | 4,094.6 | 24,534.0 |
| 1977–8 | 3,487.0 | 351.6 | 3,838.6 | 26,282.0 |
| 1978–9 | 3,620.8 | 390.4 | 4,011.2 | 27,102.8 |
| 1979–80 | 4,249.4 | 330.6 | 4,580.0 | 30,186.8 |
| 1980–1 | 4,476.1 | 413.0 | 4,889.1 | 32,076.3 |
| 1981–2 | 4,060.5 | 562.7 | 4,623.2 | 34,069.0 |
| 1982–3 | 5,090.2 | 633.6 | 5,723.8 | 36,230.8 |
| 1983–4 | 5,890.0 | 561.6 | 6,451.5 | 38,697.5 |
| 1984–5 | 6,351.6 | 514.8 | 6,866.4 | 40,554.2 |

*Notes*:
(a) From 1969–70 onwards data were collected by a revised system of returns and do not necessarily bear a direct comparison with earlier years.
(b) Reorganization of local government in April 1974 transferred responsibility for various services to regional health and regional water authorities.
*Source: Local Government Financial Statistics England and Wales 1984/5* (London: HMSO).

Table App. 5   *Local Authority Capital Income, 1923–4 to 1984–5*

| | Loans | Govern-ment Grants | Mis-cellaneous | All income | Special funds: balances at end of year[a] |
|---|---|---|---|---|---|
| **(i) England and Wales** | | | | | |
| 1923–4 | 46.5 | 3.1 | 5.0 | 54.6 | 61.8 |
| 1933–4 | 62.8 | 3.6 | 20.3 | 86.7 | 181.9 |
| 1943–4 | 17.8 | 4.6 | 5.4 | 278.8 | 295.4 |
| 1948–9 | 287.3 | 21.1 | 9.6 | 318.0 | 331.8 |
| 1953–4 | 494.8 | 19.4 | 18.8 | 533.0 | 421.4 |
| 1958–9 | 463.7 | 16.1 | 42.7 | 522.5 | 606.7 |
| **(ii) England** | | | | | |
| 1958–9 | 439.7 | 15.2 | 40.3 | 495.2 | 568.8 |
| 1959–60 | 484.1 | 16.3 | 47.8 | 548.2 | 623.1 |
| 1960–1 | 497.2 | 18.0 | 57.1 | 572.3 | 676.5 |
| 1961–2 | 607.8 | 17.7 | 61.1 | 686.6 | 724.1 |
| 1962–3 | 663.0 | 21.1 | 78.8 | 762.9 | 774.7 |
| 1963–4 | 781.1 | 26.6 | 93.7 | 901.4 | 835.1 |
| 1964–5 | 1,012.3 | 33.7 | 107.9 | 1,153.9 | 907.8 |
| 1965–6 | 1,096.8 | 32.9 | 103.6 | 1,233.1 | 991.1 |
| 1966–7 | 1,169.0 | 43.1 | 125.1 | 1,337.2 | 1,066.5 |
| 1967–8 | 1,243.1 | 75.0 | 143.7 | 1,461.8 | 1,158.5 |
| 1968–9 | 1,271.8 | 81.7 | 153.0 | 1,506.5 | 1,252.0 |
| 1969–70[b] | 1,269.6 | 88.8 | 263.3 | 1,621.7 | 1,337.7 |
| 1970–1 | 1,515.8 | 105.7 | 348.8 | 1,970.3 | 1,400.0 |
| 1971–2 | 1,605.4 | 115.8 | 421.4 | 2,142.6 | 1,524.6 |
| 1972–3 | 2,029.7 | 121.7 | 530.5 | 2,681.9 | 1,645.5 |
| 1973–4 | 2,781.2 | 143.4 | 619.0 | 3,543.6 | 1,737.0 |
| 1974–5[c] | 3,208.9 | 127.8 | 498.1 | 3,834.8 | 1,473.5 |
| 1975–6 | 3,284.8 | 177.2 | 647.0 | 4,109.0 | 2,037.4 |
| 1976–7 | 3,096.9 | 249.4 | 802.7 | 4,149.0 | n.a. |
| 1977–8 | 2,677.1 | 254.9 | 980.5 | 3,912.5 | n.a. |
| 1978–9 | 2,626.9 | 351.1 | 1,138.7 | 4,116.7 | 3,798.8 |
| 1979–80 | 2,992.3 | 385.0 | 1,367.4 | 4,744.7 | 5,037.5 |
| 1980–1 | 2,900.3 | 492.0 | 1,864.0 | 5,256.3 | 5,519.7 |
| 1981–2 | 2,527.4 | 470.3 | 2,176.7 | 5,174.4 | 6,661.5 |
| 1982–3 | 3,357.7 | 416.2 | 3,100.3 | 6,874.2 | 8,551.4 |
| 1983–4 | 3,537.9 | 379.0 | 3,293.9 | 7,210.8 | 10,457.7 |
| 1984–5 | 3,381.1 | 327.1 | 3,282.5 | 6,990.7 | 12,960.0 |

*Notes*:
(a) Funds covered have varied over the years; details for individual years may be found in the relevant *LGFS* (see source) publications. Superannuation funds are generally included. The 1923–4 figures are for sinking and redemption funds only.
(b) From 1969–70 onwards data were collected by a revised system of returns and do not necessarily bear a direct comparison with earlier years.
(c) Reorganization of local government in April 1974 transferred responsibility for various services to regional health and regional water authorities.
*Source: Local Government Financial Statistics England and Wales 1982/3* (London: HMSO).

TABLES APP. 2–APP. 5: ADDITIONAL INFORMATION

*Table App.2*
'General expenditure', 'Debt charges' and 'Revenue contributions to capital outlay' each include spending on rate fund services, Housing Revenue Account and on trading services.

*Table App. 3*
'Government grants' includes RSG, rate rebate grants, all specific grants (i.e. those relevant and none-relevant for RSG) and local taxation licence duties.

*Table App. 4*
'Expenditure on land works, etc.' includes the acquisition of land and existing buildings; new construction; vehicles; plant, machinery and equipment and other items.

*Table App. 5*
'Miscellaneous' includes sale of fixed assets, revenue contributions to capital outlay, transfers from special funds, receipts from other authorities and other receipts.

Both revenue and capital tables are affected by changes in balances.

Revenue expenditure and income tables include gross expenditure and income, including that by and from trading undertakings and the Housing Revenue Account. The expenditure figures thus produced are much larger than 'relevant', 'total', or 'current' expenditure used elsewhere.

Table App. 6 *Local Authority Capital Expenditure, 1976–7 to 1984–5 (England and Wales) (£ million)*

|  | England | Wales | England and Wales |
|---|---|---|---|
| 1976–7 | 3,397 | 206 | 3,603 |
| 1977–8 | 2,920 | 168 | 3,088 |
| 1978–9 | 2,881 | 185 | 3,066 |
| 1979–80 | 3,646 | 235 | 3,881 |
| 1980–1 | 3,515 | 245 | 3,760 |
| 1981–2 | 2,549 | 178 | 2,727 |
| 1982–3 | 2,784 | 241 | 3,025 |
| 1983–4 | 3,442 | 329 | 3,771 |
| 1984–5 | 3,556 | 242 | 3,798 |
| 1985–6 (estimate) | 3,026 | 265 | 3,291 |

*Note*: Public Expenditure White Paper uses net expenditure, while figures in Table App. 4 show gross expenditure (i.e. net expenditure plus expenditure funded by sales of assets) and use a slightly different definition.

*Source*: (i) *The Government's Expenditure Plans 1982–83 to 1984–85* Cmnd 8494 (London: HMSO); (ii) *The Government's Expenditure Plans 1985–86 to 1987–88*, Cmnd 9428 (London: HMSO); (iii) *The Government's Expenditure Plans 1986–87 to 1988–9*, Cmnd 9702 (London: HMSO).

Table App. 7   *Local Authority Income Sources, 1923–4 to 1984–5*

*(i) Revenue*
Percentage of income made up by:

| | Rates | Government grants | Miscellaneous |
|---|---|---|---|
| *(a)England and Wales* | | | |
| 1923–4 | 32.5 | 39.7 | 27.8 |
| 1933–4 | 33.3 | 27.2 | 39.5 |
| 1943–4 | 27.6 | 30.9 | 41.5 |
| 1948–9 | 32.4 | 32.4 | 35.2 |
| 1953–4 | 33.4 | 35.2 | 31.4 |
| 1958–9 | 32.4 | 36.8 | 30.8 |
| | | | |
| *(b)England* | | | |
| 1958–9 | 32.7 | 36.1 | 31.2 |
| 1959–60 | 33.7 | 35.5 | 30.8 |
| 1960–1 | 33.6 | 35.5 | 30.9 |
| 1961–2 | 33.3 | 35.9 | 30.8 |
| 1962–3 | 33.7 | 35.7 | 30.6 |
| 1963–4 | 33.6 | 36.2 | 30.2 |
| 1964–5 | 33.5 | 36.1 | 30.4 |
| 1965–6 | 33.7 | 36.5 | 29.8 |
| 1966–7 | 34.2 | 36.5 | 29.3 |
| 1967–8 | 32.7 | 38.2 | 29.2 |
| 1968–9 | 31.8 | 38.0 | 30.2 |
| 1969–70 | 27.1 | 34.2 | 38.7 |
| 1970–1 | 26.5 | 36.0 | 37.5 |
| 1971–2 | 26.5 | 35.9 | 37.6 |
| 1972–3 | 26.8 | 37.7 | 35.5 |
| 1973–4 | 24.9 | 39.1 | 36.0 |
| 1974–5 | 23.9 | 44.7 | 31.5 |
| 1975–6 | 23.9 | 46.8 | 29.3 |
| 1976–7 | 23.0 | 46.7 | 30.3 |
| 1977–8 | 23.8 | 44.9 | 31.3 |
| 1978–9 | 23.2 | 44.0 | 32.8 |
| 1979–80 | 26.5 | 48.5 | 25.0 |
| 1980–1 | 24.6 | 42.8 | 32.6 |
| 1981–2 | 26.8 | 38.4 | 34.8 |
| 1982–3 | 27.9 | 35.9 | 36.2 |
| 1983–4 | 26.7 | 39.7 | 33.6 |
| 1984–5 | 27.0 | 39.2 | 33.8 |

*Note and Source*: As for Table App. 3.

Table App. 8   *Local Authority Income Sources, 1923–4 to 1984–5*

*(ii)   Capital*
Percentage of income made up by:

|  | Loans | Government grants | Miscellaneous |
|---|---|---|---|
| *(a) England and Wales* | | | |
| 1923–4 | 85.2 | 5.7 | 9.1 |
| 1933–4 | 72.4 | 4.2 | 23.4 |
| 1943–4 | 64.0 | 16.6 | 19.4 |
| 1948–9 | 90.4 | 6.6 | 3.0 |
| 1953–4 | 92.9 | 3.6 | 3.5 |
| 1958–9 | 88.7 | 3.1 | 8.2 |
| | | | |
| *(b) England* | | | |
| 1958–9 | 88.8 | 3.1 | 8.1 |
| 1959–60 | 88.3 | 3.0 | 8.7 |
| 1960–1 | 86.9 | 3.1 | 10.0 |
| 1961–2 | 88.5 | 2.6 | 8.9 |
| 1962–3 | 86.9 | 2.8 | 10.3 |
| 1963–4 | 86.7 | 3.0 | 10.4 |
| 1964–5 | 87.7 | 2.9 | 9.4 |
| 1965–6 | 88.9 | 2.7 | 8.4 |
| 1966–7 | 87.4 | 3.2 | 9.4 |
| 1967–8 | 85.1 | 5.1 | 9.8 |
| 1968–9 | 84.4 | 5.4 | 10.2 |
| 1969–70 | 78.3 | 5.5 | 16.2 |
| 1970–1 | 76.9 | 5.4 | 17.7 |
| 1971–2 | 74.9 | 5.4 | 19.7 |
| 1972–3 | 75.7 | 4.5 | 19.8 |
| 1973–4 | 78.5 | 4.0 | 17.5 |
| 1974–5 | 83.7 | 3.3 | 13.0 |
| 1975–6 | 80.0 | 4.3 | 15.7 |
| 1976–7 | 74.7 | 6.0 | 19.3 |
| 1977–8 | 68.4 | 6.5 | 25.1 |
| 1978–9 | 63.8 | 8.5 | 27.7 |
| 1979–80 | 63.1 | 8.1 | 28.8 |
| 1980–1 | 55.2 | 6.0 | 38.8 |
| 1981–2 | 48.8 | 6.2 | 45.0 |
| 1982–3 | 48.8 | 6.1 | 45.1 |
| 1983–4 | 49.1 | 5.3 | 45.6 |
| 1984–5 | 48.4 | 4.7 | 46.9 |

*Notes* and *Source*: As for Table App. 5.

Table App. 9  *Relevant Expenditure, Total Exchequer Assistance and Grant Percentage at Settlement and Out-turn, 1967–8 to 1986–7 (England and Wales)*

| | | Relevant Expenditure | | Total Exchequer Assistance | | Grant percentage | |
|---|---|---|---|---|---|---|---|
| | | settlement | out-turn | At settlement | At out-turn | At settlement | At out-turn |
| 1967–8 | | 2,557 | 2,663 | 1,381 | 1,407 | 54 | 52.8 |
| 1968–9 | | 2,726 | 2,842 | 1,499 | 1,521 | 55 | 53.5 |
| 1969–70 | | 2,976 | 3,113 | 1,667 | 1,760 | 56 | 56.5 |
| 1970–1 | | 3,128 | 3,562 | 1,783 | 2,044 | 57 | 57.4 |
| 1971–2 | | 3,795 | 4,167 | 2,182 | 2,373 | 57.5 | 56.9 |
| 1972–3 | | 3,970 | 4,812 | 2,303 | 2,757 | 58 | 57.3 |
| 1973–4 | | 5,216 | 5,686 | 3,130 | 3,465 | 60 | 61.0 |
| 1974–5 | | 5,671 | 7,677 | 3,431 | 4,773 | 60.5 (65.3) | 62.2 |
| 1975–6 | | 8,171 | 10,056 | 5,434 | 6,694 | 66.5 | 66.4 |
| 1976–7 | | 10,461 | 11,243 | 6,852 | 7,304 | 65.5 | 65.0 |
| 1977–8 | | 11,717 | 12,124 | 7,147 | 7,539 | 61 | 62.2 |
| 1978–9 | | 12,531 | 13,542 | 7,644 | 8,287 | 61 | 61.2 |
| 1979–80 | | 14,109 | 15,686 | 8,607 | 9,454 | 61 | 59.6 |
| 1980–1 | | 15,737 | 19,181 | 9,600 | 11,131 | 61 | 58.0 |
| 1981–2 | England | 18,423 | 19,933 | 10,895 | 10,939 | 59.1 | 54.9 |
| | Wales | 1,187 | 1,233 | 871 | 873 | 73.4 | 70.8 |
| | England and Wales | 19,610 | 21,166 | 11,766 | 11,812 | 60.0 | 55.8 |
| 1982–3 | England | 20,463 | 21,765 | 11,484 | 11,242 | 56.1 | 51.2 |
| | Wales | 1,301 | 1,328 | 943 | 927 | 72.5 | 69.8 |
| | England and Wales | 21,764 | 23,093 | 12,427 | 12,169 | 57.1 | 52.7 |
| 1983–4 | England | 22,307 | 23,082 | 11,782 | 11,486 | 52.8 | 49.8 |
| | Wales | 1,385 | 1,406 | 975 | 963 | 70.4 | 68.5 |
| | England and Wales | 23,692 | 24,488 | 12,757 | 12,449 | 53.8 | 50.8 |
| 1984–5 | England | 22,883 | 23,872 | 11,872 | 11,902 | 51.9 | 49.9 |
| | Wales | 1,440 | 1,466 | 996 | 983 | 69.2 | 67.1 |
| | England and Wales | 24,323 | 25,338 | 12,868 | 12,885 | 52.9 | 50.9 |
| 1985–6 | England | 24,161 | 24,391 | 11,764 | 11,357 | 48.7 | 46.6 |
| | Wales | 1,514 | 1,522 | 1,014 | 1,009 | 67.0 | 66.3 |
| | England and Wales | 25,675 | 25,913 | 12,778 | 12,366 | 49.8 | 47.7 |
| 1986–7 | England | 25,328 | 26,644 | 11,764 | 11,815 | 46.4 | 44.3 |
| | Wales | 1,598 | | 1,067 | | 66.8 | |
| | England and Wales | 26,926 | | 12,831 | | 47.7 | |

*Notes*:
(i)   From 1981–2 England and Wales had separate RSG systems.
(ii)  Figures at 'settlement' before 1981–2 were in November prices (i.e. 1977–8 – settlement figures are November 1976 prices).
(iii) Original provision for 1974–5 was increased by the Government to assist authorities to cope with the effects of high inflation.
(iv)  Out-turn figures for 1982–3 onwards are most recent estimates, as available from RSG Reports and from the Welsh Office.

*Sources*: 1967–8 to 1980–1, Chartered Institute of Public Finance and Accountancy; 1981–2 to 1985–6, RSG Reports and Supplementary Reports for England and Wales: figures are subject to some revision at final out-turn; 1986–7, secretary of state's announcement.

Table App. 10  Rate Support Grant, Specific and Supplementary Grants, 1967–8 to 1985–6 (England and Wales) (£ million)

| | Specific grants | % of total | Supplementary grants | % of total | Domestic element | % of total | Resource element | % of total | Needs element | % of total |
|---|---|---|---|---|---|---|---|---|---|---|
| 1967–8 | 131 | 9.3 | — | 0 | 23 | 1.6 | 209 | 14.8 | 1,051 | 74.3 |
| 1968–9 | 141 | 9.2 | — | 0 | 47 | 3.0 | 222 | 14.5 | 1,126 | 73.3 |
| 1969–70 | 142 | 8.1 | — | 0 | 73 | 4.1 | 237 | 13.5 | 1,309 | 74.3 |
| 1970–1 | 168 | 8.2 | — | 0 | 100 | 4.9 | 267 | 13.0 | 1,513 | 73.9 |
| 1971–2 | 194 | 8.2 | — | 0 | 117 | 4.9 | 298 | 12.6 | 1,758 | 74.3 |
| 1972–3 | 218 | 7.9 | — | 0 | 132 | 4.8 | 340 | 12.4 | 2,056 | 74.9 |
| 1973–4 | 274 | 8.0 | — | 0 | 193 | 5.6 | 429 | 12.5 | 2,533 | 73.9 |
| 1974–5 | 429 | 9.0 | 2 | 0 | 446 | 9.4 | 1,067 | 22.4 | 2,814 | 59.2 |
| 1975–6 | 556 | 8.4 | 297 | 4.5 | 619 | 9.3 | 1,680 | 25.3 | 3,489 | 52.5 |
| 1976–7 | 685 | 9.4 | 311 | 4.3 | 640 | 8.8 | 1,838 | 25.2 | 3,817 | 52.3 |
| 1977–8 | 790 | 10.5 | 285 | 3.8 | 657 | 8.7 | 1,890 | 25.0 | 3,923 | 52.0 |
| 1978–9 | 910 | 11.0 | 302 | 3.6 | 674 | 8.1 | 2,085 | 25.1 | 4,327 | 52.0 |
| 1979–80 | 1,195 | 12.6 | 356 | 3.7 | 687 | 7.2 | 2,367 | 24.9 | 4,912 | 51.6 |
| 1980–1 | 1,421 | 12.7 | 401 | 3.6 | 700 | 6.3 | 2,816 | 25.2 | 5,844 | 52.2 |

| | | Specific and supplementary grants | % of total | Domestic rate relief grant | % of total | Block grant | % of total |
|---|---|---|---|---|---|---|---|
| 1981–2 | England | 1,930 | 17.6 | 663 | 6.1 | 8,346 | 76.3 |
| | Wales | 128 | 14.7 | 48 | 5.5 | 697 | 79.8 |
| | E & W | 2,058 | 17.4 | 711 | 6.0 | 9,043 | 76.6 |
| 1982–3 | England | 2,215 | 19.7 | 678 | 6.0 | 8,349 | 74.2 |
| | Wales | 129 | 13.9 | 25 | 2.7 | 773 | 83.4 |
| | E & W | 2,344 | 19.3 | 703 | 5.8 | 9,122 | 74.9 |
| 1983–4 | England | 2,411 | 21.0 | 686 | 6.0 | 8,389 | 73.0 |
| | Wales | 151 | 15.7 | 25 | 2.6 | 787 | 81.7 |
| | E & W | 2,562 | 20.6 | 711 | 5.7 | 9,176 | 73.7 |
| 1984–5 | England | 2,798 | 23.5 | 692 | 5.8 | 8,412 | 70.7 |
| | Wales | 172 | 17.5 | 25 | 2.5 | 786 | 80.0 |
| | E & W | 2,970 | 23.1 | 717 | 5.6 | 9,198 | 71.4 |
| 1985–6 | England | 2,604 | 22.9 | 699 | 6.2 | 8,054 | 70.9 |
| | Wales | 178 | 17.6 | 25 | 2.5 | 811 | 79.9 |
| | E & W | 2,782 | 22.5 | 724 | 5.9 | 8,865 | 71.7 |

NB Specific and supplementary grants for 1985–6 exclude transport supplementary grant hitherto paid to support revenue spending. Block grant figures for 1985–6 consequently include extra support for transport purposes.

Table App.11  Expenditure, Plans, Budgets and Out-turns, 1981–2 to 1986–7* (England only) (£ million)

| | 1981–2 | | | | | 1982–3 | | | |
| --- | --- | --- | --- | --- | --- | --- | --- | --- | --- |
| | Plan | Budget | Revised Budget | Revised Estimate | Out-turn | Plan | Budget | Revised Estimate | Out-turn |
| Current expenditure | 16,180 | 17,534 | 17,516 | 17,527 | 17,472 | 18,000 | 19,260 | 19,231 | 19,051 |
| Relevant expenditure | 18,423 | 20,071 | 20,078 | 20,047 | 19,993 | 20,463 | 21,942 | 21,717 | 21,765 |
| Total expenditure | 16,982 | 18,590 | 18,589 | 18,634 | 18,565 | 18,515 | 19,947 | 19,699 | 19,737 |

| | 1983–4 | | | 1984–5 | | |
| --- | --- | --- | --- | --- | --- | --- |
| | Plan | Budget | Revised Estimate | Plan | Budget | Revised Estimate |
| Current expenditure | 19,692 | 20,550 | 20,451 | 20,389 | 21,439 | 21,529 |
| Relevant expenditure | 22,307 | 23,070 | 23,006 | 22,883 | 23,779 | 23,872 |
| Total expenditure | 20,134 | 20,905 | 20,788 | 20,542 | 21,383 | 21,529 |

| | 1985–6 | | | 1986–7 | |
| --- | --- | --- | --- | --- | --- |
| | Plan | Budget | Revised Estimate | Plan | Budget |
| Current expenditure | 21,314 | 22,227 | 22,397 | 22,250 | 24,242 |
| Relevant expenditure | 24,156 | 24,446 | 24,391 | 25,328 | 26,644 |
| Total expenditure | 21,810 | 22,093 | 22,012 | 22,790 | 24,051 |

Comparison of plans, budgets and out-turns: % excess of budgets and out-turns over plans:

Excess of budgets over plans

| | Current | Relevant | Total |
| --- | --- | --- | --- |
| 1981–2 | 8.4 | 8.9 | 9.5 |
| 1982–3 | 7.0 | 7.2 | 7.7 |
| 1983–4 | 4.4 | 3.4 | 3.8 |
| 1984–5 | 5.1 | 3.9 | 4.1 |
| 1985–6 | 4.3 | 1.2 | 1.3 |

Excess of out-turns over plans

| | Current | Relevant | Total |
| --- | --- | --- | --- |
| 1981–2 | 8.0 | 8.2 | 9.3 |
| 1982–3 | 5.9 | 6.4 | 6.6 |
| 1983–4 | n.a | n.a | n.a |
| 1984–5 | n.a. | n.a. | n.a. |
| 1985–6 | n.a. | n.a. | n.a. |

Notes:

(i) Definitions (i.e. 'current', 'relevant', 'total') are consistent with those used in the RSG settlement in each year.

(ii) Includes both 'allocated' and 'unallocated' current expenditure in 1983–4 to 1986–7 (included in current, total and relevant expenditure).

(iii) There have been some changes in definition from year to year.

Sources: Hansard, Written Answer No. 97 (26 July 1984); RSG Reports for 1982–3 to 1985–6; secretary of state's announcement (1986–7).

Table App. 12   *Expenditure Plans, Budgets and Out-turns, 1981–2 to 1986–7 (England only) (£ million)*

Current expenditure in constant (1983–4) prices

| | | |
|---|---|---|
| 1981–2 | Plan | 18,267 |
| | Budget | 19,796 |
| | Out-turn | 19,726 |
| 1982–3 | Plan | 18,945 |
| | Budget | 20,271 |
| | Out-turn | 20,051 |
| 1983–4 | Plan | 19,692 |
| | Budget | 20,550 |
| 1984–5 | Plan | 19,528 |
| | Budget | 20,533 |
| 1985–6 | Plan | 19,580 |
| | Budget | 20,418 |
| 1986–7 | Plan | 19,012 |
| | Budget | 20,711 |

*Note*: 1985–6 and 1986–7 planned and budgeted spending excludes London Regional Transport, which was transferred from control by the Greater London Council to the Department of Transport from 1985–6. Other changes of definition have taken place from year to year.

*Sources: Hansard*, Written Answer No. 97 (26 July 1984), and RSG Reports; deflators taken from Association of County Councils, *Rate Support Grant (England) 1985–6*, table J, pt III.

Table App. 13   *Current Expenditure Out-turns, 1979–80 to 1986–7 (England only) (£ million)*

| | Cash | Constant (1983–4) prices) |
|---|---|---|
| 1979–80 | 12,976 | 20,111 |
| 1980–1 | 15,682 | 19,893 |
| 1981–2 | 17,472 | 19,726 |
| 1982–3 | 19,051 | 20,051 |
| 1983–4 | 20,451 (revised estimates) | 20,451 |
| 1984–5 | 21,439 (budgets) | 20,533 |
| 1985–6 | 22,227 (budgets) | 20,418 |
| 1986–7 | 24,242 (budgets) | 20,711 |

*Note*: 1985–6 spending excludes London Regional Transport, which was transferred from control by the Greater London Council to the Department of Transport from 1985–6. Other changes of definition have taken place from year to year.

*Sources: Hansard*, Written Answer No. 40 (12 May 1983), and Written Answer No. 97 (26 July 1984); deflators taken from Association of County Councils, *Rate Support Grant (England) 1985–6*, table J, pt III.

Table App.14   Average Rate Poundage, by Class of Authority (England and Wales)

| | England | | | | | | Wales | | | | | | |
| | London boroughs Inner | London boroughs Outer | County boroughs | Non-county boroughs | Urban districts | Rural districts | County boroughs | Non-county boroughs | Urban districts | Rural districts | England | Wales | England and Wales |
|---|---|---|---|---|---|---|---|---|---|---|---|---|---|
| 1966-7 | 50.8 | 57.9 | 61.3 | 61.3 | 59.2 | 54.2 | 66.3 | 70.4 | 71.3 | 62.5 | 57.9 | 67.5 | 58.3 |
| 1967-8 | 55.8 | 60.4 | 63.8 | 63.8 | 61.3 | 56.3 | 67.1 | 74.6 | 74.6 | 65.8 | 60.0 | 70.0 | 60.4 |
| 1968-9 | 60.8 | 66.7 | 66.3 | 66.7 | 64.6 | 59.2 | 70.4 | 77.9 | 77.9 | 68.3 | 62.5 | 73.3 | 62.9 |
| 1969-70 | 66.4 | 72.3 | 70.8 | 70.0 | 67.9 | 62.5 | 72.5 | 85.0 | 82.1 | 72.9 | 67.1 | 77.5 | 67.1 |
| 1970-1 | | | 76.4 | 74.8 | 72.2 | 65.4 | 77.4 | 92.7 | 88.6 | 77.8 | 71.8 | 83.2 | 72.2 |
| 1971-2 | 78.0 | 78.9 | 87.2 | 85.8 | 82.9 | 74.9 | 91.3 | 105.3 | 104.4 | 88.6 | 82.0 | 96.5 | 82.5 |
| 1972-3 | 88.6 | 90.6 | 96.1 | 94.9 | 92.3 | 82.9 | 102.4 | 107.8 | 111.2 | 92.3 | 91.5 | 102.7 | 91.5 |
| 1973-4 | 36.1 | 41.1 | 45.0 | 40.8 | 39.8 | 35.2 | 47.6 | 49.5 | 50.4 | 41.9 | 40.1 | 46.9 | 40.3 |

| | London boroughs Inner | London boroughs Outer | Metropolitan districts | Non-metropolitan districts | England | Wales | England and Wales |
|---|---|---|---|---|---|---|---|
| 1974-5 | 42.7 | 51.9 | 58.9 | 53.2 | 51.6 | 63.5 | 52.0 |
| 1975-6 | 63.4 | 75.1 | 71.8 | 65.7 | 67.4 | 80.0 | 67.9 |
| 1976-7 | 69.2 | 74.8 | 75.4 | 71.6 | 72.1 | 86.9 | 72.7 |
| 1977-8 | 75.8 | 77.3 | 83.9 | 79.9 | 79.4 | 93.6 | 80.0 |
| 1978-9 | 77.9 | 78.5 | 89.7 | 86.8 | 84.4 | 100.3 | 85.0 |
| 1979-80 | 84.7 | 91.0 | 102.8 | 98.7 | 95.5 | 116.2 | 96.2 |
| 1980-1 | 107.3 | 111.0 | 129.3 | 119.1 | 117.5 | 140.9 | 118.4 |
| 1981-2 | 139.6 | 141.9 | 164.0 | 134.2 | 142.0 | 162.1 | 142.4 |
| 1982-3 | 157.0 | 156.0 | 186.6 | 152.6 | 160.6 | 167.2 | 160.8 |
| 1983-4 | 173.9 | 168.8 | 195.1 | 160.5 | 170.0 | 168.2 | 170.9 |
| 1984-5 | 181.9 | 176.2 | 204.9 | 170.3 | 180.2 | 182.0 | 180.2 |
| 1985-6 | 187.1 | 192.4 | 228.8 | 182.1 | 193.1 | n.a. | n.a. |

Sources:

(i)   1966-7 to 1973-4 taken from Rates and Rateable Values in England and Wales, (London: HMSO) for each year from 1966-7 to 1973-4.
(ii)  1974-5 to 1980-1 taken from Local Government Financial Statistics England and Wales 1978-79 (London: HMSO).
(iii) 1981-2 to 1984-5 taken from Local Government Financial Statistics England and Wales 1983-84 (London: HMSO).

Table App. 15    *Local Authority Employment in England and Wales (thousands)*

|  | Old series coverage (a) | | | New series coverage (b) | | |
|  | Full-time | Part-time | Total full-time equivalent | Full-time | Part-time | Total full-time equivalent |
|---|---|---|---|---|---|---|
| 1966 | 1,350 | 539 | n.a. | | | |
| 1967 | 1,422 | 579 | n.a. | | | |
| 1968 | 1,451 | 618 | n.a. | | | |
| 1969 | 1,466 | 658 | n.a. | | | |
| 1970(c) | 1,468 | 694 | n.a. | | | |
| 1971 | 1,506 | 728 | n.a. | | | |
| 1972 | 1,570 | 770 | n.a. | | | |
| 1973 | 1,629 | 825 | n.a. | | | |
| 1974(d) | 1,599 | 845 | n.a. | | | |
| 1975 | 1,660 | 896 | 2,011 | 1,716 | 907 | 2,072 |
| 1976 | 1,682(e) | 892(e) | 2,035(e) | 1,733 | 903 | 2,091 |
| 1977 | 1,668(e) | 888(e) | 2,020(e) | 1,712 | 899 | 2,069 |
| 1978 | 1,665(e) | 903(e) | 2,021(e) | 1,708 | 914 | 2,069 |
| 1979 | 1,682 | 924 | 2,045 | 1,736 | 935 | 2,104 |
| 1980 | 1,661 | 903 | 2,018 | 1,717 | 914 | 2,079 |
| 1981 | 1,625 | 879 | 1,975 | 1,683 | 891 | 2,038 |
| 1982 | 1,598 | 877 | 1,948 | 1,656 | 889 | 2,010 |
| 1983(f) | 1,599 | 890 | 1,953 | 1,658 | 901 | 2,017 |

*Notes*:
(a)    Education, construction, transport, social services, police and other departments.
(b)    Includes civilians, cadets and traffic wardens employed by police forces, employees of magistrates' courts and probation and after-care committees, and agency staff.
(c)    About 19,000 employees were transferred from local authorities to passenger transport executives between 1969 and 1970.
(d)    The reorganization of local government led to an estimated total of 90,000 employees being transferred from local authorities to regional water authorities, the National Health Service and passenger transport authorities.
(e)    Includes some temporary employment programme staff. These are excluded in the new series figures.
(f)    Provisional.

Figures shown are for June each year.
    *Sources: Local Government Financial Statistics England and Wales 1979–80* (London: HMSO), table B1; Joint Manpower Watch Press Notice; *Employment Gazette*, Various issues, table 1.7.

1   In relation to the council of a non-metropolitan county, a metropolitan district or the Council of the Isles of Scilly –

*(a)*   The number of acres comprised in their area minus a number equivalent to 0.05 times the population of their area;

Multiplying that number by £2.898

*(b)*   The number of acres comprised in their area minus a number equivalent to 1.5 times the population of their area (if the resultant number is a positive number);

Multiplying that number by £4.466

*(c)*   The number of acres comprised in their area minus a number equivalent to 3.0 times the population of their area (if the resultant number is a positive number);

Multiplying that number by £1.584

*(d)*   In relation to the council of a non-metropolitan county, the sum of the respective products of the number of persons per acre in the area of each district in the county and the population of that district, and, in relation to a metropolitan district or the Council of the Isles of Scilly, the number of persons per acre in their area multiplied by the population of their area;

Multiplying that number by £0.4997

*(e)*   The number of persons in their area living in parishes or wards or parts of parishes or wards whose density exceeded 50 persons per hectare at the date of the 1971 census, multiplied by the population of their area on 30 June 1978 and divided by the population of their area at the date of the 1971 census;

Multiplying that number by £3.900

*(f)*   The number of new permanent dwellings started in their area during the period from 1 January 1976 to 31 December 1978, in so far as it exceeds 0.59 per 100 of the population of their area;

Multiplying that number by £319.5

*(g)*   The number by which the population of their area on 30 June 1968 exceeded that on 30 June 1978;

Multiplying that number by £19.32

*(h)*   The number by which the population of their area on 30 June 1973 exceeded that on 30 June 1978, multiplied by one-thousandth of the population of their area;

Multiplying that number by £0.0318

*(i)*   The number of men 65 years of age or over and women 60 years of age or over living alone in their area at the date of the 1971 census, multiplied by the number of persons 65 years of age or over living in their area on 30 June 1978 and divided by the numbers of persons 65 years of age or over living in their area at the date of the 1971 census, in so far as the resultant number exceeds 2.9 per 100 of the population of their area;

Multiplying that number by £396.8

*The Politics of Local Government Finance*

Table App.16   *Needs Element Factors, 1980–1 (cont.)*

| | | |
|---|---|---|
| *(j)* | The number of persons in their area living in permanent or non-permanent buildings in households without the exclusive use of hot water supply, fixed bath or inside water closet at the date of the 1971 census, in so far as it exceeds 1.74 per 100 of the population of their area; | Multiplying that number by £97.10 |
| *(k)* | The number of persons in their area living in permanent buildings with a density of occupation greater than 1½ persons per room at the date of the 1971 census, in so far as it exceeds 1.03 per 100 of the population of their area; | Multiplying that number by £131.8 |
| *(l)* | The number of persons in their area living in shared households in permanent buildings at the date of the 1971 census, in so far as it exceeds 0.15 per 100 of the population of their area; | Multiplying that number by £41.87 |
| *(m)* | The number of lone parent families with dependent children in their area at the date of the 1971 census, in so far as it exceeds 0.73 per 100 of the population of their area; | Multiplying that number by £4756.0 |
| *(n)* | The number of primary school pupils living in their area, in so far as it exceeds 6.88 per 100 of the population of their area; | Multiplying that number by £572.0 |
| *(o)* | The number of secondary or special school pupils under 16 years of age living in their area, in so far as it exceeds 6.35 per 100 of the population of their area; | Multiplying that number by £747.5 |
| *(p)* | The number of secondary or special school pupils 16 years of age or over living in their area, in so far as it exceeds 0.36 per 100 of the population of their area; | Multiplying that number by £673.8 |
| *(q)* | The number of pupils under 16 years of age who are attending direct grant grammar schools at the expense of the council; | Multiplying that number by £617.4 |
| *(r)* | The number of pupils 16 years of age or over who are attending direct grant grammar schools at the expense of the council; | Multiplying that number by £471.6 |
| *(s)* | The number of further education students, full time or full time equivalent, living in their area, in so far as it exceeds 0.65 per 200 of the population of their area; | Multiplying that number by £748.6 |
| *(t)* | The number of persons in their area unemployed and registered for employment, in so far as it exceeds 0.86 per 100 of the population of their area; | Multiplying that number by £342.2 |
| *(u)* | In relation only to the council of the counties of Bedfordshire, Berkshire, Essex, Hampshire, Hertfordshire, Kent, Oxfordshire and Surrey, the amount of the labour cost differential in their area multiplied by the population of their area; | Multiplying that amount by £5.066 |

Table App.16  *Needs Element Factors, 1980–1 (cont.)*

---

| | | |
|---|---|---|
| *(v)* | In relation only to the council of the county of – | Multiplying that number by |
| | Hertfordshire | £2.677 |
| | Kent | £0.358 |
| | Powys | £7.575 |
| | and to the council of the metropolitan district of – | |
| | Manchester | £0.247 |
| | the population of their area; | |
| *(w)* | The number of the population of their area. | Multiplying that number by £6.4150 |

## A. PEOPLE IN THE AREA
A 1 Residents
A 2 Daytime net inflow
A 3 Visitor nights

CHILDREN
A 4 Aged under 5
A 5 Aged under 11
A 6 Aged 11–15
A 7 Aged 11–17

SCHOOL PUPILS
A 8 Primary age
A 9 Secondary aged under 16
A10 Aged 16 and over
A11 Non-advanced further education students
A12 People aged 16–24
A13 People aged 25–44
A14 People aged 45–64
A15 People aged 18–64
A16 Elderly people aged 65 and over

## B. PHYSICAL FEATURES OF THE AREA
B1 Area
Sparseness of school population:
B2(i) a Primary education
B2(i) b Secondary under 16
B2(i) c Secondary 16 and over
B2(ii)a Primary education
B2(ii)b Secondary under 16
B2(ii)c Secondary 16 and over

DENSITY OF SETTLEMENT
B3a(i) Ward-weighted density – general
B3a(ii) Ward-weighted density – refuse collection
B3b Simple density

DEPARTMENT OF TRANSPORT ROADS
B4 Motorways
B5 Trunk roads in built-up areas
B6 Trunk roads in non-built-up areas

LOCAL AUTHORITY ROADS
B7a Principal roads in built up areas: 1984
B7b Principal roads in built-up areas: 1981
B8 Principal roads in non-built-up areas
B9a Other roads in built-up areas: 1984
B9b Other roads in built-up areas: 1981
B10 Other roads in non-built-up areas
B11 Road maintenance usage adjustment
B12 Road maintenance weather adjustment

PROPERTIES
B13 Number of non-domestic properties
B14 Number of domestic properties
B15 Floorspace of shops and restaurants

DEVELOPMENT
B16 Building regulations
B17 Planning applications

OTHER
B18 Protected coastline

## C. SOCIAL AND ENVIRONMENTAL PROBLEMS

ADDITIONAL EDUCATIONAL NEEDS
C 1 Under 5s
C 2 Primary
C 3 Secondary
C 4 Pupils in families receiving supplementary benefit
C 5 Youth unemployment
C 6 Children aged 11–17 in less advantaged areas
C 7 People in private rented accommodation

C 8 Effect of area's social
conditions
C 9 Total unemployment
C10 Public transport factor
C11 Recreation unit cost
adjustment
C12 Concessionary fares factor

## D. COSTS OF PROVIDING SERVICES

D 1 Higher costs in the London
area
D 2 Isles of Scilly special costs

## E. SPECIAL REQUIREMENTS OF PARTICULAR SERVICES

CRIME
E 1 Notifiable offences recorded by
the police

DEFENDANTS PROCEEDED AGAINST AT
MAGISTRATES' COURTS
E 2 Indictable offences
E 3 Summary offences

FIRE
E 4 Number of fires
E 5 Areas of high fire risk

VARIOUS EXPENDITURES
E6a Expenditures on mandatory
student awards, education
pools, rate rebates, rent
allowances and rebates and
land drainage

E6b Passenger transport debt
charges

HOUSING
E 7 Notional HRA deficit

CEMETERIES AND CREMATORIA
E 8 Deaths

NEW CAPITAL
E 9 Financing of new capital
expenditure

PASSENGER TRANSPORT
E10 Local rail networks

HOME OFFICE SERVICES
E11 Adjustments for police and
probation authorities

PERSONAL SOCIAL SERVICES
E12 Social services for children
under 5
E13 Social services for children
5–17
E14 Social services for elderly
people
E15 Adjustment for elderly
residential care
E16 Income adjustment for elderly
home-help services
E17 Other social services

OTHER ADJUSTMENTS
E18 Leasing charges
E19 Interest receipts and
contributions to special
and capital funds
E20 Rounding adjustment

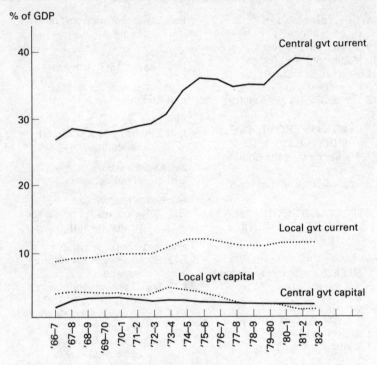

% of GDP

Central gvt current

Local gvt current

Local gvt capital

Central gvt capital

Figure App. 1    Local and central government as a proportion of gross domestic product, 1966–7 to 1982–3.

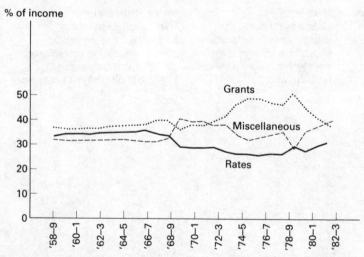

% of income

Grants

Miscellaneous

Rates

Figure App. 2    Proportion of local authority revenue income made up by rates, grants and other sources, 1958–9 to 1982–3 (England).

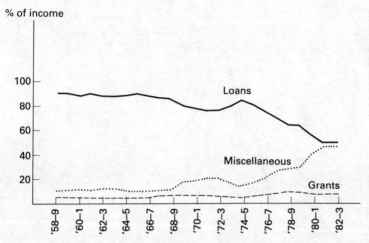

Figure App. 3   Proportion of local authority capital income made up by loans, grants and other sources, 1958–9 to 1982–3 (England).

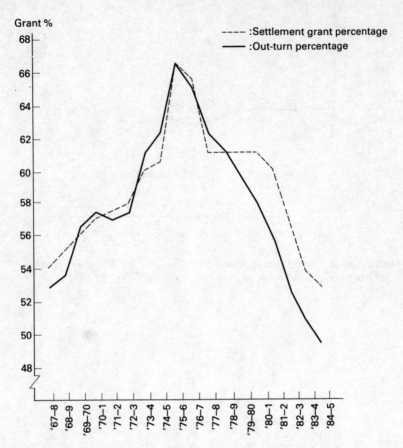

Figure App. 4    Grant percentage: settlement and out-turn, 1967–8 to
1984–5 (England and Wales).

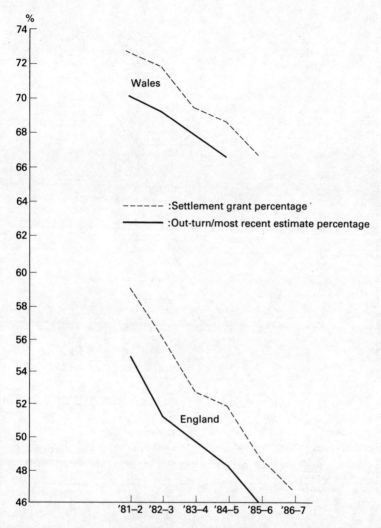

Figure App. 5    Grant percentage; settlement and out-turn, 1981–2 to
1985–6 (England and Wales).

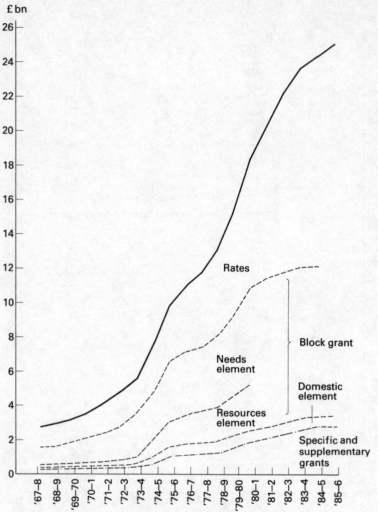

*Note*: Rate income may be slightly different to the figure shown because of the need to fund small amounts of 'non-relevant' expenditure

Figure App. 6   Income sources for relevant expenditure, 1967–8 to 1985–6 (England and Wales).

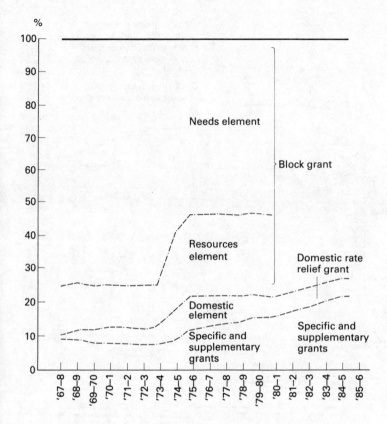

Figure App. 7   Grant as a proportion of aggregate Exchequer grant,
1967–8 to 1985–6 (England and Wales).

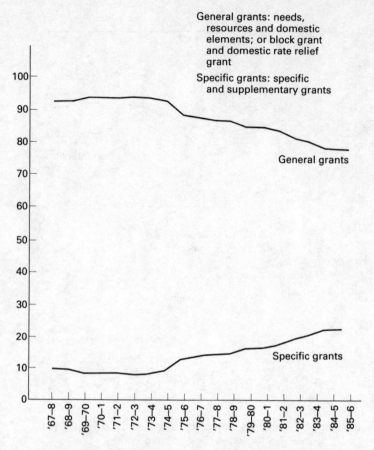

Figure App. 8  Aggregate Exchequer grant: proportion devoted to specific and general grants, 1967–8 to 1985–6 (England and Wales).

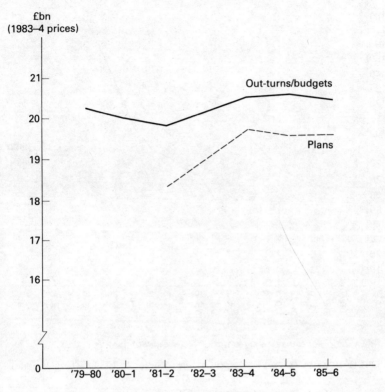

Figure App. 9   Local authority current expenditure: plans and out-turns,
1979–80 to 1985–6 (England).

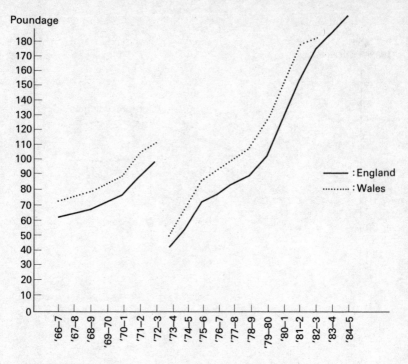

(Revaluation of rateable values from 1973–4 onwards)

Figure App. 10  Average rate poundages, 1966–7 to 1984–5 (England and Wales)

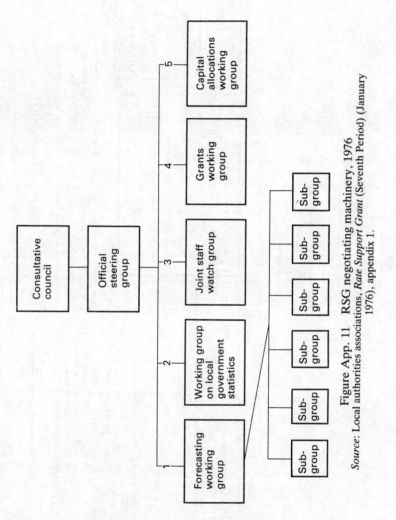

Figure App. 11    RSG negotiating machinery, 1976
*Source:* Local authorities associations, *Rate Support Grant* (Seventh Period) (January 1976), appendix 1.

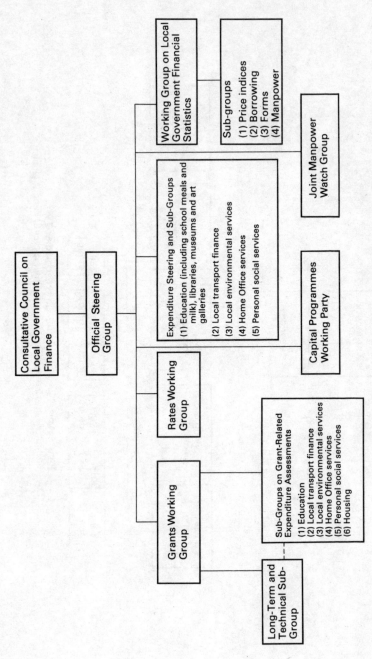

Figure App. 12   RSG negotiating machinery, 1984

# INDEX